SHIRAZ MAHER

Salafi-Jihadism

The History of an Idea

PENGUIN BOOKS

PENGUIN BOOKS

UK | USA | Canada | Ireland | Australia
India | New Zealand | South Africa

Penguin Books is part of the Penguin Random House group of companies whose addresses can be found at global.penguinrandomhouse.com.

Penguin Random House UK

First published in Great Britain by C. Hurst & Co. (Publishers) Ltd. 2016
Published in Penguin Books 2017
001

Printed in Great Britain by Clays Ltd, St Ives plc

A CIP catalogue record for this book is available from the British Library

ISBN: 978–0–141–98626–5

www.greenpenguin.co.uk

FSC www.fsc.org MIX Paper from responsible sources FSC® C018179

Penguin Random House is committed to a sustainable future for our business, our readers and our planet. This book is made from Forest Stewardship Council® certified paper.

for Maryam

CONTENTS

ACKNOWLEDGEMENTS

The study of Salafism as an idea, movement and religious doctrine in the English speaking world was done a great service by the edited collection of essays put together by Roel Meijer in *Global Salafism*. Over the last five years this work has inspired a cluster of academic and scholarly works exploring the idea even further. Important texts on some of modern Salafism's intellectual forbears such as Ibn Taymiyya and 'Abd al-Wahhab have since emerged but, as Meijer himself notes, there remains a lack of studies specifically focusing on Salafi-Jihadi thought. This is curious given the not unsubstantial body of primary source material that is in circulation from leading theorists of the movement.

For a moment it seemed as if militant Salafism might have been in decline with the United States killing both Osama bin Laden and Anwar al-Awlaki. At the same time ostensibly peaceful uprisings gathered momentum across North Africa, particularly in Tunisia and Egypt. Bashar al-Assad changed all that, with his brutal repression galvanising global support for militant millenarian movements.

My research into the contours of Salafi thought began in late 2010, several months before the Syrian crisis began. Throughout this time I have been based in the Department of War Studies at King's College London, where I am a Senior Fellow at the International Centre for the Study of Radicalisation (ICSR). My sincerest thanks must first go to the Chairman, Henry Sweetbaum, and the trustees: Sir David Sieff, Jonathan Sacher CBE, the Rt. Hon. Kim Campbell and H.E. Omar Saif Ghobash for the tremendous opportunity they have extended me. King's College London has also supported me immensely. For this, I must thank Sir Lawrence Freedman, Theo Farrell, Joe Maiolo and Michael Rainsborough, who have consistently offered invaluable advice.

This book is essentially my PhD thesis and I am therefore extremely grateful to my supervisor, mentor and friend, Peter Neumann, who oversaw the whole thing. He waited with varying degrees of patience and frustration as I kept telling him "just one more chapter to go, then it's done," when, in truth, there were probably three or four left to write at the time. He has helped me refine many of my ideas, reorganised lots of the material presented here, and ultimately trusted me to conduct my own research. He has also been my boss at ICSR throughout this time, which has been a fantastic base from which to work on issues relating to militant Salafism. I am grateful to him for all of it.

I have been lucky enough to work with many friends during this time, particularly John Bew, Alexander Meleagrou-Hitchens and Martyn Frampton. On my day-to-day activities I was supported by the best team of Syria analysts anywhere in the world, colleagues who enlightened the study of an otherwise dour subject matter. I am indebted to Joseph Carter, Melanie Smith ("Millie"), Audrey Alexander and Nick Kaderbhai—the dream team. I must also thank my other ICSR colleagues Aaron Zelin, Scott Kleinmann, Christina Mitsiali and Katie Rothman. Antoine Barthe provided accommodation and generous hospitality when I collected research materials in the United States.

I have benefitted from numerous exchanges over the years with distinguished and brilliant scholars whose opinions, insights and generosity have helped shape my views. I thank Gilles Kepel, William McCants, Thomas Hegghammer, Joas Wagemakers, Brynjar Lia, Lorenzo Vidino, Mark Stout, Gary Ackerman, Magnus Ranstorp and Sayed Khatab. For their detailed and considered comments on this manuscript, I am grateful to David Martin Jones and Edwin Bakker. The two anonymous peer-reviewers who checked my work prior to publication provided me a great service with their forensic feedback. They saved me from a number of embarrassing howlers, for which I thank them. Mitchell Reiss also gave me an opportunity to work on this project while I was a visiting lecturer at Washington College. I thank him and the students for a most enjoyable experience.

Special mention must be given to Thom Dyke, one of my oldest friends, who agreed to be my guinea pig. As an intelligent non-specialist I hoped he would be able to follow and enjoy the content of this book. He generously sacrificed several weekends to meticulously check the manuscript, commenting on style, language and structure. I am hugely grateful to him. Samar Batrawi slapped my wrists when I made basic errors with Arabic texts and was always ready to answer rudimentary questions on Arabic grammar and prose (and much else besides)—a walking, talking version of Hans Wehr. Dave "L-Squad" McAvoy was also extremely helpful in this regard, always insightful, always funny. Aymenn Jawad Ali al-Tamimi is a polyglot and never refuses an opportunity to discuss all things jihad. Thank you.

For their friendship and support while I wrote this book I would also like to thank Marcus and Lucy Appleton, Pete and Alex Johnson, Dan and Joey Segelman, Ben and Kate Scott, Alex Glenister, John Kenyon, Dominic Chastney, David Toube, Duncan Gardham and Laura Kramer.

My publisher, Michael Dwyer, has been a pleasure to work with throughout this process as have his team at Hurst. My agent, Rachel Conway, expertly walked me through the process of getting the first book out and only sent me harassing emails when absolutely necessary.

Much of the research in this book was funded by a generous grant from the Gerda Henkel Stiftung. I'm very grateful to them for backing my research.

My greatest debt is to my family: my parents, Ehsan and Rubina; my sister, Madiha; and Ayisha. They have sacrificed and endured much to get me where I am today, and I hope this book goes some way towards repaying that debt. Finally, this book is dedicated to my wonderful, brilliant daughter, Maryam.

NOTE ON TRANSLITERATION

I have transliterated Arabic terms in this book using the conventions of the *International Journal of Middle East Studies* (IJMES) with diacritic markings. There are, however, some exceptions to this. IJMES rules state that "words found in Merriam–Webster's should be spelled as they appear there and not treated as technical terms. They should have no diacritics, nor should they be italicised." This applies to terms such as jihad, mujahideen and shaykh (and many others). There are some exceptions to this which preserve *'ayn* and hamza, in words such as: Qur'an, shari'a, 'ulama', and Ka'ba. All of them appear in this book and consequently conform to this rule. A full list of such terms is available online in the 'IJMES Word List,' which I have also used throughout my text.

As the convention dictates, there are no diacritic markings for personal names, place names, names of political parties and organisations. Where an author has published works in English, I have respected their choice of how their name is rendered (e.g. Abdul instead of 'Abd al-). The same applies for renderings of common Arabic words that appear in book or journal titles. For example, the notes show *shariah*, *sharia* and *shari'a*; or *umma* and *ummah*. Finally, I have partially derogated from the IJMES convention on transliteration regarding Arabic names. Names of Salafi scholars, Islamic clerics, and those otherwise having prominence within that milieu are transliterated according to the IJMES system (e.g. 'Abd al-'Aziz) although those who would be known to the general reader and have widely accepted English spellings of their names (e.g. Osama bin Laden, Gamal Abdel Nasser) are given those terms for ease of reference and familiarity. The only other derogation in this regard relates to al-Qaeda, for which I have used this common rendering. The 'IJMES Word List' recommends that it be presented as al-Qa'ida, although this is too removed from what would be familiar to the general reader. Finally, the plurals of some Arabic terms, such as *aḥadīth*, have been simplified with English plurals to make it easier for general readers (e.g. *ḥadīths*).

Although I have worked with a broad range of Arabic texts in this book, none of the translations are my own. I have therefore noted the English translations I consulted (many of which were often read in parallel or in conjunction with the identical Arabic text). Solitary Arabic texts I consulted are noted accordingly and where translations appear, the relevant translator is acknowledged in the notes. Urdu texts, where they appear, are my own translations unless alternative translations were available (again, these are acknowledged and noted accordingly).

GLOSSARY

Amīr	Denotes a leader or ruler or someone in authority. It can also can have suffixes such as *Amīr al-Mu'minīn*—"leader of the faithful."
'Aqīda	Doctrinal creed, referring to the essential and core components of the Islamic belief system.
Bid'a	Heretical or deviant innovation. Taken to mean a prohibited and sinful religious innovation.
Fatwa	Non-binding juristic opinion.
Fiqh	Islamic jurisprudence, of which there are numerous types. Therefore the term "*fiqh*" is often accompanied by a suffix such as *fiqh al-muwāzanāt*, the jurisprudence of balances (weighing up the relative benefits and harms of a particular action).
Ḥadīth	Collections of teachings, sayings, actions, and traditions attributed to the Prophet Muhammad. The *ḥadīth* are collected in volumes, of which the most famous collections are: Bukhari, Muslim, Daud, and Tirmidhi.
Ḥākimiyya	The rule of Allah; securing God's sovereignty in the political system.
Ḥalāl	Permissible.
Ḥarām	Forbidden.
Ḥukm (plural, aḥkām)	Islamic rulings derived from jurisprudence (*fiqh*).

Ijmāʿ al-Ṣaḥāba	Consensus of the Prophet's companions. Regarded as a source of law in several normative schools of Islamic jurisprudence.
Ijtihād	Independent juristic reasoning by a competent scholar who uses scriptural sources to deduce a legal ruling.
Īmān	Belief in Islam, typically tied to the acceptance of six core articles of faith: God, prophets, angels, divine books, the day of judgement, and predestination.
Iṣlāḥ	Reform, to improve.
Jihad	Literally and linguistically means to struggle or exert effort, although it has a legal meaning which relates to combat and fighting.
Khawf	Literally means to be fearful or scared, but in the religious context refers to fearing Allah alone. None of creation is to be feared.
Madhhab (pl. madhāhib)	Refers to a school of jurisprudential thought of which there are four in normative Sunni Islam. These are the Hanafi, Shafiʿi, Hanbali, and Maliki schools.
Mafhūm al-mukhālafa	Jurisprudential principle meaning "the understanding of the opposite." Applied in situations where scholars believe the opposite of a positive command can be taken as law.
Manhaj	The methodology employed to achieve a particular ideal or virtue.
Mushrik (pl. mushrikūn)	Polytheist.
Muwaḥḥid	A true believer in the oneness of God; someone who accepts *tawḥīd*; a monotheist.
Naṣīḥa	Morally corrective advice promoting reform.
Naskh	The Islamic principle of abrogation where some earlier verses of the *Qur'an* are deemed to have been abrogated by later ones.
al-Qaḍā' wa-l-qadr	Divine will and predestination, one of the six articles of *īmān*.

Qiṣāṣ	The principle of equal retaliation, retaliation in kind, or *lex talionis*. Part of Islamic criminal jurisprudence allowing the victim to seek retribution in kind against the perpetrator of a particular crime.
Rāfiḍī (pl. *rawāfiḍ*)	Literally means "rejecter" or "splitter" and is used as a pejorative term by some Sunni Muslims—particularly Salafis—to refer to Shi'a who reject the first three companions of the Prophet Muhammad who succeeded him in leading the Caliphate: Abu Bakr, Umar ibn al-Khattab, and Uthman ibn Affan.
Ṣahāba	Companions of the Prophet Muhammad.
Ṣaḥwa	Literally means "awakening," and refers to a number of different revivalist movements in the Gulf, Levant and North Africa.
al-Salaf al-ṣāliḥ	The "pious predecessors" of the Prophet Muhammad. This refers to the first three generations that surrounded the Prophet Muhammad.
Shari'a	The Islamic legal system derived from the *Qur'an*, *sunna* and supplementary sources of jurisprudence such as *ijmā' al-Ṣahāba*.
Shirk	Denying the unitary oneness of God; engaging in polytheism or denying God altogether. Considered to be the worst of sins.
Sunna	The teachings, sayings, actions, experiences and omissions of the Prophet Muhammad. This constitutes a source of law alongside the *Qur'an*. The *sunna* are recorded in the *ḥadīth*.
Tābi'īn	The generation which followed the *Ṣahāba*, and one of the generations which forms the *al-salaf al-ṣāliḥ*.
Tābi' tābi'īn	The generation which followed the *tābi'īn*, and the last of the generations which forms the *al-salaf al-ṣāliḥ*.
Ṭā'ifa al-manṣūra	The victorious group. A reference to normative Muslim belief that Islam will divide into a

	number of sects, of which only one will ascend to heaven.
Takfir	Excommunication of other Muslims, banishing them from the faith.
al-Taṣfiya wa-l-tarbīya	Purification and education, a quietist Salafi method which aims to perfect personal discovery of the *'aqīda*.
Tatarrus	Military doctrine relating to the status, rights, and use of human shields.
Tawakkul	Having absolute faith and reliance on Allah alone.
Tawḥīd	The unitary oneness of God; the core component of Islam and the single most important factor in Salafism.
'Ulama' (s. 'ālim)	Religious scholars or clerical authorities.
Uṣūl	Refers to the various sources of jurisprudence.
al-walā' wa-l-barā'	To love and hate for the sake of Allah; loyalty and disavowal.

INTRODUCTION

1

INTRODUCTION

The Prayer Hall Putsch

On 4 July 2014 the leader of Islamic State, Abu Bakr al-Baghdadi, defiantly ascended the pulpit of the Mosul Grand Mosque, slowly and deliberately, leading with his right foot. "Your brothers, the *mujahideen*, were blessed with victory by Allah," he told congregants listening to his Friday sermon. "After long years of jihad, patience, and fighting the enemies of Allah, he guided them and strengthened them to achieve this goal. Therefore they rushed to establish the Caliphate."[1] Baghdadi was confirming a statement made several days earlier by Islamic State's spokesman, Abu Muhammad al-Adnani, who first announced the revival of the Caliphate as a fulfilment of the "promise of Allah."[2] It had been timed to coincide with the start of Ramadan, the Muslim holy month of fasting and penance. "Today the nations of *kufr* [disbelief] in the West are terrified. Today the flags of Satan and his party have fallen. Today the flag of *tawḥīd* [monotheism] rises with its people. Today the Muslims are honoured," declared Adnani in a triumphalist audio recording on behalf of Islamic State. "Now the *khilāfa* [Caliphate] has returned, humbling the necks of the enemy. Now the *khilāfa* has returned in spite of its opponents. Now the *khilāfa* has returned."[3]

It was the first time since 1924 that a Sunni Muslim leader could make such a claim with any credibility. Other groups had claimed smaller patches of land as enclaves or emirates over the last half-century, but none could realistically claim to have revived an actual Caliphate. Perhaps the most serious claims to the institution came from Mulla Muhammad Omar, who previously led the Taliban, when he gave himself the honorific title of *Amīr al-Mu'minīn*, or leader of the faithful. Although the title emerged by chance during the reign of the second Caliph, Umar ibn al-Khattab (583–644), it has endured ever since and is generally regarded as a marker for claims to the Caliphate.[4]

Even for the group that has called itself the Islamic State of Iraq and Syria (ISIS) before rebranding to Islamic State (IS), a distinction is made between statehood and the Caliphate. Its members regard the former as a necessary precursor to the latter and believe statehood can be achieved simply by capturing parcels of land. For the Caliphate, however, an additional series of conditions must be satisfied before it is declared. Before ISIS consolidated control across large parts of eastern Syria and pushed into northern Iraq to grab major urban centres like Mosul, they only considered themselves worthy of statehood. Now that the group enjoyed a substantial powerbase and territorial control which reached into significant parts of Syria and Iraq, they convened a meeting of their legal scholars to assess whether the conditions of a Caliphate had been met. "The Islamic State, represented by the *ahl al-ḥal wa-l-'aqd* (its people of authority), consisting of its senior figures, leaders, and the *shūrā* [consultation] council—resolved to announce the establishment of the Islamic *khilāfa*," Adnani declared.

That announcement has been a controversial one, even within the community of militant Salafism to which the fighters of Islamic State belong. Whatever his detractors argue, few figureheads in recent history can make such strong claims to the institution of the Caliphate as Abu Bakr al-Baghdadi. Certainly, none has so dramatically or effectively captured its essence. His Caliphate has defied the odds and represents the revival of "an obligation that was abandoned for centuries."[5] It is the most dramatic physical manifestation of Salafi-Jihadi doctrine in the modern era, serving a dualistic purpose between temporal and cosmic ends. Baghdadi explained the group's worldly aims when he declared, "Allah created us to practise *tawḥīd*, worship him, and establish his religion."[6] In that sense, the Caliphate represents a forgotten duty where God's sovereignty is both supreme and absolute. The wider ambitions of Islamic State are more eschatological and involve hastening the day of resurrection, *yawm al-qiyāma*, when all of mankind will account for its actions.[7] The group's purpose can therefore appear contradictory: practically constructive insofar as it wishes to engage in the process of state building, yet philosophically destructive in its desire to precipitate the end of the world.

Islamic State is a Salafi-Jihadi movement, although the broader soteriology of Salafism from which it is derived remains poorly understood by the public. Salafis are typically viewed with suspicion and are often characterised as extremists because of their religious conservatism and aesthetic conformity. For men this would typically include a long and unkempt beard with a robe that stops just short of covering the ankle. For women in public it is most closely associated with the *niqab*, an enveloping veil which reveals only the eyes. To reduce Salafism to this alone is to compress a vast and complex tradition into a few lazy caricatures.

Recent events in the Middle East have been accompanied by a wider unravelling of world order. This turbulence has stimulated public interest not just in the political dimensions of the crises currently engulfing the Levant and North Africa, but also in the ideas which drive millenarian militants on the ground. That much is clear from the extraordinary reception to Graeme Wood's hugely influential essay for *The Atlantic* in February 2015, titled "What ISIS Really Wants."[8] The magazine's commissioning editors can be forgiven for having assumed that an article on the religious and theological dimensions of ISIS might attract only a niche audience, choosing to first publish it online before making it their cover story the following month. It was an instant success. Wood's piece is now the most read article in *The Atlantic's* almost 160-year history and was the most read digital story of 2015—receiving more than one million page views the day it was published online.[9] After the Paris attacks in November 2015 it received just under two million hits in 24 hours.

Wood set himself the task of examining the religious roots of Islamic State by asking, "What is the Islamic State? Where did it come from, and what are its intentions?" These are basic but important questions. What he found is that "the Islamic State is no mere collection of psychopaths. It is a religious group with carefully considered beliefs."[10]

There is clearly an urgent need to better understand those beliefs, not least because they partly inform the activities of so many groups currently redefining the contours of power in the Middle East. Yet, the ideology of Islamic State is neither new nor entirely novel, and its intellectual framework appears to sit within the mainstream tradition of Salafi-Jihadi thought. This might seem unusual given that Islamic State has captured global attention in a way that not even al-Qaeda was able to achieve. Where it does differ from other groups is in its style and approach. Yes, Islamic State is more brazen and ruthless than its predecessors but the ideas that guide it are well established in radical Sunni thought. Their roots are grounded in the experiences of Sunni Islam over the last century and beyond. That is the real purpose of this book: to examine and explain the evolution of Salafi-Jihadi soteriology. This is a broad and varied ecosystem of dense Islamic jurisprudence that has licensed the actions of militant movements across the word. Islamic State is just the latest and most successful group it has spawned.

To that end, this is not a book about Islamic State per se—nor is it about any group in particular. What this book does is explain the core concepts of an idea that has motivated groups around the world, from Nigeria and Sudan to the Levant and the mountains of Mindanao in the Philippines. The book consequently assembles scholarship from theorists across the spectrum of Islamic history to explain how we have arrived at the situation in which we find ourselves today. It is the prequel to the horror that we find so hard to understand, an explanatory backstory accounting for how we got to where we are, what the actors involved want to achieve, and precisely what is guiding their behaviour.

The history of an idea: who are the Salafis?

Salafism occupies a peculiar place in our lexicon as one of those exotic terms imported from the Orient, frequently used but rarely understood. This is not entirely surprising. As an idea it relates to a reactionary soteriology which first emerged from the deserts of Arabia before growing in very different ways. This book aims to clarify and explain the word, providing both the history and the anatomy of an idea. "The term Salafi, and those it designates," wrote Bernard Haykel, "remains ill-defined and often misunderstood in the literature on this movement, and in studies on Islamism more generally."[11] In its simplest construction, Salafism "refers to the righteous predecessors of the first three generations of Muslims," according to the Permanent Committee for Scholarly Research and Fatwas, Saudi Arabia's highest clerical authority.[12] Salafism is therefore a philosophical outlook which seeks to revive the practices of the first three generations of Islam, who are collectively known as the *al-salaf al-ṣāliḥīn*, or "pious predecessors." The *salaf* consist of three components: the first are the prophet's contemporary companions who are known as the *Ṣaḥāba*, the last of whom died around 690. The next generation are known as the *tābi'īn*, the last of whom died around 750. They were followed by the *tābi' tābi'īn*, the last of whom died around 810.[13] These three generations are held to constitute a golden age of authenticated and orthodox Islam, based on a *ḥadīth* of the Prophet Muhammad in which he was asked about the characteristics of the best Muslims. He described them as follows:

> Of the generation to which I belong, then of the second generation (generation adjacent to my generation), then of the third generation (generation adjacent to the second generation).[14]

Viewed in this way, Salafism is a philosophy that believes in progression through regression. The perfect life is realised only by reviving the Islam of its first three generations. Taken as markers of both authenticity and purity, the legacy of the *al-salaf al-ṣāliḥīn* provides the praxis for contemporary Salafism. The message is consequently a revivalist one, seeking to bring Muslims back to what is regarded as the "authentic" and "pure" Islam of its early generations. Their doctrine is principally concerned with the realisation of God's unity, *tawḥīd*, and maintenance of doctrinal purity, *'aqīda*. By attempting to emulate the practices of Islam's supposedly golden era, Salafis believe that only they constitute the so-called "victorious group" (*ṭā'ifa al-manṣūra*) or "saved sect" (*al-firqa al-nājiya*). This comes from a reference in another *ḥadīth* which states Islam will splinter into various movements of heresy and deviance. Only one faction will practise Islam as God intended and will consequently be saved.[15]

It is therefore best to think of Salafism as a redemptive philosophy based around an idealised version of Islam that enshrines both authenticity and purity. There are plenty of ways to realise that vision, with different scholars outlining various methods (*manhaj*) for its realisation.[16] This distinguishes the Salafi philosophy about key issues such as *tawḥīd* and *'aqīda* from *manhaj* which, according to shaykh Salih ibn Fawzan is, "more general than the '*aqīda*," meaning that greater degrees of variance and divergence are tolerated.[17]

Scholars such as the Yemeni cleric Ibn Qayyim al-Jawziyyah or the Indian scholar Shah Wali Allah (1703–1762) have articulated different approaches for the realisation of Salafi philosophy.[18] Perhaps the most popular *manhaj*, however, comes from Muhammad ibn 'Abd al-Wahhab whose followers are sometimes referred to as "Wahhabis"—a label they themselves do not subscribe to, regarding it as a pejorative term.[19] His works and legacy are of huge importance to contemporary Salafis across the world. The former Grand Mufti of Saudi Arabia, 'Abd al-'Aziz bin Baz, described Wahhab as a *mujaddid* (reviver of the faith) who "brought back the strength, purity, and power of Islam to the Arabian Peninsula."[20] The use of *mujaddid* as an appellation here is invested with profound significance because it refers to a *ḥadīth* in which the Prophet Muhammad stated that God will send a *mujaddid* in every century to revive and preserve the religion. The corollary is unmistakable—that we should view 'Abd al-Wahhab's doctrines as being divinely mandated.

Yet, his is a contested and disputed message. Some have argued it is the wellspring of contemporary Islamic terrorism, whereas others have noted its importance to the modern Saudi state, where it provides stability and informs the quietist approach of the official clerical establishment.[21] Madawi al-Rasheed argues that Wahhab's legacy is continuously contested within Saudi Arabia, with radicals and quietists both claiming to be its rightful heirs.[22] Intra-Salafi competition in this respect is not just limited to Wahhab, but also extends to other scholars such as Ibn Taymiyya.

Salafi-Jihadism: typologies and definitions

Any examination of Salafism quickly reveals that its adherents are far from constituting a monolithic bloc. Quintan Wiktorowicz notes: "the community is broad enough to include such diverse figures as Osama bin Laden and the Mufti of Saudi Arabia. Individuals and groups within the community reflect varied positions on such important topics as jihad, apostasy, and the priorities of activism."[23] These variances are not limited to those within its community but also include the effects of Salafism: from being a source of state stability in Saudi Arabia to a great force of instability and barbarism in countries like Syria. In fact, the rise of Islamic State in recent years has only further complicated this picture because even within the milieu of radical and millenarian Salafi groups, its jurisprudential opinions are regarded as esoteric and eccentric. Nonetheless, Wiktorowicz has argued that Salafis can be divided into three broad categories: purists, politicos, and jihadis.[24] This method of categorisation has been widely used and accepted by other scholars ever since he first published it in 2006, although occasional efforts to refine it have been attempted. For example, Muhammad Hafez accepts Wiktorowicz's distinctions but rejects the label of "purist," preferring instead the term "apolitical" or "conservative".[25] Jarret Brachman has taken this a step further by arguing that Salafis can actually be divided into eight different categories based on his study of the Canadian Salafi preacher Dr Tariq Abdelhaleem.[26]

The Wiktorowicz system of classification is undoubtedly helpful but it is not without its problems. Thomas Hegghammer points out that Salafism is a "theological, not a political category."[27] As a result, "it says very little about the political preferences of the actors described as Salafis."[28] That much is true. Yet, although Salafism is a theological distinction, divisions within the tradition are best understood with reference to its fault lines, which principally cut across cleavages of power. This makes the relationship between Salafism and power iridescent, a kaleidoscopic philosophy producing different results based on how its adherents choose to view it.

Herein lies the principal problem with the Wiktorowicz model—it is too broad to capture the relationship between how these actors view their connection to power and the manner in which they wish to engage with, or change it. These two factors must be considered in isolation and are expressed in the table below.

This approach helps to better understand the different ways in which Salafi actors manifest themselves politically. For example, the official clerical body in Saudi Arabia known as the Council of Senior Scholars (*Majlis Hay'at Kibār al-'Ulama'*) advises the House of al-Sa'ūd in private, but eschews public dissent or open challenge to the government.[29] Members of this council can therefore be thought of as being quietist-advisors who prioritise *al-taṣfiya wa-l-tarbīya* (purification and education) over politics.

Table 1: Categorisations of Salafi political preference

Method for change	*Violence*	*Activism*	*Quietism*
Attitude towards the state or international order	Reject	Challenge	Advise

By contrast, the Saudi Awakening movement (*ṣaḥwa*) produced a cadre of scholars who operated as activist-challengers by publicly airing their disagreements with the government and calling on it to reform.[30] They are more directly engaged with the political process, lobbying and campaigning for organic change in accordance with Islamic precepts. Moreover, their belief in maintaining social order and unity leads them to reject radical or revolutionary upheaval. A number of Salafis who could be described as activist-challengers have been critical of the Arab uprisings which began in 2011 for causing unrest, whilst simultaneously expressing sympathy for the underlying conditions which first gave rise to them (Salman al-ʻAwda is one example of someone who has argued precisely this. His views are explored in the chapter on *ḥākimiyya*).

Yet, not every challenger to the state is an activist. Groups such as the Islamic Salvation Front (abbreviated to FIS after its official French name, Front Islamique du Salut) started life as activist-challengers by contesting elections and urging acts of civil disobedience (such as general strikes) to bring about social change. This changed in 1993 when the FIS moved towards armed resistance after military officials had annulled their electoral successes the previous year.[31] Having taken up arms, it is best to think of the FIS as violent-challengers because they had not rejected either the state or the international order at this stage. Their political agenda was Islamist in orientation but their horizons were nonetheless confined to Algeria's borders. The same might be said of the Syrian opposition group Ahrar al-Sham which is currently fighting against Bashar al-Assad's regime. It has adopted violence against the Syrian state, but its Islamist ambitions are limited to Syria's borders. Its political agenda, though conservative, is not one which fundamentally seeks to overturn the entire existing order either within the country or abroad.[32] Other groups have periodically moved between different categories. The Egyptian group Takfir wal Hijra, which splintered from the Muslim Brotherhood in the 1960s, was initially quietist-rejectionist when its members withdrew from society and moved to wholly isolated communes in the mountains. When the Egyptian state later moved against the group, it responded with violence—taking a former government minister hostage and executing him—perhaps marking a move towards violent-rejectionism, although the group was resoundingly crushed shortly afterwards.[33]

Finally, violent-rejectionists are irreconcilably estranged from the state, regarding it as a heretical and artificial unit. The entire notion of the modern nation-state is a heterodox affront to Islam whereby temporal legislation usurps God's sovereignty. The system therefore needs radical overhaul and reordering while its agents must be confronted. "We believe that the ruler who does not rule in accordance with God's revelation, as well as his supporters are infidel apostates," al-Qaeda declared. "Armed and violent rebellion against them is an individual duty on every Muslim."[34] Until recently al-Qaeda was the most prominent of the violent-rejectionist groups, with others including al-Shabaab and Boko Haram. Today it has been surpassed by Islamic State which goes further than merely rejecting constitutional politics or the international system by actually enacting policies that defy even civilizational standards. This was seen most dramatically when the group revived slavery after capturing scores of Yazidi women in Iraq. It also adopts highly sectarian characteristics and rejoices in the slaughter of its opponents.

Under the formulation offered above, only violent-rejectionists are considered Salafi-Jihadis for the purposes of this book. This is because although many violent-challengers are undoubtedly Salafis who also believe in jihad (and practise it in many cases), their worldview does not believe in the absolute reconstruction of either the international order or the nation-state. To put it another way, were they to achieve power, they would largely behave as a consensus state within the international framework. For ease of reference, the term Salafi-Jihadi will be used when discussing adherents of the violent-rejectionist grouping and it is specifically adherents of this particular part of the Salafi spectrum that are the focus of this book.

There is much to study. Salafi-Jihadi movements have dominated the jihadi landscape over the last two decades and have provided the greatest challenge to established power structures. In the eyes of Frazer Egerton this makes it "one of the most significant movements in politics today."[35]

In this book I aim to demonstrate tensions within the movement by highlighting intra-Salafi debates and disputes over orthodoxy. These differences are most noticeable when Salafi-Jihadi theorists clash with their counterparts who are operationally active in the field. While theorists have the luxury of time, which allows for the reflection and gestation of different ideas, fighters in the field are driven by a real-time, ad hoc form of jurisprudence that is borne of both the privations and exigencies of war.

Roel Meijer explains how this causes divergences by noting that while Abu Muhammad al-Maqdisi legitimises jihad from within a Wahhabi tradition, Abu Musab al-Suri has created "a secularised, political jihad without the religious paraphernalia, geared to fighting the enemy by the most efficient means."[36] In other words, his is a more practical—almost *realpolitik* or pragmatic—approach to getting the job done. This is even more apparent in the works of other operational figures such as the former leader of al-Qaeda in Saudi Arabia, Yusuf al-'Uyayri. Meijer notes that he combines aspects of classical Salafi doctrine "with a sharp and ruthless analysis of reality, geared to the implementation (*taṭbīq*) of a jihadi strategy, thus producing a Salafist activist concept of praxis that is comparable to Leninism."[37]

The first three concepts explored in this book deal explicitly with the operational aspects of Salafi-Jihadi belief, clearly revealing intra-Salafi tensions between jihadi theorists and practitioners. There appears to be greater uniformity of opinion among Salafis on issues which are less concerned with actual fighting. In this respect, Eli Alshech makes an important observation regarding the manner in which operational Salafi-Jihadis are empowered because of the way in which they understand the relationship between belief, knowledge, action, and spiritual legitimacy. The interrelatedness of these concepts means that dogmatic and zealous devotion is not just a necessity, but also serves as a marker of religious authority. Alshech argues:

It is important to note that Salafi-Jihadis pursue legal knowledge not for the sake of erudition per-se but rather for the sake of application (*taṭbīq*). Their writings invoke the classical notion that "knowledge should be sought for sake of practice" (*al-'ilm li'l-'amal*). By contrast, neo-*takfiris* consider uncompromising zeal to constitute perfect piety. For them, a person who is not zealous lacks religiosity and authority. Indeed, al-Zarqawi's followers considered his piety as a legitimate and sufficient basis for religious authority. Erudition and scholarship were secondary. In the eyes of al-Zarqawi's followers, a Muslim's spiritual level and thus his authoritative position are determined by strict religious practice and not by knowledge.[38]

Defining Salafi-Jihadism

Although Salafi-Jihadism is the focus of this book, it is just one part of a much broader Salafi spectrum. Different scholars have contested precisely what characteristics or underpinnings define the Salafi-Jihadi movement as a whole. For example, Muhammad Hafez argues that contemporary Salafism is defined by five characteristics: *tawḥīd*, *ḥākimiyya*, a rejection of *bid'a* (heretical innovations), *takfir*, and jihad.[39] Jarret Brachman argued something similar to Hafez, agreeing that *tawḥīd*, *takfir*, and jihad are necessary characteristics of the movement, but then rejected both *ḥākimiyya* and *bid'a*. Instead, he replaced those concepts with *'aqīda* and *al-walā' wa-l-barā'*.[40] However, neither Hafez nor Brachman offered any substantial explanation of how or why they came to regard these particular aspects of Salafi-Jihadism as constituting its essential features.

In identifying the essential and defining features of Salafi-Jihadism for the purposes of this book, the lists suggested by Hafez and Brachman provide an important starting point, but it is also necessary to go further and consider the wider range of other jurisprudential concepts deemed to be of importance to contemporary Islamic movements. These can be classed as practical, theoretical, or ritualistic concepts. Of the practical concepts there are *irtidād*/*ridda* (both are used for apostasy), *bid'a* and *ḥisba* (meaning accountability, in line with the Islamic injunction to "command good and forbid evil"). Yet, none of these could really be considered as being unique to Salafi-Jihadism because there are several Muslim traditions that are concerned with the prevention of *bid'a*. Similarly, *ḥisba* is practised by a range of different groups while opposition to apostasy is usually subsumed under public morality laws (typically related to *ḥisba* initiatives).

A similar view was taken towards theoretical concepts such as *'aqīda* and *īmān* (faith). Again, all Muslims concern themselves with *'aqīda* and *īmān*, as these are two of the most basic cornerstones of religious acceptance. While Salafis interpret these two ideas somewhat differently from other Muslim traditions, there is nothing particularly unique about the Salafi-Jihadi understanding of them when compared to other Salafis. For this reason, neither was included as an essential feature of the movement. Finally, two ritualistic concepts involve *dhikr* (remembrance of God) and *shafa'a* (intercession). Both are much more heavily pronounced, communally ritualised, and widely practiced by Sufi Muslims rather than Salafis. Indeed, many Salafis regard communal displays of *dhikr*—which is typically accompanied by singing and dancing—as constituting *bid'a*. Meanwhile, in its broadest constructions, *shafa'a* is seen as constituting *shirk*, or polytheism, because it establishes intermediaries between an individual and God. Therefore, this issue would be better subsumed within a discussion of *tawḥīd*. None of the concepts listed above are sufficiently important, or unique, to Salafi-Jihadism to be included in its defining characteristics.

This book argues that there are five essential and irreducible features of the Salafi-Jihadi movement: *tawḥīd*, *ḥākimiyya*, *al-walā' wa-l-barā'*, jihad, and *takfir*. These five features appear repeatedly in literature from both ideologues and groups which espouse a Salafi-Jihadi ideology. The literature consistently references these ideas and demonstrates they have undergone significant ideational mutation in Salafi-Jihadi understanding. Whilst all of these ideas exist within normative Islamic traditions, and there is nothing particularly unique or special about them, what makes them relevant in this context is that the contemporary Salafi-Jihadi movement has interpreted and shaped them in unique and original ways. Explaining *what* they have done to those ideas and *how* they have done it is the overriding aim of this book.

For example, Abu Muhammad al-Maqdisi offers a cursory but panoptical overview of Salafi belief in a short book, *This is our 'aqīda*.[41] He dedicates a chapter to each of the issues identified as one of the defining features of Salafi-Jihadism above, with the exception of *al-walā' wa-l-barā'* although that concept is pervasive throughout his work. "We declare *barā'* [disavowal] from the *mushrikūn* [polytheists], their helpers, and their allies," Maqdisi writes. "We hate them and we declare our *barā'* from what they worship besides Allah, and we disbelieve in their methodologies, their religions, and their false paths that oppose the *dīn* [religion] of Allah."[42] A declaration of principles released by al-Qaeda also touches on all of the same issues.[43] There are several points in the declaration which talk about the importance of *tawḥīd*, *ḥākimiyya* (and the "tribulation" of democracy), *takfīr*, *al-walā' wa-l-barā'*, and jihad. "We believe that the victorious faction is a faction of knowledge and jihad," the document states.[44]

Osama bin Laden was critical of other Muslims who did not embrace all of these things. He denounced a group of Saudi intellectuals who attempted to promote coexistence between Muslims and the United States in the aftermath of 9/11, supposedly because their interpretation of Islam lacked the five defining features central to the Salafi-Jihadi project. "The Islam preached by [moderates] does not contain [the doctrine of] loyalty and disavowal [*al-walā' wa-l-barā'*], nor does it contain jihad, nor the boundaries established by the *shari'a* [e.g. *takfīr*]," he wrote, "since it is these very doctrines that worry the West most."[45]

This explains the basis on which the five defining characteristics of Salafi-Jihadism were selected. By reference to their own works, ideas were selected based on: their importance to the movement, the centrality of those ideas to their aims, and objectives, and the extent to which those ideas were sufficiently cultivated in a particularly unique or different way to inform the Salafi-Jihadi worldview.

The five defining characteristics are therefore principally concerned with two things—protection and promotion. Protection of the faith comes through jihad, *al-walā' wa-l-barā'*, and *takfīr*; while its promotion is linked to *tawḥīd* and *ḥākimiyya*. It is the first part of this equation that interests Salafi-Jihadis the most because it is battlefield-related, providing the *raison d'être* for their modus operandi. The doctrine of Salafi-Jihadism is therefore one of millenarian change, with each of its constituent components driving towards that goal. The nomenclature of theology and jurisprudence that surrounds it relates to issues of rightful authority, legitimacy, obedience and rebellion (*bughāt*).

All of the five essential characteristics of Salafi-Jihadism identified here relate to those questions in some way. The doctrine of *al-walā' wa-l-barā'* establishes lines of loyalty and disavowal; *takfīr* delineates Islam against everything else and protects it against insidious corruption from within; *tawḥīd* and *ḥākimiyya* explain what legitimate authority should look like and who it should serve; and jihad prescribes the method for this particular revolution.

Salafi-jihadism as a neologism

Having identified the essential characteristics of the movement, it remains that Salafi-Jihadism is somewhat of a neologism. Thomas Hegghammer notes that the word first emerged in academic literature in 1998 when Gilles Kepel and Kamil al-Tawil wrote about the Algerian Civil War in separate studies.[46] He argues, however, that the first known reference to a "jihadi Salafi movement," came from the current leader of al-Qaeda, Ayman al-Zawahiri, in 1994.[47] Alison Pargeter argues that the term is "more akin to a current of thought that … individuals may well subscribe to and should not be confused with a specific group as such."[48] That is one of the key things this book attempts to demonstrate—that Salafi-Jihadism is a thought, or ideological strain, with which individuals can identify. It does not belong to a particular group or movement although there are certain actors (such as Maqdisi) who have been particularly influential in the formation of certain ideas.

The Moroccan Salafi preacher, Abdelwahhab al-Rafiki, told Pargeter the term Salafi-Jihadi "is a media and security term because I don't know anybody who claims to represent that current…wherever there is a group of Muslims who are declaring jihad and making the word of Allah higher, we support them. If this is the meaning of *salafiyya jihadia*, then we are *salafiyya jihadia*."[49] The rise of Salafi-Jihadism as an idea—and in many respects, its establishment as an ideal—followed the decline of political Islam at the start of the 1990s. Islamism appeared to be in retreat across much of North Africa, the Levant, and Central Asia at the time. The most dramatic example of this came with the outbreak of the Algerian Civil War, but it was not the only case. The Muslim Brotherhood had been crushed in Egypt and was effectively wiped out in Syria, the Tunisian Islamists of the Ennahda Party also suffered a brutal crackdown, and leaders of the Saudi *ṣaḥwa* movement were being rounded up and sentenced to lengthy prison terms. Only the Taliban appeared to be winning—and were doing so through force, not constitutionalism. Other insurgencies were also taking place, in Algeria, Bosnia and Chechnya. It certainly seemed as if ostensibly non-violent Islamists were incapable of delivering results and that if Islam was going to be politically empowered, it would also have to assert itself physically and militarily. All of this prompted both Gilles Kepel and Olivier Roy to separately argue that a "post-Islamist" phase was taking hold, one where the political initiatives of Islamist actors had failed.[50]

The Second Gulf War (2003–2011) becomes the crucible of Salafi-Jihadi thought

The use of Salafi-Jihadi as a term has grown not only in academic and popular discourse, but also among those who would self-identify as such today. Although the incipient phases of what we now recognise as Salafi-Jihadism first began to emerge during the Algerian Civil War, it was really during the Second Gulf War that something more concrete, coherent, and discernable appeared. This is when jihadi groups on the ground, principally led by al-Qaeda in Iraq, began issuing a large body of carefully considered literature to explain, justify and vindicate their activity. There is an important point to appreciate here. The violence of groups like al-Qaeda and associated movements is neither irrational nor whimsical. For every act of violence, they will offer some form of reference to scriptural sources—however tenuous, esoteric, or contested—to explain their actions. It therefore follows that this is when the most output was produced, as jihadis fighting Western coalition forces in Iraq sought to explain themselves to an otherwise uncertain Muslim audience in the Middle East and beyond. In many senses, the intellectual development of jihadist thought in this period lends further credence to Trotsky's now hackneyed observation in the 1922 *Report on the Communist International*, that war is the locomotive of history.

The 2003 invasion of Iraq was instrumental in giving shape and definition to what is recognised as Salafi-Jihadism today. Understanding the importance of ideological coherence is what matters here. There is an important difference in degree between those groups that were inspired by, or conceived during, this time and those which had come before, such as Islamic Jihad, al-Jama'a al-Islamiyya, and even the Algerian GIA. The same also applies to those foreign fighters who had travelled to earlier conflicts in Afghanistan, Bosnia, or Chechnya. They were all influenced to varying extents by Salafism and practised jihad but none of these combat environments brought together all of the various aspects of what is today recognised as Salafi-Jihadi ideology into a consolidated and coherent belief structure. For example, in 2001 Quintan Wiktorowicz argued that:

> Salafi thought has influenced the ideological orientation of many practicing Muslims and some of the most well-known Islamic organisations in the Muslim world... These "jihadi" Salafis identify themselves as adherents to the Salafi *manhaj* [method] and use well-known Salafi identity markers.[51]

What Wiktorowicz is talking about is jihadis who happen to be Salafis—or Salafis who also engage in jihad. This is precisely the point shaykh Omar Haddouchi made during an interview with Alison Pargeter regarding what he called the "imagination of the atheist media" whom he blamed for creating the Salafi-Jihadi neologism. "We pray, so why don't they call us *salafiyya* praying, we go to pilgrimage and they don't call us *salafiyya* pilgrimage," he argues. "We believe in jihad for the sake of Allah, like any Muslim on the earth, so why do they describe us as *salafiyya jihadia*?"[52] This ambiguity arose from the absence of a coherent ideology to which one could point.

It should be noted, however, that the process of intellectual development within Salafi-Jihadi thought was taking place for several years before the Second Gulf War. This is when different ideas were being developed, largely in response to the state of flux in which the global jihad movement found itself at the time. A number of Arab *mujahideen* had regrouped in Sudan under the leadership of Hasan al-Turabi and watched as their countries imploded in different ways. Saudi Arabia suffered an unprecedented identity crisis when the House of al-Sa'ūd entered into a military alliance with the United States to repel Saddam Hussein from Kuwait. When civil unrest followed in opposition to this alliance, celebrated and highly popular Salafi clerics from the Saudi *ṣaḥwa* movement were harassed and arrested. This was arguably one of the most important civic episodes in the development of a Salafi-Jihadi ideology. Elsewhere, Algerian Islamists with the GIA were engaged in a bitter civil war at home, as were members of the Libyan Islamic

Fighting Group. Hosni Mubarak had also launched another crackdown against political Islamists—the Muslim Brotherhood in particular—which increased already simmering tensions between the government and Islamic activists.

It was in this environment, fuelled by the exigencies of war, repression, and detention, that Salafi theorists began producing abstract adumbrations about what a future Salafi-Jihadi movement should look like in practice and what *manhaj* it should adopt to realise its vision. These ideas were later given expression by al-Qaeda after its key members were expelled from Sudan and forced to regroup in Afghanistan. Divorced from their primary arena of activity in the Arab world, the group began quite consciously cultivating a transnational agenda which decoupled Muslim identity from geography and culture. Instead it created a transcendental identity which overcame these strictures by appealing to an imagined community, the *umma*. It is no coincidence that of the five defining characteristics of Salafi-Jihadism identified above, al-Qaeda speaks most about the three which relate to the protection of Islam: jihad, *al-walā' wa-l-barā'*, and *takfir*. These are the more "operational" aspects of Salafi-Jihadi belief which are of practical consequence on the battlefield—compared to those concepts which are linked to the "promotion" of Islam, such as *tawḥīd* and *ḥākimiyya*.

Al-Qaeda appears less concerned with these aspects of Salafi belief because it regards existing scholarship as already well established and sufficient. There are consequently no detailed books from al-Qaeda or its leadership regarding *tawḥīd* or *ḥākimiyya*, although both concepts are frequently referenced in passing. The former leader of al-Qaeda in Iraq, Abu Musab al-Zarqawi, gave one of the clearest expositions of the consolidated Salafi-Jihadi worldview when his group published a document about "our creed and methodology," in March 2005.[53] It is as full a statement of principles as exists regarding Salafi-Jihadi belief, encompassing the full spectrum of the group's worldview. It also underscores al-Qaeda's Salafi credentials by heaping encomium on the *Ṣahāba*, the Prophet Muhammad's companions. "We are pleased with the entire companions and we speak well of them," Zarqawi states. "It is a duty to love them and hypocrisy to hate them. We do not discuss their disagreements. They are the best ancestors."[54]

Yet, the Second Gulf War also created serious divisions within the global jihad movement, principally between theorists and those actively engaged in battle. Some of the main ideologues involved in these debates included Abu Muhammad al-Maqdisi, Abu Hamza al-Masri, Abu Qatada al-Filastini, and Abu Basir al-Tartusi who—along with others—had previously helped develop and theorise the ideas that gave rise to the contemporary movement. All of their most significant works are explored in this book, although it is worth observing that none of them have actively participated in jihad since the 1980s (with the exception of Tartusi). This means they take a more considered and detached approach to jihadi jurisprudence (*fiqh*) than their counterparts engaged in actual fighting, exposing important areas of ideological dissonance.[55] By surveying the approach of both active jihadist movements and theoreticians, this book demonstrates how Salafi-Jihadi ideology is like any other: subject to the inherent friction in transitioning from abstract theory to practical implementation.

Intellectual history

Militant Islamic groups have proved themselves to be committed, dangerous and resilient. They have endured decades of domestic repression and an international "War on Terror," but have nonetheless flourished in both North Africa and the Levant following the Arab uprisings of 2011. The behaviour of the groups and individuals operating in these environments, although sometimes brutal and distasteful, is not irrational. All of it is grounded, somewhere, in a particular reading of scripture. This is not to make subjective value judgements by suggesting that one interpretation is inherently "correct" while others are not. The theological positions presented by all Muslim participants in this debate—between jihad and quietism; fundamentalism and liberalism—are deeply contested. The approach adopted in this book is therefore to merely present the fault lines of these debates with dispassionate observation.

This has been done before, albeit in different ways. When Josef Van Ess studied the formation of political ideas in early Islamic thought he argued that scholars should examine the proposed models and theories while offering explanations of what has happened.[56] Historians have thus far shied away from the study of contemporary jihadism, instead leaving its pursuit to political scientists, linguists, and religious and area studies specialists. Consequently, there remain glaring blind spots in our knowledge of the movement. "The number of studies on the ideological development of al-Qaeda and jihadi Salafism has been relatively limited compared to the enormous amount of attention paid to their operational capacity," noted Roel Meijer.[57] This book is presented as an antidote to the dearth of historical inquiry into the intellectual culture of militant Salafism by exploring the expansive body of Salafi-Jihadi literature which explains its *'aqīda*, *manhaj* and *fiqh*. Leading members of al-Qaeda have already stated that this body of work constitutes the foundations of their distinct worldview. During an interview with al-Qimmah, a now defunct internet forum previously run by members of al-Shabaab, al-Qaeda's late financial officer, Mustafa Abu al-Yazid (also known as Saeed al-Masri) stated that:

> ...[our] ideology is spreading, thank Allah, and all the young people of the *umma* [Islamic nation] are receptive to this ideology which is, as we said, the ideology of Islam, not just the ideology of al-Qaeda.[58]

In many respects, the ideological nature of the Salafi-Jihadi creed accounts for the resilience of the movement it has spawned. Being based around an idea, rather than a particular leader or personality, it is extremely difficult to undermine Salafi-Jihadism decisively. When senior members of these groups are killed, their networks largely carry on as before. Consider the eulogy of Abu Musab al-Zarqawi, the former leader of al-Qaeda in Iraq:

> They [the American Armed Forces] think that we fight for money and prestige—and what they do not understand is that our arteries are filled with the ideology of jihad. Even if they managed to reach Zarqawi, praise be to Allah, we have a million more Zarqawis because our *umma* is the *umma* of jihad, and jihad is at the top of our religious hierarchy.[59]

This is not an atypical statement from the group following the assassination of one of its leaders. When American Special Forces killed Osama bin Laden in Pakistan, al-Qaeda reaffirmed the enduring ideological aspect of its message:

> Are the Americans able to kill what shaykh Osama lived and fought for, even with all their soldiers, intelligence, and agencies? Never! Never! Shaykh Osama did not build an organisation that would die with him, nor would end with him.[60]

A similar message of ideological defiance followed the assassination of Anwar al-Awlaki, when al-Qaeda in the Arabian Peninsula (AQAP) declared, "America has killed shaykh Anwar, but they can never kill his ideology."[61] AQAP understood this better than most, having done more than any other chapter of al-Qaeda to proliferate the group's message to a global audience. Perhaps the greatest manifestation of this came with the rise in so-called "lone wolf" terrorism, a doctrine first theorised by Abu Musab al-Suri who served in al-Qaeda's central leadership, before it was spread by Awlaki.[62] Lone wolves are typically those individuals who have no, or negligible, direct contact with al-Qaeda. They have not trained in its training camps. They are not connected to any discernible network. Nonetheless, they are sufficiently inspired by its cause that they choose to act in its name. Their connection to the movement in this regard comes from both proximity to and empathy (in varying degrees) with its worldview. This is not to suggest that motivations for lone wolf terrorism can be explained by reference to ideology alone, but its role in the process of binding individuals to a cause larger than themselves cannot be dismissed.[63]

Defining the historical method

The primary aim of this book is to produce an intellectual history which explores the development of ideas and intellectual trends within a particular context over time.[64] This is a contentious area of historical inquiry, as Peter Gordon notes:

> Intellectual history is an unusual discipline, eclectic in both method and subject matter and therefore resistant to any single, globalised definition. Practitioners of intellectual history tend to be acutely aware of their own methodological commitments; indeed, a concern with historical method is characteristic of the discipline. Because intellectual historians are likely to disagree about the most fundamental premises of what they do, any one definition of intellectual history is bound to provoke controversy.[65]

Disputes over precisely what methodology or approach should be adopted as best practice are pervasive within the field. Indeed, they even stretch to what the discipline should be called—intellectual history or the history of ideas?

The latter of those phrases is now regarded as dated by most historians and is most closely associated with Arthur Lovejoy, an American philosopher who began practising history later in his career. For Lovejoy, the history of ideas concerned itself with the examination of large concepts which could be boiled down to 'unit-ideas,' constituent building-blocks on which bigger ideas rested.[66] Lovejoy was careful to note that unit-ideas must be reduced to their most fundamental level to have meaning. Therefore, it is not enough to use a concept such as that of "God" as a unit-idea because of the inherently vast and varied ways the notion of supernatural and extra-human deities have been conceived over different times and contexts. "The idea of God is not a unit-idea," Lovejoy writes. "I do not mean merely the truism that different men have employed the one name to signify superhuman beings of utterly diverse and incongruous kinds; I also mean that beneath any one of these beliefs you may usually discover something, or several things, more elemental or more explanatory, if not more significant, than itself."[67] One of the reasons why such an approach is no longer popular is that it can give rise to a Platonist approach.[68] This would suggest that ideas can somehow exist beyond the physical world (or even in its absence) as absolutist abstractions that merely contort themselves to the contours of temporality.

Intellectual history is regarded as a somewhat different endeavour to that of the history of ideas. Intellectual historians believe ideas are birthed of experience; products that are shaped by the anvil of events. The potential contributing circumstances are wide ranging: economic, political, social, demographic, natural, artificial, and genealogical.[69] The point is that each of these factors—and many others besides—can be considered to varying degrees of relevance and utility. Yet, the sum of human experience is clearly too divergent and iridescent for such an approach to be meaningful. The job of the historian is to set the boundaries, define the lines of delineation, and provide a compelling rationale for how and why they have been set as such. For the purposes of this study it is necessary to engage with both political and social theory, theology, and contemporary Middle East history—the most relevant disciplines with which the overriding themes of this book engage.

This book will therefore focus on the ideas of militant Islam insofar as they have informed the jihadi aspect of the Salafi religious tradition. The methodology will draw on the work of John Dunn and Quentin Skinner who have influenced the field of intellectual history dramatically, with their own approach to the matter now commonly referred to as "the Cambridge school," where both have been members of staff.[70]

Consideration must be given when examining the corpus of Salafi-Jihadi literature to a broad set of questions which establish the foundations of this inquiry. For whom was the text written? Why does the author choose to speak, and in this manner, and style, and at this moment? Why are they silent at other times? Was the document intended for a public audience? What purpose does it serve? All of these factors play a significant role in helping to uncover the meaning of a text when posited within its broader social context. The following example highlights this in a practical way. After the 7/7 terrorist attacks in London, Tony Blair vowed to ban the Islamist group Hizb ut-Tahrir (whose name means "party of liberation"). Arguments put forward by the group in their defence highlight—albeit unintentionally—the very issues Dunn and Skinner were driving at. In an article for the "Open Democracy" website, executive committee member Abdul Wahid argued:

> ...some who do challenge our political views often resort to partial understandings of individual texts that are detached from context—either of the Muslim world or of global history in general. For example, the war rhetoric prevalent in Europe fifty years ago was full of derogatory epithets and proud declarations, but these are no longer seen as appropriate.
>
> Winston Churchill's "fight them on the beaches" is relevant to Normandy in 1944, not Barbados in 2005; the language of "freedom" used in campaigns for independence today differs between Scotland and Aceh. It would be ridiculous to assume that rhetoric relevant to a population that sees itself under occupation is symptomatic of the viewpoint of Muslims generally, and Hizb ut-Tahrir specifically ... In fact, the decision to remove some of our overseas literature from our British website was a considered response to the legitimate proposition that people who read it out of its context might see it as offensive.[71]

The contextual understanding of Churchill's "fight them on the beaches" speech is the Second World War, but proponents of the Cambridge School would argue this only offers a limited understanding of what is important here. To understand the phrase in its fullest context the Cambridge School would look to the work of the late John

Austin, a philosopher of language at Oxford University.[72] Austin argued that words had to be broken up into their "locutionary," "illocutionary" and "perlocutory" forces.[73] The locutionary force is simply the utterance consisting of phonetic, syntactic and semantic features. To put it baldly, this means what was said. By contrast, the illocutionary force reveals what the author meant, or was implying, with their speech. In this context the locutionary act is to say "fight them on the beaches" whereas the illocutionary force reveals a spirit of defiance and determination to succeed in the war effort against the Nazis. What the illocutionary force really says is: "we will fight to the very end, we won't surrender, we will win." To illuminate that meaning, of course, it is necessary to first appreciate the context in which Churchill was speaking, underscoring the importance of adopting these approaches in unison when studying a relevant text.[74] The perlocutory force relates to the psychological force or consequences behind the words: to inspire, scare, enliven, or depress. In this context the message is simultaneously meant to inspire and uplift the British masses while intimidating their enemies.

Ideology

A brief note on ideology is also needed given that it forms the cornerstone of what is being examined here. In its most basic construction, ideology is distinct from the political way of thinking by attempting to bring together a series of speculative abstractions into a coherent doctrine in the pursuit of utopia or, at the very least, a better way of living. The classical theorist on totalitarianism and ideology, Hannah Arendt, argued that "ideologies are *isms* which to the satisfaction of their adherents can explain every occurrence by deducing it to a single premise."[75] Others have defined ideology less restrictively. For example, Ian Adams argues that it is more diffuse and that "there is little agreement about the nature of ideology."[76] This is argued by those who regard conservative strains of thought about political organisation (particularly in some of its postmodern forms) to be more concerned with power than ideology, where the world is not explained through *longue durée* or catchall reasoning. There is no "single premise," but a series of independent, occasionally concentric, silos of understanding.[77]

In this regard, much of the contemporary scholarship on ideology and its uses can be traced back to the pioneering work of Karl Mannheim who argued that ideological thoughts can be divided along cleavages of interest into *particular* and *total* forms.[78] The former relates to special interests within a group where one necessarily competes against the other for the protection of its interests, whilst the latter applies to society or a particular era as a whole. Conceptual ambiguities arise, of course, when considering precisely what the whole is to constitute in those circumstances. For example, Salafi-Jihadism could be seen as a *particular* ideology, competing within Islamic precepts for dominance of its theological outlook. Alternatively, it could also be seen as a *total* ideology, given the universality of its nature—based, not least, on Islamic universalism—towards a desire to consume and aggregate the entirety of both human existence and organisation within its systems.

This aspect of Salafi-Jihadi belief makes it similar to totalitarian strains of political thinking. In many senses, its ascendancy in the post-modern world can be attributed to what Leo Strauss identified as the inherent arcing of liberal societies towards one of two different forms of nihilism.[79] His basic proposition was that liberal societies erode culture, customs, history, tradition and memory, replacing these with relativist mores. It is in these environments that nihilisms then arise. The first of these is what Strauss termed *brutal* nihilism, such as Nazism or Marxism, where the impulse to wash-away relativist ambiguities with authoritarian social control and order licences force. The second, equally undesirable form, is *gentle* nihilism, of the kind that is now pervasive in Western societies. This is where the primacy of selfhood comes to replace society as a whole, or where individual silos of self-interest subordinate collectivism. Strauss therefore concluded that social customs would be fully eroded by the nihilism of a rudderless and unanchored society that stood for nothing and which encouraged an environment of "permissive egalitarianism."[80] He argued:

> The core of permissive egalitarianism is the individual with his urges...the man who wants to indulge his urges does not have the slightest intention to *sacrifice* his life and hence his urges...this is the moral decline which has taken place.[81]

This explanation may well help account for the rise of Salafi-Jihadism as an ideology within certain contexts and with reference to particular ideas within its belief structure, such as *ḥākimiyya*. For example, Salafi belief is unsentimental about the nomenclature of tradition or history, except where it concerns ritual authenticity. Everything else is therefore a distraction at best or, at worst, *bid'a* or *jāhiliyya*. To this end, it exhibits a tendency towards *brutal* nihilism with its desire to forcibly replace everything other than itself. Its adherents also recoil at the "permissive egalitarianism" of contemporary societies, seeking a return to more assured—albeit absolutist—times.

In this sense, Salafi-Jihadism follows a very modern ideological pathology of the type that Eric Voegelin would have once described as political religion (although Thierry Gontier has shown that he eschewed the term later in his career).[82] Voegelin shared the ideas of Arendt and Strauss insofar as he believed liberalism ignored the need for meaning in public life. Individuals attempting to find meaning for themselves would therefore create the conditions in which politics would serve as religion. Satiating ideologies consequently provide their adherents with a form of common cause, a unifying mission, and sense of purpose for bringing society together. Much has been written about totalitarianism as political religion—Strauss's *brutal* nihilism—where absolutist political constructs provide social meaning and cause.[83] For Jones and Smith, this tendency first emerged from an "ersatz religious purpose that informed the European totalitarian movements of the 1930s."[84] This saccharine piety is not just limited to the experiences of twentieth-century Europe, but is also flourishing in the Middle East today where reactionary political movements based on Islam have found dramatic expression. Of these, this book examines one: Salafi-Jihadism, which can be considered Islam's latest—and perhaps most successful—political religion.

JIHAD

2

THE OBLIGATION OF FIGHTING

The virtues of jihad

Jihad is the most well-known and yet least understood Islamic concept in public consciousness today. Over the last fifteen years its proponents have challenged established power structures, spawned a massive security industry in the West and overrun large parts of the Levant. It is also one of the most enduring features of Islam. Although jihadist groups have captured the public imagination ever since 9/11, practitioners of Islamic holy war have been around in one form or another ever since the *Qur'an* first mandated it. Of course, the idea did not exist during the initial phases of Islamic revelation when the Prophet Muhammad and his companions resided in Makkah despite facing intense persecution and oppression. It was only when the Prophet migrated to Medina after the first thirteen years of Islam that jihad was sanctioned, as a means of both protection and territorial conquest. The Prophet Muhammad subsequently participated in 27 *ghazwat*, or battles, himself while his companions engaged in countless more.[1] This history is celebrated within Salafi traditions, as are warrior-scholars who have followed later. For example, Imam Ahmad ibn Hanbal, whose scholarship largely established the framework for Salafi jurisprudence, was consistently at odds with the Abbasid leadership of the Caliphate before being imprisoned by the Caliph. Ibn Taymiyya, who also retains huge significance to contemporary Salafis, similarly fought the Mongols, whilst Muhammad ibn 'Abd al-Wahhab was crucial in sanctioning Ibn Sa'ūd's battles of conquest against rival tribes in the Arabian Peninsula with the express purpose of restoring *tawḥīd*.

As an idea, jihad is iridescent and opaque. Muslims contest both its legal and linguistic meaning, while also arguing over how it should be implemented and practised. The word itself comes from the root verb '*jahada*' which means to labour, struggle, or exert effort. The leader of the Arab-Afghan *mujahideen* in the 1980s, 'Abdallah 'Azzam, argued that whilst the linguistic meaning was important it did not inform the distinct and very specific legal meaning of the word.[2] He noted that when all of the four normative schools of Islamic jurisprudence had considered the legal definition of jihad, they had agreed it meant *al-qitāl*, or fighting.[3] Part of the reasoning for this is that the *Qur'an* quite frequently couples it with the phrase *fī sabīl Allah* (in the path of Allah), thereby linking *al-qitāl* to the very entity in whose name it is to be conducted.[4] This legal definition also undermines those who insist that jihad principally refers to a struggle against oneself, emotions or desires (*jihad al-nafs*) which is sometimes also referred to as "the greater jihad" (*jihad al-akbar*).[5] It is not the purpose of this book to investigate the veracity of these competing claims or to apportion credibility to them. It is sufficient for present purposes to adopt the Salafi-Jihadi interpretation of the concept in order to explore the Salafi-Jihadi understanding of it.

At its core the contemporary Salafi-Jihadi movement regards physical struggle in the cause of God as the pinnacle of Islam, its zenith and apex. It is the vehicle by which the religion is both defended and raised. This chapter explores the importance attached by Salafi-Jihadi theorists to the idea particularly with regards to the virtues of combat and its link to the concept of worship itself. Viewed in this way, jihad in the path of God is '*ibāda*, an act of worship akin to ritualistic acts such as prayer (*ṣalāa*), pilgrimage ('*umra*), or fasting (*ṣawm*). This chapter also explores mainstream Salafi-Jihadi positions on defensive jihad before explaining how the global jihad movement appropriated these opinions to license its war against the West as a legitimate and necessary defensive measure.

One of the most revered scholars of antiquity who retains popularity among the contemporary jihad movement is Abu Zakaryya al-

Dimashqi al-Dumyati (better known as "Ibn Nuhaas") who died in 1411. He wrote the *Book of Jihad*, which 'Abdallah 'Azzam had distributed among the Arab *mujahideen* in Afghanistan, describing it as "the best book on jihad."[6] It continues to influence fighters today and has been celebrated by notable figures within al-Qaeda, including Anwar al-Awlaki who provided a commentary on the book to inspire a new generation of *mujahideen*.[7] Ibn Nuhaas explained that jihad should constitute an article of faith, *īmān*, in its own right:

> If it weren't for Allah checking the nonbelievers through the believers and giving the believers authority to protect Islam and break the armies of disbelief, [then] disbelief would have reigned on earth and the true religion would have been eliminated. This proves that whatever is in this status [i.e. jihad] deserves to be a pillar of *īmān*.[8]

He was actually paraphrasing and building on a quote from the *Qur'an* itself which states: "and if it were not for Allah checking [some] people by means of others, the earth would have been corrupted, but Allah is full of bounty to the worlds."[9] 'Azzam read that verse in a similar fashion to Ibn Nuhaas and titled his first major fatwa on the war in Afghanistan *The defence of Muslim lands: the first obligation after īmān* (faith).[10] This is a remarkable statement. Whereas Ibn Nuhaas argued that jihad is a pillar of the faith, 'Azzam elevated its position to make it the foremost obligation after arriving at a belief in Islam itself. This was not entirely unprecedented. 'Azzam was largely parroting a statement attributed to Ibn Taymiyya where he said "the first obligation after *īmān* is the repulsion of the enemy aggressor who assaults the religion and the worldly affairs."[11]

A great deal of importance has been attached to jihad throughout Islamic history, with a number of classical works continuing to inspire the contemporary Salafi-Jihadi movement. In a clear attempt to emulate his predecessors, the first leader of al-Qaeda in Iraq, Abu Musab al-Zarqawi, argued that "next to faith, there is nothing more important than repulsing an assailant enemy who ruins the religion and the world."[12] Similarly, the current leader of al-Qaeda, Ayman al-Zawahiri, underscored just how much the group prioritised jihad by arguing that it "takes precedence over feeding the hungry, even if the hungry would starve as a result."[13]

Jihad as enduring worship

Abu Qatada argued that the entire notion of jihad is inextricably intertwined with the overriding purpose of creation itself—that God created man to worship him exclusively. In this context, disbelief and disobedience erode virtue, thereby affronting God while simultaneously challenging all those who serve him. Only jihad can stem the corrosive tide of defiance while safeguarding Islamic principles. "Jihad is a legislated, divine commandment for the establishment of the religion of Allah on the earth," writes Abu Qatada, "and to vanquish *fitna* from the earth."[14]

A number of theorists have argued that as a consequence jihad should not be seen as something anomalous, but should instead be considered an ordinary act of worship within the typical rubric of ritual Islamic practice. 'Abdallah 'Azzam was a key proponent of this view, having written that "neglecting jihad is like abandoning fasting and praying."[15] While reflecting on his experiences in Afghanistan, he also argued, "jihad is the most excellent form of worship, and by its means the Muslim can reach the highest of ranks [of paradise]."[16] Given that worship must be consistently featured in a devotional life, the duty to fight could not be regarded as something transient or exceptional. 'Azzam reiterated his opinion that jihad is bound together with the fundamental purposes of faith itself, arguing that it "cannot be separated from the constitution of this religion."[17] To underscore its enduring nature, he quoted from Sayyid Qutb's seminal work, *In the shade of the Qur'an*, which argued:

> If jihad had been a transitory phenomenon in the life of the Muslim *umma*, all these sections of the *Qur'anic* text would not be flooded with this type of verse! Likewise, so much of the *sunna* of the Messenger of Allah, would not be occupied with such matters. If jihad were a passing phenomenon of Islam, the Messenger of Allah would not have said the following words to every Muslim until the Day of Judgement, 'Whoever dies neither having fought (in jihad), nor having made up his mind to do so, dies on a branch of hypocrisy.'[18]

Similar ideas about the primacy of jihad and its spiritual dimensions are found in the work of Ibn Nuhaas. He stressed its importance by recounting an incident where three companions of the Prophet

Muhammad were sitting adjacent to his pulpit shortly before Friday prayers while comparing the virtues of serving pilgrims with those of jihad.[19] During their discussion, Muslims believe that Allah instructed the angel Gabriel (known as Jibrīl in Islam) to reveal the following verse of the *Qur'an*:

> Have you made the providing of water for the pilgrim and the maintenance of al-Masjid al-Haram [the sacred mosque] equal to [the deeds of] one who believes in Allah and the last day and strives in the cause of Allah? They are not equal in the sight of Allah. And Allah does not guide the wrongdoing people.[20]

Ibn Nuhaas consequently reasoned that no act of worship in Islam could be equivalent to jihad and that it constitutes "the pinnacle of Islam."[21] Similar views pervade contemporary thinking among Salafi-Jihadis. The first leader of al-Qaeda in Saudi Arabia was Yusuf al-'Uyayri, a cleric from Dammam who argued that jihad is not just an enduring feature of Islam but is also one of its rituals that has remained relatively unchanged over time.[22] Abu Musab al-Zarqawi therefore declared, "jihad will continue until the day of judgement."[23] Giving a sense of just how important this concept remains within Salafi-Jihadi thinking Abu Qatada concluded, "jihad is the identity of the Muslim in his existence."[24]

Authorising defensive declarations of jihad

The nature of jihad falls under two categories: offensive and defensive. It is generally accepted within both normative Islam and Salafi-Jihadi circles that only a rightful authority, such as the Caliph, can sanction the former. Defensive jihad is different. Alternative rules apply in this case because the situation is reactive—sparked in response to external aggression or occupation. There is historical precedent for this. Hulagu Khan led the Mongol siege of Baghdad and killed the last of the Abbasid Caliphs, al-Musta'sim Billah, after his troops finally overran the city in 1258.[25] The urgencies of the Mongol invasions meant that another Caliph was not appointed for the next three years until al-Mustansir assumed the title and moved the seat of the Caliphate from Baghdad to Cairo.[26] This break in succession from one Caliph to the next did not prevent physical resistance to the Mongols, with irregular and voluntary campaigns persisting until al-Mustansir was able to raise an army of his own.

Defensive jihad is borne of necessity and circumstances which, left unaddressed, would pose a threat to the community of Islam. Few derogate from this position, although a notable voice of dissent from within the Salafi community comes from Muhammad Nasir al-Din Albani who advocates an ultra-passive approach towards defensive jihad. While he does not dismiss the notion of jihad outright, he argues that it should be suspended in all circumstances if no *amīr* is present. "If the Muslims had no leader they stay away from all groups," he says.[27] For Albani the absence of a rightful leader is indicative of more serious and underlying problems with the Muslim *umma* itself—a lack of education and purification; *al-taṣfiya wa-l-tarbīya*.

This passive characteristic is precisely what defined the first thirteen years of Islam when the Prophet Muhammad spread his message of monotheism and personal perfection in Makkah before making *hijra* (migration) to Medina. It was only after the migration that divine injunctions relating to jihad began to emerge. "To do this jihad we need an *amīr*, to get this *amīr* we must work on the *taṣfiya* and *tarbīya*," Albani reasoned.[28] The absence of an appropriate authority to authorise jihad stems from personal shortcomings and imperfections, factors that must be addressed before jihad can be initiated. There is an important point to note about Albani's cautiousness here. He is not challenging the role of jihad in Islam, but is instead arguing for its suspension while people strive for better self-realisation:

> Jihad is, without doubt the pride of Islam and the basis of Islam, and the verses and *ḥadīths* regarding this are known to everybody inshallah [God willing]. But this jihad has its [own] conditions and introductions.[29]

Albani regarded the political and temporal decline of Muslim fortunes as stemming from their inability to realise the virtues of the *'aqīda* through *al-taṣfiya wa-l-tarbīya*. He therefore prioritised this ahead of everything. Taking this view to its most logical—albeit extreme—conclusion, Albani even issued a controversial and esoteric fatwa calling on Palestinians to leave the West Bank and Gaza because he reasoned they could not practice Islam properly under Israeli occupation. One of his students, Muqbil bin Hadi al-Wadi'i, similarly argued that the independence of Southern Yemen from British rule was undesirable because it resulted in a communist government that denied religion and killed Muslims.[30] These are exceptional views and are shared by only a very small number of Salafi scholars who otherwise regard defensive jihad as being automatically sanctioned once attacked by a foreign enemy.

Defensive jihad as necessity in Salafi-Jihadi thought

'Abdallah 'Azzam dismissed the type of reasoning advocated by Albani outright, although his work does not reference or refute him directly. Nonetheless, 'Azzam considered the issue of defensive jihad and its legitimacy in the absence of an *amīr* in his fatwa regarding the war in Afghanistan. One of the reasons given for Arab unwillingness to assist the Afghans stemmed from perceptions that they lacked an appropriate level of Islamic observance by smoking or wearing talismans. 'Azzam responded with two arguments. The first was practical and noted the impossibility of striving for perfection. Waiting for something that is unattainable before initiating jihad would be tantamount to effectively removing it from Islam. His second response was more theological and involved a principle known as the jurisprudence of balances, *fiqh al-muwāzanāt*. He asked readers:

> We must choose from two evils. Which is the greater evil: that Russia takes Afghanistan, turns it into a *kafir* country and forbids *Qur'an* and Islam for it, or jihad with a nation with sins and errors?[31]

'Azzam's argument was simple: the harm incurred by neglecting jihad far outweighed any shortcomings of the Afghan people. This chimed with the general consensus (*ijmā'*) of Islamic scholars which suggests that jihad is legitimate in such circumstances because its principal aim is to safeguard both Islam and Muslims. 'Azzam reasoned that the threat posed to Islamic practice in Afghanistan from the Soviet Union was so acute that the duty to resist it had become personally incumbent upon every individual Muslim (*farḍ al-'ayn*). "The first obligation after *īmān* is the repulsion of the enemy aggressor," 'Azzam wrote, quoting Ibn Taymiyya.[32] Saudi scholar 'Abdallah al-Ghunayman expressed similar sentiments:

> If the enemy attacks a land, everyone who is able is obliged to defend it, even the women are also obliged to fight. This was stated by the *fuqahā'* [jurists], because this is an individual obligation; the role of the leader is to

> organise. If there is a leader, all well and good; if there is no leader, the Muslims are still obliged to fight.[33]

This is where the specific aims of defensive jihad must be carefully understood. Whereas offensive jihad is a considered and deliberate act designed to win territorial acquisitions, defensive jihad arises organically and spontaneously in response to external political events. This might include foreign invasion, civil unrest, or another series of events resulting in the breakdown of social order. In these circumstances the aim is to remove whatever it is that endangers life or causes oppression. This is what Ghunayman explains above, pointing out there is no need to wait for an *amīr*. His presence is merely incidental, a bonus, "all well and good."

The premium attached to protecting the wider Muslim community is so great that it overrides a number of obligations that would otherwise govern inter-personal relationships. "No permission is required from the husband for the wife, the parent for the child, the creditor for the debtor," 'Azzam wrote. "The *umma* is called to march forward to protect its religion."[34] It follows that jihad is therefore licenced without an *amīr*. His absence "does not annul the obligation of fighting in the defence of Muslim lands," 'Azzam said.[35] He also reasoned that fighting in the defence of Islam would actually help foster the circumstances in which a Caliphate might emerge, given that jihad was helping to unify different nationalities under a common Islamist cause. He argued:

> We do not wait for the Caliphate to be restored because the Caliphate does not return through abstract theories, amassed knowledge and studying. Rather, jihad is the right way to reform the divided authorities to the ultimate authority of the Caliphate.[36]

The experience of the Abbasid Caliphate against the Mongols resonated particularly strongly for 'Azzam in this regard. After all, military resistance persisted even after al-Musta'sim Billah's death and arguably precipitated the restoration of a Caliph under Mamluk rule. Although history in itself is not a source (*uṣūl*) of *shari'a*, 'Azzam believed the story was instructive. Moreover, the lack of any serious scholarly condemnation of those who had continued to fight despite the absence of a Caliph could be seen as implying a consensus from religious authorities (*ijmā' al-a'imma*).

Within the contemporary jihad movement this concept was developed further by Anwar al-Awlaki who argued that God is the only *amīr* required for jihad because it is fought *fi sabīl Allah*, in the path of Allah. Linking jihad to an individual therefore risked negating, or at least diminishing, the role of God. "If we believe that jihad depends on individuals, then this leads to the weakening of *'aqīda* on jihad," he wrote. "It will alter the idea that jihad will continue until the Day of Judgement."[37]

Jihad would consequently have to exist independently of human agency in order to remain an enduring and constant principle of Islam in Salafi-Jihadi thought. Tethering it to an individual or titular position such as an *amīr* was not just wrong, but constituted an improper understanding of Islam itself—negating one of the faith's most important obligations: the command to fight; a duty that exists beyond both human agents and worldly consequences. Whether intentional or not, this view later satisfied a strategic necessity for al-Qaeda and affiliated groups by allowing them to promote "leaderless" or "lone wolf" acts of jihad.

Conclusion

Jihad occupies an important place within Salafi-Jihadism as something that represents the lifeblood of Islam, with its purpose being to simultaneously defend and promote the religion. This was how the concept first emerged and how the Prophet Muhammad originally encountered it. When he lived in Makkah during the first thirteen years of Islamic revelation, the religion existed without any warring doctrine despite the extreme persecution faced by Muhammad and his companions. Martyrdom was instead limited to a more passive form of the kind traditionally associated with the oppression of the early Christian Church by the Romans.[38] It is interesting to note that Islam's first martyr was a woman, Sumayyah bint Khayyat, who was killed by Abu Jahl, a prominent leader from the Quraysh—the tribe principally responsible for trying to suppress Islam during its incipient phases.[39]

The *hijra* to Medina changed all this. Arriving as a conqueror of sorts, the Prophet Muhammad was empowered through his status as the ruler of an early city-state, allowing him to adopt a more muscular approach towards his enemies. This explains the context of verse 22:39 which states: "Permission [to fight] has been given to those who are being fought, because they were wronged. And indeed, Allah is competent to give them victory."[40] Ibn Kathir has identified this as the first verse of jihad in the *Qur'an*.[41]

Given that jihad emerged as a response to persecution, it has traditionally enjoyed an elevated position within Islam. The first major confrontation is known as the Battle of Badr (624) and was an offensive campaign where the Prophet Muhammad led a group of fighters to ambush a series of caravans from the Quraysh. Muslims who survived the battle were called *badriyyun*, an appellation that marked them out. Relatives of those who died were comforted with assurances about the virtues of martyrdom which involve a long list of cosmic rewards including: immediate absolution, entry into the highest levels of paradise, salvation for family members, and exemption from *'adhāb al-qabr* (torment of the grave). Perhaps most importantly, Badr established a shift in the notion of martyrdom away from the passive and towards the active, where dying for the sake of God was not just something imposed on individuals, but could also be actively sought out.

Having won the battle, Muhammad was transformed. He found himself leading an emerging force in the Arabian Peninsula that was now empowered and willing to shape its own fortunes. They would confront and challenge the threats to their security, a point that was underscored by the killing of Abu Jahl in Badr—retribution for Sumayyah nine years after her murder. It was a jubilant moment for the *badriyyun* who were now, as Barnaby Rogerson has argued, "an exultant and heroic force."[42]

There were broader implications too. Badr and the latter history of Muhammad's experiences in Medina established jihad as an integral component of the faith. This is especially relevant in cases where the Islamic community finds itself under attack. Jihad becomes a decentralised concept at this point, requiring no central authority or agency. Legitimacy instead resides in the hands of individual actors, allowing Salafi-Jihadis to invoke precisely this principle in order to establish their authority and legitimise their activities.

3

APPLYING JIHAD IN SALAFI THOUGHT

Attacking the far enemy as a defensive measure

The idea of a non-state and irregular force of volunteer fighters marching off to become *mujahideen* gained popular traction in the modern era during the Afghan-Soviet war in the 1980s. Afghanistan had come under communist assault which, if successful, would have eradicated Islam from public life as it had already done in Central Asia. A small coterie of principally Sunni Arab men committed themselves to aiding the resistance. Arguments about defensive necessity were straightforward enough in that case, but required increasing sophistry as veterans of that conflict later began turning their hostility towards the West. Current jihadist movements have established a chain of causation which leads from episodes of oppression and tyranny in the Muslim world back to Western nations. The same line of reasoning has licenced attacks against both the Western and Muslim worlds.

The theological contortions of Salafi-Jihadi theorists became apparent after the 2003 invasion of Iraq, when militant Sunni groups felt compelled to explain their brutality—not just against Western coalition forces, but against fellow Muslims too. They achieved this by interpreting the laws on fighting (*qitāl*) and killing, equal retaliation (*qiṣāṣ*), and human shields (*tatarrus*) in expansive new ways. A novel doctrine of vicarious liability also emerged, where private individual citizens are held responsible, and punished, for the supposed crimes of their governments. This reasoning is informed by the consensual nature of the social contract in democratic states, where officials derive their authority to rule by a direct licence from their constituents. A standing government therefore rules only with the on-going and tacit approval of its citizens—prompting some Salafi-Jihadis to argue they can be held responsible for its shortcomings and excesses.

Redefining the nature of self defence

When 'Abdallah 'Azzam led the Arab Afghans during the 1980s he was not particularly enamoured with the United States, but did not regard it as an enemy either. Along with one of his closest associates, Tamim al-Adnani, he even undertook several trips to America during the war in order to raise funds for the Afghan *mujahideen*.[1] All this would change after 'Azzam's death in 1989 when some of the fighters who surrounded him took refuge first under Hasan al-Turabi in Sudan and then Mulla Omar in Afghanistan. These fighters reasoned that Western governments indirectly controlled Muslim countries through local proxies. All of the contemporary problems of the Muslim world including corruption, nepotism, political instability and repression were therefore the products of a Western conspiracy to contain Islam and keep Muslims in check.

Western support provided sustenance for these governments, explaining why the jihad movement had been unable to overrun them in places like Egypt, Libya and Syria despite years of trying. Whereas earlier theorists such as Muhammad 'Abd al-Salam Faraj had called for a direct confrontation with local Muslim rulers, the newly emerging jihad movement instead committed itself to focusing on the power behind the throne. For them, there was no need for Hulagu Khan's army to have marched on Baghdad in the thirteenth century, or for the Soviet Union to have invaded Afghanistan in the twentieth. The West was at war with Islam through more amorphous and insidious means. The recalibration of Salafi-Jihadi enmities that followed principally took shape from 1992–1996, when the 9/11 Commission believes Osama bin Laden first began turning his attention towards the United States.[2] This refocusing of priorities has been described as a decision to confront the "far enemy."[3]

War served as the catalyst for this change. Saddam Hussein's invasion of Kuwait had a transformative effect on radical Salafi thinking because it brought American troops physically in to the Gulf, thereby confirming the malignant motives of Western machinations, to the Salafi-Jihadi mind. During an interview in 1996 with Abdel Bari Atwan, editor of the London based Arabic newspaper *Al-Quds al-Arabi*, Osama bin Laden explained:

> We believe that the US Government committed the biggest mistake when it entered a peninsula which no non-Muslim nation has ever entered for 14 centuries despite the presence of imperialist forces in the region. They all feared to enter the two holy mosques area and remained in the fringes, such as Yemen and Oman. The British and others respected the feelings of more than 1 billion Muslims, which is why they did not occupy the land of the two holy mosques… [America's] entry was arbitrary and a reckless action. They have entered into a confrontation with a nation whose population is 1 billion Muslims.[4]

Bin Laden also condemned the former Grand Mufti of Saudi Arabia, 'Abd al-'Aziz bin Baz, as "irresponsible" for sanctioning the presence of Western troops in the Arabian Peninsula; a move he claimed had "insulted the dignity of the nation and smeared its honour, and denigrated its sanctities."[5] For many Salafis, the arrival of American troops in Saudi Arabia represented a belligerent move by the United States. By contrast, the more politically inclined Salafis of the *ṣaḥwa* (awakening) movement took a different approach. One member who was later exiled to Britain, Muhammad al-Massari, explained, "The U.S. did not invade Saudi Arabia. It was invited in by the Saudi royal family. The regime invited the U.S. and [therefore] it has to pay the price."[6]

These diverging views explain the bifurcation of approaches between Salafi-Jihadis and those of a more activist-challenger orientation. For the latter, the decadence of Muslim regimes remained their own. Yes, the West may have a relationship with corrupt Muslim rulers, but it is the regimes themselves that remain the principal causes of oppression and wrongdoing. Remove them and the rest will follow. By contrast, Salafi-Jihadis concluded that the West was the root cause of all suffering in the Muslim world. They also saw the entire global system such as international law and banking, development aid, and the United Nations, as being the tools of modern colonialism.

The malignancy of this Western international order was confirmed by events. The 1990s produced a flurry of activity in Arab-Israeli relations and, for a moment at least, the prospect of genuine peace seemed likely. Israeli and Palestinian representatives met in Norway in 1993 and signed the Oslo Accords, while Yasser Arafat—once the emblem of Arab resistance—agreed to recognise Israel and renounced violence. Elsewhere, the Jordanians and Israelis were also inching towards normalisation, signing a peace treaty the following year. The apparent acquiescence of these Arab leaders, underscored by their willingness to broker deals with Israel, only confirmed the treachery of their agenda. "A generation has come to realise that the U.N. is nothing but an instrument in the hands of the Jews and Crusaders to exterminate, and rob, the wealth of Muslims," Bin Laden wrote in June 1994.[7]

Events the following year only reaffirmed this view. The United Nations declared its first ever 'Safe Zone' in Srebrenica during the Bosnia War and deployed a United Nations Protection Force (UNPROFOR). Scores of Muslim refugees moved there in the expectation of security only to be massacred by Serb fighters once they overran the town in July 1995. The United Nations had not only failed to prevent the fall of Srebrenica but then sat by idly while the subsequent massacre took place. Within a matter of weeks Osama bin Laden wrote another letter explaining how the U.N. was nothing but "a tool to implement the Crusaders' plan to kill the causes of the Islamic nation and its people."[8]

In this way a chain of causation was established, whereby the West orchestrated Crusader plots to undermine Islam. Sometimes it would assert itself directly—as was the case in Saudi Arabia where the United States established military bases. Elsewhere, however, and much more often it would favour indirect measures to secure its interests from afar, such as the Oslo Accords or the Israeli-Jordanian Peace Treaty. "All of this is done in the name of American interests," Bin Laden said.[9] Based on this logic there is barely any difference between the Soviet invasion of Afghanistan in the 1980s and Bill Clinton's attempts to sponsor peace deals in the Middle East. Their tactics may have differed—dialogue and diplomatic influence instead of war and direct control—but the aims remain the same: subjugating the Muslim world and its interests.

This belief would pervade the Salafi-Jihadi worldview and has been one of its most enduring characteristics. The targeting of American interests began in earnest. Osama bin Laden issued a remarkably frank and forthright fatwa in 1996 declaring war against the United States. Magnus Ranstorp argues that it (and a subsequent fatwa in 1998) presented "a sophisticated mixture of religious legitimation for jihad… coupled with an astute political analysis of accumulated Muslim grievances."[10] In the first document, Bin Laden explained:

> The people of Islam have been afflicted with oppression, hostility, and injustice by the Judeo-Christian alliance and its supporters. This shows our enemies' belief that Muslims' blood is the cheapest and that their property and wealth is merely loot. Your blood has been spilt in Palestine and Iraq, and the horrific images of the massacre in Qana in Lebanon are still fresh in people's minds. The massacres that have taken place in Tajikistan, Burma, Kashmir, Assam, the Philippines, Fatani, Ogaden, Somalia, Eritrea, Chechnya, and Bosnia-Herzegovina send shivers down our spines and stir up our passions. All this has happened before the eyes and ears of the world, but the blatant imperial arrogance of America, under the cover of the immoral United Nations, has prevented the dispossessed from arming themselves. So the people of Islam realised that they were the fundamental target of the hostility of the Judeo-Crusader alliance.[11]

When two American embassies were simultaneously bombed in Kenya and Tanzania in 1998, Osama bin Laden explained away the attacks with blithe indifference. "My word to American journalists is not to ask why we did that but ask what their government has done that forced us to defend ourselves," he said.[12] "These people are resisting the forces of world infidelity that occupied their land. Why should the United States get angry when the people resist its aggressions?"[13] Almost half a decade later Osama bin Laden touched on the very same issues in his *Letter to the American People*, which attempted to rationalise the 9/11 attacks. Al-Qaeda attacked the United States, he suggested, because "you attacked us and continue to attack us."[14] He proceeded:

> Under your supervision, consent and orders, the governments of our countries, which act as your agents, attack us on a daily basis; these governments prevent our people from establishing the Islamic *shari'a*, using violence and lies to do so.[15]

This passage clearly illustrates the growing belief in Bin Laden's mind that the United States controls Muslim lands by proxy. It is the original source of all hostility against the Islamist project to overthrow local regimes and replace them with an Islamic system. "End your support of the corrupt leaders in our countries," Osama bin Laden warned the American people, "do not interfere in our politics and method of education."[16]

The rules of *qitāl*

Although jihadist violence is often characterised by nihilistic brutality it is neither whimsical nor irrational. Instead, there is a broad framework of laws which govern the rules of jihad, constituting the *jus in bello* of Islamic war. The framework is broad and overarching, protecting the lives of civilians, the weak, elderly, women, non-combatants, animals, livestock, and woodland.[17] This is well established in normative Islamic law and is also underscored by the consensus of the Prophet Muhammad's companions, known as *ijmā' al-Ṣahāba*—a source of law in Sunni jurisprudence. When the first Caliph, Abu Bakr al-Siddiq, dispatched an army to Syria shortly after the Prophet's death he codified a series of rules for combat which were universally agreed upon by his contemporaries. Soldiers fighting on his behalf were told:

> Stop, oh people, that I may give you ten rules for your guidance in the battlefield. Do not commit treachery or deviate from the right path. You must not mutilate dead bodies. Neither kill a child, nor a woman, nor an aged man. Bring no harm to the trees, nor burn them with fire, especially those which are fruitful. Slay not any of the enemy's flock, save for your food. You are likely to pass by people who have devoted their lives to monastic services, leave them alone.[18]

Niaz Shah argues that verse 2:190 of the *Qur'an* informed this view by establishing the ethos of the Islamic conduct of war.[19] "Fight in the way of Allah those who fight you but do not transgress," it states. "Indeed, Allah does not like transgressors."[20] This verse imposes firm limits and draws a line against excesses, making it clear that God will punish those who overstep the bounds.

The status of non-Muslim civilians as 'protected persons'

Within the framework of these prohibitions, militant theorists had never given much serious consideration to the status of non-Muslim civilians. Their previous military campaigns were principally focused against government targets in Muslim countries like Algeria or Egypt, where non-Muslims did not feature in a prominent way. Those campaigns therefore focused on ideas such as *al-walā' wa-l-barā'*, *takfīr*, and *bughāt* (rebellion)—which are discussed later in the book. It was only when the Salafi-Jihadi movement later began diverting its attention towards the West that this issue came under serious discussion.

Two of the most important books that explore the status of non-Muslim civilians were produced by al-Tibyān Publications in 2004 and offer a vivid insight into Salafi-Jihadi thinking on the topic. They argue that the general rule (*aṣl*) in Islam is that the blood, wealth and honour of non-Muslims is not protected from assault.[21] To arrive at this conclusion they use the jurisprudential principle of *dalālāt*, which relates to textual implications and allows for inferences to be drawn from divine texts. A crucial subsection of this jurisprudential field is called *mafhūm al-mukhālafa*, which is a principle that relates to "the understanding of the opposite," meaning there are situations where the opposite deduction of a positive command can be taken as law.[22] The books from al-Tibyān consequently use various *ḥadīths* to justify their belief about the general permissibility of attacking non-Muslims. For example, one of the *ḥadīth* they use states the following:

> Whoever says *'lā ilaha illā-Allah'* and disbelieves in what is worshipped besides Allah, then his wealth and his blood are unlawful (i.e. protected) and his account is for Allah.[23]

Using the principle of *mafhūm al-mukhālafa*, the authors conclude that "it is the characteristic of *īmān* [faith] which protects the blood and wealth of the believers, and this is what distinguishes them and their inviolability from the disbelievers."[24] Thus, despite the absence of anything in the text regarding non-Muslims, the principle of opposite deduction leads to the conclusion that only Muslim life enjoys sanctity and the right of inviolability. "The characteristic of disbelief is what permits the blood and wealth of the disbelievers," it states in al-Tibyān's *Essay Regarding the Basic Rule of the Blood, Wealth, and Honour of the Disbelievers*.[25]

Restrictions on mafhūm al-mukhālafa

The use of *mafhūm al-mukhālafa* as a jurisprudential tool is deeply contested and generally discouraged. Shafi'i scholars argue that it can only be used in very limited cases where it supports or gives credence to a positive statement found elsewhere in Islamic scripture.[26] Its role is therefore merely to affirm a positive command found elsewhere within the body of Islam's divine texts. The Hanafi school prohibits its use altogether for examining the *Qur'an* and *sunna*. Instead, they argue that it can only be used to inform deductive reasoning with regards to *ijtihād* (independent juristic reasoning) or *ḥukm* (commands).[27]

Even contemporary Salafi-Jihadis believe that *mafhūm al-mukhālafa* should not be used without some constraints. Thus, while they believe the lives of non-Muslims are not generally protected, they also recognise a number of exceptions to this rule. This includes exemptions for women, children, and the elderly—provided, of course, they are non-combatants. "They have protection due to the [religious] texts excluding them from the original ruling," says Yusuf al-'Uyayri.[28] This view is supported by other clerics from within the contemporary jihad movement such as Sayyid Imam al-Sharif.[29] He argues that although there is a general ruling in place which protects them, there are also additional securities (*amān*) which can further safeguard their blood in certain circumstances.

This can include the payment of a tax for protection (known as the *jizya* or *amān al-thimma*); when a non-Muslim is seeking knowledge about Islam (*amān al-jawār*); when there is a treaty between two nations (*amān al-ṣulḥ*); or when a Muslim lives as a minority among non-Muslims and enjoys a covenant of security (*'aqd al-amān*) with them.[30] Taken together, these caveats provide a series of impediments against the whimsical or wanton killing of disbelievers and pose a practical challenge to the actions of militants who desire to launch attacks in overwhelmingly non-Muslim countries. To overcome this some Salafi-Jihadi theorists have argued that these restrictions are neither absolute nor rigid, but are instead malleable and subject to change. Al-Tibyān publications explains:

> Protection is not absolute, nor is it unrestricted. Because, indeed, there are circumstances in which it is permissible to kill them [non-Muslims] both intentionally and unintentionally. In these situations the restriction is removed and...[they] revert back to the original ruling of the people of *kufr* [disbelief].[31]

Al-Qaeda traditionally used four main arguments when indiscriminately targeting civilians in the West, two of which relate to deliberate and intentional targeting while the others arise in circumstances where the deaths of "protected" persons arise out of necessity.[32] All of these arguments were outlined in a document published in 2004 which explained the "mandate of the heroes and the legality of the operations in New York and Washington."[33] These arguments, which al-Qaeda has used to justify 9/11 and which it has popularised ever since, are explored in turn below. They include the belief: (a) that ordinary citizens of Western states are neither innocent nor civilians, because they are vicariously liable for the actions of their governments; (b) that civilian deaths are justified under the law of equal measures, *qiṣāṣ* or equal retaliation; (c) the use of human shields, *tatarrus*, sanctions the targeting of civilians; and (d) it is not always practical or possible to distinguish between civilians and combatants when an assault is obligated. The practical outgrow of these arguments is that the definition of "non-combatant" is constructed through narrow strictures, while those who can be classed as combatants—or, at least, considered legitimate targets—are conceived of in the broadest of brushstrokes.

Qiṣāṣ: the law of equal retaliation

"It is allowed for Muslims to kill protected ones among unbelievers as an act of reciprocity," al-Qaeda stated as justification for the 9/11 terrorist attacks. "If the unbelievers have targeted Muslim women, children, and the elderly, it is permissible for Muslims to respond in kind and kill those similar to those whom the unbelievers killed."[34] This argument is based on the Islamic principle of *qiṣāṣ*, or retaliation in kind, and is commonly used by members of the global jihad movement to justify the targeting of civilians.[35]

A comparable idea within the Christian tradition would be the principle of *lex talionis*, or "an eye for an eye."[36] The concept of *qiṣāṣ* works in the same way and is an established part of the Islamic penal code alongside other punishments such as *ḥudūd* and *ta'zīr*.[37] The *ḥudūd* (singular: *hadd*) applies to crimes for which a specific punishment is stipulated in the *Qur'an* or *ḥadīth*, for which perpetrators have no worldly recourse to clemency or pardon. This includes crimes such as fornication, adultery, theft and drinking alcohol. *Ta'zīr* punishments, by contrast, are entirely discretionary and apply in cases where neither the *ḥudūd* nor *qiṣāṣ* are applicable. *Qiṣāṣ* typically relates to cases of murder, manslaughter, or acts involving physical mutilation (such as the loss of limbs) and creates a framework for the victim (or their families) to seek retributive justice.[38] *Qiṣāṣ* is therefore concerned with achieving equity between individuals, providing restitution between criminals and their victims. This is enshrined within the *Qur'an* itself. Verse 2:178 states:

> O you who have believed, prescribed for you is legal retribution for those murdered—the free for the free, the slave for the slave, and the female for the female.[39]

And 5:45 which states:

> We ordained for them therein a life for a life, an eye for an eye, a nose for a nose, an ear for an ear, a tooth for a tooth, and wounds for wounds as legal retribution.[40]

The contemporary Salafi-Jihadi movement has been particularly innovative with the concept of *qiṣāṣ* in two ways. Firstly, they have taken an instrument of justice intended for private individuals and have applied it to international affairs. Yusuf al-'Uyayri explained this in his important work, *Ḥaqīqat al-ḥarb al-Ṣalībiyyah al-Jadīda* (The Truth of the new Crusader War) by arguing that *qiṣāṣ* has a political dimension based on the principle of *mafhūm al-muwāfaqa* which means "the understanding of compliance," a concept that is related to *mafhūm al-mukhālafa* (see above).[41] This states that a logical inference can be drawn from scriptural rulings provided it builds on an explicit and unambiguous command already found within Islamic texts. 'Uyayri therefore argues that because *qiṣāṣ* offers restitution for individuals then "it is even more correct and more worthy to deal with the *kāfir ḥarbī* [belligerent/warring disbeliever]."[42] It is worth noting that *mafhūm al-muwāfaqa* is a jurisprudential tool rejected by most scholars—including those from a Salafi background—but is one that is frequently cited in al-Qaeda's literature.

Secondly, *qiṣāṣ* is traditionally restricted to cases where the aggressor is known. Retribution is carried out only against the specific individual guilty of having inflicted the original harm, not against their families, spouse, or offspring. By contrast, when militants apply *qiṣāṣ* as an instrument of international law they hold every citizen-stranger of an enemy state liable for the actions of their government. "The blood pouring out of Palestine must be equally revenged," wrote Osama bin Laden in 2002. "You must know that the Palestinians do not cry alone; their women are not widowed alone; their sons are not orphaned alone."[43] The implication was that Bin Laden intended to widow Israeli women and orphan their children with random and indiscriminate attacks. By attributing the suffering of Muslims in Palestine, Iraq, Sudan, Kashmir, Bosnia, and the Philippines to the United States, Yusuf al-'Uyayri argued that under the rules of *qiṣāṣ*, "it would be perfectly permissible for us [al-Qaeda] to kill around 10 million American civilians."[44]

The idea that *qiṣāṣ* should apply as a means of redress in cases of modern warfare is well established among Salafi-Jihadi theorists. A number of clerics including Hamud al-Shu'aybi, 'Ali al-Khudair, Abu Jandal al-Azdi, 'Abd al-'Aziz al-Jarbu, and Abu Qatada al-Filastini all ruled that 9/11 was justified based on *qiṣāṣ*.[45] None of them were active members of al-Qaeda, but instead belonged to the broader intellectual milieu of Salafi-Jihadi thought. Yet it is not just Salafi-Jihadi theorists who have applied *qiṣāṣ* as a tool of retribution in international affairs. In the late 1990s Muhammad bin Salih al-'Uthaymin also endorsed this view, despite being a Salafi preacher rooted firmly within the Saudi clerical establishment. He had even held a number of official positions including one on the Council of Scholars and regularly preached at the Masjid al-Haram in Makkah before his death in January 2001. "They kill our women, we kill their women," he told a gathering in Saudi Arabia. "This is justice."[46] The emphatic endorsement of *qiṣāṣ* in this way reveals the extent to which the idea had become normalised within Salafi circles by the late 1990s.

Methods of retaliation

Not only has *qiṣāṣ* been expanded into a concept enveloping international affairs, but so too have the methods by which retaliation can be sought. For example, al-Tibyān Publications argues that anything is permissible when seeking retribution provided the act does not constitute something which is expressly forbidden within Islam. For example, they cite an absolute prohibition against inflicting death by sodomy as a form of retribution because of Islamic injunctions against the practice.[47] This view was taken to its logical—and most extreme—conclusion by the Saudi cleric Nasir ibn Hamad al-Fahd in a now infamous book justifying the use of Weapons of Mass Destruction against enemy states. "Anyone who considers America's aggressions against Muslims and their lands during the past decades," wrote Fahd, "will conclude that striking her [with WMD] is permissible merely on the basis of the rule of treating as one has been treated [*qiṣāṣ*]. No other arguments need to be mentioned."[48]

Ayman al-Zawahiri adopted this view and developed it half a decade later in *The Exoneration*—a long, rambling book which is ostensibly a rebuttal of accusations levelled against al-Qaeda by a former member and theorist, Sayyid Imam al-Sharif. "Is it not all the more proper for us to use such means [WMD] by way of equivalence?" he asks. "To bomb them as they are bombing us and blow them up as they are blowing us up."[49] To support this position, both Fahd and Zawahiri used verses of the *Qur'an* such as 2:194 which states, "whoever has assaulted you, then assault him in the same way that he has assaulted you."[50] There are also other verses such as 42:40 and 16:126 which stipulate similar injunctions. Based on similar reasoning, Osama bin Laden argued that al-Qaeda should be free to use whatever means it chooses against its enemies. In a statement issued in January 2004 he declared:

> We do not differentiate between those dressed in military uniforms and civilians. American history does not distinguish between civilians and military, not even women and children. They are the ones who used [nuclear] bombs against Nagasaki. Can these bombs distinguish between infants and the military?[51]

The Algerian war: the first use of qiṣāṣ *as a military tool*

The first practical application of *qiṣāṣ* as an instrument of war in the modern era emerged during the Algerian civil war (1991–2002). Fighters returning from the Afghan-Soviet conflict employed it as a guiding principle there: first against government troops, and then against the French after the Islamic Salvation Front (FIS) was prevented from seizing power.[52] The Groupe Islamique Armé (GIA), conducted this campaign, having emerged as one of the main armed opposition groups in 1993.[53] Osama bin Laden supported the cause by donating funds to Qamar al-Din Kharban, a contemporary from the Afghan war.[54] Kharban enjoyed more than just financial aid. He was also being supported by a small number of foreign fighters and was offered theological advice from clerics who identified with the more militant aspects of Salafi thought.[55]

The GIA adopted a confrontational posture from the outset. Its leader, Cherif Ghousmi, had close ties with the al-Qaeda theoretician Abu Musab al-Suri throughout much of the war and even declared a Caliphate in Algeria, appointing himself as the *amīr al-mu'minīn*. Suri was responsible for encouraging Ghousmi to attack France, offering an early insight into how al-Qaeda was beginning to rationalise the use of *qiṣāṣ* as a retributive instrument against Western states deemed to be hostile to Islam. He recollected:

> I recommended to the GIA *amīr* at the time, Abu 'Abdallah Ahmad [Ghousmi] and his leadership that they strike deeply in France in order to deter and punish her for her war against the GIA and for the French support for the dictatorial military regime [in Algeria]... To strike against France is our right. We are at war, and we do not play games, and our enemies should know that.[56]

All of the necessary components for *qiṣāṣ* are present here. France had assailed the rights of Algerian Muslims by "waging war against the GIA" and "supporting the dictatorial military regime." Suri therefore concluded that the GIA was justified in retaliating against France, both as a punishment and deterrence. Although Ghousmi's leadership of the GIA was short lived, his successor persisted in trying to make Suri's vision into reality. Djamel Zitouni (1994–1996) began aggressively targeting French civilians, taking the Algerian war into the French public space. The most dramatic attack he orchestrated was the hijacking of Air France flight 8969 in December 1994. According to the *Al-Ansar Newsletter*, a GIA magazine published in London, the group had initially planned to crash the plane into the Eiffel Tower although this aspect of the plan proved too challenging. The group maintained its assault against the French throughout 1995, planting a series of bombs across Paris—seven in total—resulting in a handful of civilian fatalities.

The use of Suri's advice by the GIA perfectly captures three of the central issues already discussed in this chapter. These are that the

French government is to blame for the problems in Algeria because it supported the cancellation of elections which brought the FIS to power; that French civilians are to be held responsible for the actions of their government; and that *qiṣāṣ* stipulates both the scope and method of redress.

Dissent within the Salafi-Jihadi movement regarding qiṣāṣ

The use of *qiṣāṣ* as a tool of generalised and indiscriminate attacks is not universally accepted among Salafi-Jihadi scholars. Notable examples of dissent have come from Abu Basir al-Tartusi and Sayyid Imam al-Sharif, both of whom, despite their connections to militant groups, grew weary of the promiscuous manner in which *qiṣāṣ* was being used by the mid-2000s. Despite having been a member of al-Qaeda, the abuse of *qiṣāṣ* was one of things Sharif highlighted when he later turned against the group.[57]

Tartusi shared those concerns. He had moved to London after the Afghan-Soviet war but maintained close links with the leadership of the GIA, just as Abu Musab al-Suri had.[58] Tartusi did not express any serious concerns over the GIA's attacks in France, but broke publicly with Salafi-Jihadi consensus after the 7/7 attacks in 2005 when the London public transport system was targeted by four suicide bombers. There are four arguments he used in order to rebuke those who endorsed and supported the attacks.[59]

The first argument he advanced was that it is unacceptable to use *mafhūm al-mukhālafa* (the understanding of compliance) to justify indiscriminate attacks against civilians. The evidence for its use as a jurisprudential tool was too weak for Tartusi. He argued that such attacks contradict explicit textual commands which prohibit the killing of civilians, which cannot be derogated from merely on the basis of *mafhūm al-mukhālafa*. "The *shari'a* texts have stringently forbidden targeting the children and women of the polytheists with any type of killing or fighting, no matter what the reasons and causes for doing so," he wrote.[60] To reinforce this view he argued that there are no precedents from the Prophet Muhammad's life to support the view that civilians can be killed indiscriminately.

Secondly, Tartusi argued that Salafi-Jihadis have misinterpreted verse 2:194 of the *Qur'an*, which states, "whoever has assaulted you, then assault him in the same way that he has assaulted you."[61] For Tartusi, this verse does not allow for unfettered or unchecked responses. Retaliation must still be in accordance with *shari'a* guidelines. This was a view Sharif had echoed in his own work. He argued that al-Qaeda only offered a partial consideration of verse 2:194 of which the latter part goes on to state, "But fear Allah, and know that Allah is with those who restrain themselves."[62]

This latter part of the verse cannot be decoupled from the former. Yes, retaliation is permitted—but only within a prescribed and regulated framework. Tartusi also argued that any act that is ordinarily *ḥarām* limits what can be done under *qiṣāṣ*. There is an important distinction here from the limits stipulated in the al-Tibyān publication. For them, it is only an act of *kufr*—rather than one which is *ḥarām*—that acts as a bar. The difference is one of degrees, but is crucial nonetheless. *Ḥarām* actions are those which are forbidden and consequently result in sin, whereas those which are *kufr* are of such magnitude that they lead to disbelief. Tartusi and Sharif were therefore challenging the view that *ḥarām* acts can become *ḥalāl* in cases where *qiṣāṣ* applies.

Thirdly, Tartusi and Sharif argued that the laws of *qiṣāṣ* can only be used to provide restitution or retaliation against a specific individual who has been tried in a court of law. Applying the principle indiscriminately punishes random people for crimes not committed by them and which were not necessarily committed in their name. Tartusi used verse 6:16 from the *Qur'an* to support this view, with the verse stating that "none shall carry the burdens of another."[63] Similarly, Sharif argued that al-Qaeda was simply killing people on the basis of nationality alone. This, he insisted, is a "monstrosity," which "makes three hundred million Americans equivalent to a single individual [the President]."[64]

The fourth bar to killing civilians focused specifically on children. "Children are not to be killed, because according to the *shari'a*, they are pure souls," Tartusi argued.[65] This is an expression of the Islamic view that all children are born free of sin and have a *fiṭra*, natural inclination, which predisposes them towards the *tawḥīd* of Allah. This makes them free of any liabilities until puberty, after which accountability begins, and then free will leads them either towards the servitude or disobedience of God. As Islam does not hold children accountable for their actions, Tartusi argued it was wrong to target them, because they "do not have the slightest intent or understanding in regards to the actions of their fathers."[66]

The reception to these views was frosty and, at times, provoked a fierce debate on jihadi internet forums.[67] Within a month of the 7/7 attacks Tartusi had been forced to issue three separate statements clarifying his position, revealing the intensity of the backlash against him. Sharif's criticisms also provoked a flurry of activity, not least with the publication of a lengthy treatise from Ayman al-Zawahiri, *The Exoneration*, in which he attempted to refute his claims. The real aim of both Tartusi and Sharif was to restore the balance of Salafi-Jihadi thinking on *qiṣāṣ*. The laissez-faire manner in which it had been deployed in the mid-2000s was mistaken rather than monstrous. Crucially, they still accepted the principle, but insisted it must operate within a highly structured and measured legal framework.

Vicarious liability

After 9/11 a group of sixty American public intellectuals wrote a letter expressing their support for the "War on Terror," prompting two responses from Osama bin Laden. The first was to Saudi intellectuals who had urged their American counterparts to embrace a more balanced doctrine of peaceful coexistence. The second was to the authors of the letter themselves, and was titled, "Why we are fighting you." It is a straightforward and rather matter-of-fact document citing a litany of well-known grievances. "You attacked us," Bin Laden wrote, noting American involvement in Palestine, Iraq, Saudi Arabia, Kashmir, Chechnya, and Somalia.[68] His complaints were numerous: American support for anti-jihadist elements in some countries, its relationship with Muslim dictators in others, and seemingly lopsided trading agreements in other places. "You may dispute that the above [grievances] do not justify aggression against civilians for crimes they did not commit and offences in which they did not partake," wrote Bin Laden, before explaining:

> This argument contradicts your continual repetition that America is the land of freedom, and freedom's leaders in this world...the American people have the ability and choice to refuse the policies of their government and even to change it if they want.[69]

In this way the democratic process became the mechanism through which al-Qaeda began holding ordinary citizens responsible for the actions of their government. Their culpability was further compounded through taxation which "funds the planes that bomb us."[70] This view does not discriminate between those who actively participate in the mechanisms of the state and those who do not. An apathetic non-voter who pays no tax is therefore just as culpable as an evangelical partisan who canvases for, and financially supports, his elected leader. What matters is that both individuals have the ability and opportunity to influence the policies of their government, and are accordingly held responsible for its actions. "The Americans deserve what they're getting," Ayman al-Zawahiri told al-Sahab, al-Qaeda's media production wing, in 2007. "They chose this liar [George W. Bush] two times, so let them pay the price for their choice."[71]

This was an entirely novel development even within the radical strictures of the Salafi-Jihadi movement. Prior to 9/11 militant Islamist campaigns had largely been confined to Muslim countries such as Syria, Egypt, Libya and Algeria. Those conflicts were often framed around the doctrine of *būghat* (rebellion) which has its roots in the principle of *takfir* (see chapter 4). Indeed, it can be said that just as the development of *takfir*—and associated ideas—were a necessary precursor towards licensing intra-Muslim violence, so it was that the principles of vicarious liability first allowed transnational jihadist groups to focus their attention on the West. That idea was already being popularised by Osama bin Laden as early as 1997 when he told CBS News, "all Americans are our enemies, not just the ones who fight us directly but also the ones who pay their taxes."[72] Views like this were well entrenched among Salafi-Jihadi clerics who used it to express support for the 9/11 attacks. The Saudi scholar Hamud al-Shu'aybi offered the clearest elucidation of how al-Qaeda's supporters viewed the matter, arguing:

> We should know that whatever decision the non-Muslim state, America, takes—especially critical decisions which involve war—it is taken based on opinion poll and/or voting within the house of representatives and senate, which represent directly, the exact opinion of the people they represent—the people of America—through their representatives in the Parliament [sic]. Based on this, any American who voted for war is like a fighter, or at least a supporter… [The victims] may be part of those who

> did not participate directly in the war but helped with their wealth or opinions, these cannot be called "innocent," nay they are among the fighters and part of the strength of the enemy.[73]

Shu'aybi's views are important in so far as they give an insight into how adherents of the Salafi-Jihadi worldview regarded 9/11. He was not a member of al-Qaeda but nonetheless accepted the view that ordinary Americans could not be deemed "innocent" and were therefore legitimate targets for attack. In this respect, Shu'aybi was emblematic of the movement as a whole.

Vicarious liability and jus in bello *principles*

These views ostensibly place Salafi-Jihadi beliefs at odds with normative Islamic theology regarding *jus in bello* principles which hold that the lives of protected non-combatants are inviolable. To reconcile this, jihadi theorists exploit ambiguities arising from one of Ibn Taymiyya's most important works on the relationship between private citizens and the state in *al-Siyāsa al-Shari'a* (the political *shari'a*).[74] Ibn Taymiyya offers a substantive digression into the religious and moral doctrine of jihad in one passage, explaining:

> As for those who cannot offer resistance or cannot fight, such as women, children, monks, old people, the blind, handicapped and their likes, they shall not be killed, unless they actually fight with words and acts… We may only fight those who fight us when we want to make the religion of Allah victorious… The reason is that Allah has [only] permitted to shed blood if that is necessary for the welfare of the creation… The unbelief of those who do not hinder the Muslims from establishing Allah's religion is only prejudicial to themselves.[75]

The definition of civilian in this passage is sufficiently ambiguous to allow for various constructions of its meaning because their non-combatant status is linked to their capacity. Only those "who cannot offer resistance" are exempted, although there is no objective standard by which to measure this. Moreover, words alone are enough to constitute fighting, further blurring the distinction between civilians and combatants. Osama bin Laden seized on this in the aftermath of 9/11 and argued, "it is allowed for Muslims to kill protected ones among unbelievers on the condition that the protected ones have assisted in combat, whether in deed, word, mind, or any other form of assistance."[76] By the reasoning already explored above, this encompasses almost every citizen of non-Muslim countries because of their day-to-day activities.

Human shields (*tatarrus*)

The doctrine relating to human shields, *tatarrus*, is complex but nonetheless important to understanding another way in which militants have justified the deaths of civilians. "It is allowed for Muslims to kill protected ones among unbelievers when the enemy is shielded by their women or children," al-Qaeda argued when it sought to provide a rationale for the 9/11 attacks.[77] It is important to distinguish precisely what constitutes a human shield in this context because the way it is used in Islamic legal discussions is different from its ordinary everyday meaning. For present purposes a human shield is someone who is caught up as an unintended victim of an attack, or someone who might popularly be referred to as "collateral damage." An example is illustrative here.

A terrorist group might place a bomb on a public transit system with the intention of killing civilian commuters. They would justify this with reference to *qiṣāṣ* by arguing that the enemy had bombed their urban centres and killed civilians, so this was an act of retaliation in kind. By contrast, the same group might place a bomb next to a government building intending to kill a prominent politician or employees of the state in response to their policies. In the process, a neighbouring school is also destroyed and the children inside are killed. In this case, fatalities in that building would be explained away with reference to the laws of *tatarrus*. In essence, the rules relating to *tatarrus* apply whenever and wherever civilians are intermixed with legitimate targets. They are killed typically due to misfortune or because they cannot be reasonably distinguished and separated out from the intended target.

When considered in this way the rules of *tatarrus* mirror—albeit unintentionally—the doctrine of military necessity, distinction, and proportionality as it relates to collateral damage in international humanitarian law. This is, after all, the primary concern of *tatarrus*: establishing a framework in which the calculus for collateral damage can be assessed while also limiting its frequency. By challenging the way in which *tatarrus* has been traditionally viewed by scholars, contemporary militant movements have sought to broaden and dilute the threshold of acceptability for killing human shields.

Arguments for the permissibility of killing human shields

To justify the killing of human shields, militant theorists frequently cite two incidents from the life of the Prophet Muhammad. The first comes from the Siege of Taif in 630 which followed the Battle of Hunayn. After Hunayn was overcome, a group of fighters had managed to escape from the town and fled to Taif, which was a heavily fortified redoubt.[78] The Prophet's men pursued the fighters but were unable to breach the city's defences. To overwhelm the fighters inside they erected a mangonel—an ancient military catapult—which bombarded those inside until they were subdued.[79] This was a crude and indiscriminate device incapable of distinguishing between combatants and the civilians among whom they were taking refuge. The second incident relates to night raids launched by the Prophet Muhammad where his soldiers would raid unsuspecting enemy tribes by surprise at night. There is a *ḥadīth* recorded in the collection of Muslim (the name by which one of the six major collections of *ḥadīth* are known) which states that the Prophet Muhammad was asked about the safety of women, children, and the elderly during these raids. "They are from them," the Prophet replied.[80]

There are important caveats to both incidents. With regards to the first, it is not clear that a mangonel was actually used. The most authentic collections of *ḥadīth* and *sīra* such as Bukhari, Muslim and Ibn Kathir do not mention its use. Reference to it is only found in the work of al-Tabari.[81] With the second incident, some contemporary scholars have pointed out that the *ḥadīth* is unclear. For example, the Egyptian cleric Ibn Hajar al-Asqalani argued that the *ḥadīth* is devoid of any context and it is unclear whether the women, children, and elderly were non-combatants.[82] Imam Shafi'i takes this a step further in his *risāla*. He argues that even if the killing of women, children, and the elderly was permitted at that time, that this ruling was later abrogated (*naskh*) by more explicit verses in Islamic scripture which categorically prohibited their murder.[83] This is an important argument because normative Islamic jurisprudence frequently employs the concept of abrogation, noting that while some things were allowed at the start of Muhammad's Prophethood they were then later forbidden. A notable example of this relates to alcohol, where Muslims were originally allowed to drink before God abrogated this rule and prohibited its consumption.

The development of tatarrus *by the contemporary Salafi-Jihadi movement*

Despite recognising barriers against the unfettered killing of human shields, al-Qaeda and associated groups have used both of the incidents above to initiate a broad practice of indiscriminate killing. What is most surprising, however, is that whilst doing so their literature neither dismisses nor refutes any of the cautionary points regarding the Taif incident or the night raids. One of the most important and authoritative texts to discuss al-Qaeda's opinion on this comes from Abu Yahya al-Libi in *al-Tatarrus fi al-Jihad al-Mu'āsir* (human shields in modern jihad).[84] Libi starts by reaffirming the classical view on *tatarrus* and argues that the restraint urged by previous clerics is neither invalid nor misguided. "Jihad should not imply non-respect for the sanctity of blood," he explains, "it does not dispense with the correct legal weighting."[85]

Two words from the title of Libi's book explain how he could square that opinion with al-Qaeda's actions in the battlefield: *jihad al-mu'āsir*, or modern jihad. Libi forwarded two arguments revolving around necessity and modernity. The first was a point of almost Benthamite utilitarianism where he argued that there are circumstances in which the benefit achieved by killing women and children outweighed the harm, thus making it permissible. This is neither a particularly exciting nor innovative point. Al-Qaeda has frequently employed this kind of principle—the lesser of two evils—or the *fiqh* of balances (*fiqh al-muwāzanāt*) to validate its doctrines. Libi explained:

> ...when the unbelievers attack the houses of Islam, major harm is afflicted on Muslims if jihad is given up. This leads to the hegemony of the unbelievers and their destroying [our] religion and existence.[86]

The terminology is loaded and emotive. Not only is Islam under attack, but the consequences of inaction potentially include the "destruction of religion and existence." For Muslim jurists considering this in the context of choosing between the lesser of two evils, it is important to note that normative Islamic jurisprudence holds that the fundamental purpose of the *shari'a* is to achieve the security of five things: lineage, property, intellect, religion, and life.[87] These are known as the *maqāṣid al-shari'a*. It is the last two goals that Libi argues are under threat unless the West is confronted. From here it follows that attacks against Western interests, including in urban centres where civilians will inevitably be among the victims, is an act born of defensive necessity. Given that impermissible acts become permissible in Islamic law in cases of existential threat, this allowed Libi to broaden the circumstances in which human shields could be legitimately killed.[88] "Whenever it is not possible to prevent harm to Muslims without killing those used as shields, it becomes permitted," he argued.[89] This view was also propagated by a large number of Salafi-Jihadi theorists sympathetic to al-Qaeda such as Abu al-Mundhir al-Shinqiti, a Mauritanian cleric closely associated with Abu Muhammad al-Maqdisi.[90]

Ayman al-Zawahiri also argued that the necessity of jihad trumped other considerations in a substantial essay titled: *Jihad, Martyrdom, and the Killing of Innocents*.[91] He asked his readers: "Is jihad, which is assigned to us, to be abandoned on account of...protected blood?"[92] Zawahiri recognised three distinct types of jurisprudential opinion concerning what should happen when the *mujahideen* attack an area where human shields might be killed. The first group argue for a total prohibition against attacks in those circumstances; the second state that such attacks are allowed, but only if "blood money," or compensation is paid to relatives of the victims; while the last allows for such attacks without the need for any compensation. "This [final] view is the one that we hold to," Zawahiri explained.[93]

He arrived at this opinion, not through expediency, but compulsion. Compared to its adversaries, al-Qaeda is a weak and irregular force confronting an enemy who enjoys overwhelming military superiority. "It has become next to impossible to confront them in open warfare," he argued.[94] It follows that the only practical means available to the group are asymmetrical ones, using tactics that are often crude and indiscriminate. This view was given further legitimacy when viewed from their perspective of being forced into a defensive campaign against a belligerent foe. "Forfeiting the faith is a much greater harm than forfeiting money or lives," Zawahiri explained.[95] Although he displays a callous and blithe indifference towards civilian casualties throughout much of the text, Zawahiri does end by stating that al-Qaeda would mitigate civilian deaths wherever possible. This was, however, a secondary consideration. A proposed attack would always goes ahead regardless of humanitarian considerations because, "expediency makes it so."[96]

In this context there are two different types of human shield: those who are forcibly compelled to be present alongside legitimate targets; and those who are there voluntarily (*ikhiyāri*). Libi argued that both could be legitimately killed.[97] This approach found its most dramatic application in Iraq under the insurgency led by Abu Musab al-Zarqawi when he spearheaded a violent campaign against Shi'a Muslims. Zarqawi explained his actions in a highly sectarian pamphlet directed towards Iraqi Shi'a titled, *Wa 'aād ahfad Ibn al-'Alqemi* (The Grandchildren of Ibn Al-'Alqemi Have Returned).[98] 'Alqemi was a Shi'a minister under the Abbasid Caliphate who, according to Sunni tradition, conspired with the Mongols when they ransacked Baghdad in the thirteenth century. The reference was therefore a pejorative one aimed at suggesting the country's Shi'a community were once again conspiring with a belligerent outsider—this time the United States—to undermine Iraqi sovereignty.

Libi made two arguments about the Shi'a which he argued justified their slaughter. The first was that they should not be considered as Muslims at all. They should instead be seen as *rawāfiḍ*, renegade heretics whose blood is valid under the rules of *takfir*. If this was in dispute, he argued, then their murder was nonetheless legitimate under the general rules of *tatarrus* because they mixed freely with the occupying "crusaders." Nibras Kazimi has called this kind of sophistry "the triumph of battlefield logic over theology."[99]

The second of Libi's arguments against classical opinions on *tatarrus* involved a rejection of the entire premise on which the existing debate is based. Although he accepted that the classical theology is not incorrect, it was nonetheless outmoded, impractical, and therefore could not be applied to the "modern jihad"—*jihad al-mu'āsir*. Libi and Zawahiri both made this case forcefully. They argued that advances in modern weaponry made it increasingly difficult to adhere to rules about minimising civilian casualties. As non-state actors with limited resources they were also unable to acquire the most technologically advanced weapons that might otherwise achieve this. Libi explained that the group inadvertently killed civilians because it is forced "to use the kinds of weapons that cause large numbers of deaths because [we] cannot find better and more efficient ones in such cases."[100] The classical rules on *tatarrus* were therefore not incorrect, but simply out-dated.

Zawahiri and Libi also considered the issue with specific reference to non-Muslim civilians and argued that modern migration patterns made it impossible to minimise the threat against them. Zawahiri explained:

> [Previously] Muslims resided in the realm of Islam and the infidels in the realm of war. In the realm of Islam a *dhimmi* [protected non-Muslims living in Muslim lands] could be distinguished from a Muslim by his appearance. Nowadays there is no such thing and the people are mixed together. This is a new and different situation and, as such, requires caution when one consults the writings of the early *'ulama'* and makes judgement on people.[101]

The absence of essentially homogenous societies therefore makes it harder, if not impossible, to distinguish between combatants and civilians, Muslims and non-Muslims. "It is difficult to separate [combatants and civilians] in distinct cases such as the ones cited by the scholars of Islam in the distant past," Libi argued. "The enemies live among the Muslims, settle their military camps and bases in Muslim quarters and move in their streets."[102]

The role of intention in tatarrus

Both Zawahiri and Libi were agreed that while every effort should be made to distinguish between Muslim civilians and combatants, the practical realities of warfare in the modern age made this practically impossible. The issue therefore becomes one of intention. When al-Qaeda attacked the United States, London and Madrid, or bombed crowded public areas in Iraq following the 2003 invasion, its stated aim was to hurt "the crusaders." Civilians killed in these events were unfortunate victims, or collateral damage, caught in an otherwise targeted attack with a specific aim and purpose behind it. Quoting imam Abu Bakr al-Sarakhsi, a classical scholar from antiquity, Libi explained, "The Muslim hit-man has to target the unbeliever, because if he can actually distinguish between him and the Muslim, that becomes his duty; if he is unable to do it, he has to distinguish by his intention."[103] Zawahiri reasoned that, whatever the case, it was not actually al-Qaeda killing civilians but God himself. Their obligation was merely to wage jihad to the best of their abilities. The rest was up to God. "We can kill Muslims used as human shields to safeguard jihad. When we let the hungry die or the human shields die in this case, they die by God's hand," he wrote.[104]

These arguments explain how al-Qaeda viewed the issue of *tatarrus*. For them, the traditional rules governing its practice were outpaced by modernity and therefore needed updating in order to accommodate the new reality. What they proposed was a more aggressive and deadly doctrine borne of pragmatism and necessity.

Salafi-Jihadi criticisms of killing Muslim human shields wantonly

Al-Qaeda produced a very modern theological framework for *tatarrus* which found popular expression amongst its followers in the aftermath of 9/11. Indeed, much of the literature on this topic has been produced recently and it does not appear to have been a significant issue for Salafi theorists in the past. Algerian and Egyptian jihadists tended to use arguments of *takfir* (albeit to varying degrees) to justify killing Muslim civilians rather than *tatarrus*. This was precisely how Algerian fighters explained their assassination campaign against secular intellectuals including Tahar Djaout, Abdelkader Alloula, and Mahfoud Boucebci for supposed apostasy.[105] Djaout's assassins even said they had targeted him because he "wielded a fearsome pen that could have an effect on Islamic sectors."[106] The GIA similarly explained their attacks in Paris with reference to the laws of *qiṣāṣ*. *Tatarrus* did not feature as a factor. This seems reasonable enough given that the Arab Afghan fighters had been very disciplined in not targeting civilians. Tamim al-Adnani, one of 'Abdallah 'Azzam's closest associates, explicitly condemned the targeting of civilians during a trip to the United States in 1988, saying:

> We are Muslims—we do not touch women, we do not touch girls—and those who are hijacking [planes], are going completely against Islam. All

> *mujahideen* leaders are against hijackings—we do not believe in hijackings. As Muslims we think that these hijackings are not fair at all. You are killing innocent people!
>
> [...]
>
> [People] think *mujahideen* are people who just attack people and hijack planes and aircrafts—like those who hijacked a Kuwaiti aircraft—we are completely against this. This is not jihad—this is nonsense![107]

Even among Salafi-Jihadi clerics al-Qaeda's views on *tatarrus* have been controversial.[108] As we saw earlier, both Sayyid Imam al-Sharif and Abu Basir al-Tartusi have become important voices of dissent within this community of theorists, often providing contrarian views. Both have been extremely critical of the casual manner in which some militant groups have explained away civilian casualties. Sharif argued that the entire issue is a contentious one and therefore needs to be approached with caution. The *Qur'an*, for example, does not state anything about killing human shields and the only *ḥadīths* which exist on the topic are ambiguous at best. This means there is an absence of definitive textual sources on the matter. He argues:

> There is no text that allows the killing of a Muslim human shield, but [it] is interpretive judgment and [it] is not legitimate...it is *ijtihād* [independent juristic reasoning] that allows the spilling of innocent blood.[109]

Although Sharif only discusses Muslim human shields in this passage, his work suggests the same ruling would also apply to non-Muslims too. Sharif also argued that because the textual sources are ambiguous regarding *tatarrus*—stemming from the siege of Taif and night raids—the concept is one that relies heavily on *ijtihād*. This makes it subjective, debatable, and open to interpretation. As a practise it lacks definitive proof and is born of the human mind—not scripture. To further underscore this view, Sharif cited the opinions of classical Islamic authorities such as Imam Malik and al-Ghazali, both of whom urged caution with regards to *tatarrus*.

Paul Kamolnick argues that when Sharif rebuked al-Qaeda for its liberal application of the principle he was really condemning the movement for having produced "a self-serving, deviant, and lawless 'killing en masse' doctrine."[110] Disputes like this drove the bitter feud between Sharif and Zawahiri which produced a series of public claims and counter-claims between 2006–2008. Sharif essentially accused Zawahiri of degrading jihad and embracing nihilism while using flimsy theological reasoning to license his position. Even in cases where Zawahiri was capable of producing jurisprudential evidence, Sharif argued that he was still guilty of misapplying it or exaggerating its scope.[111]

Abu Basir al-Tartusi was less emphatic than Sharif but nonetheless argued that *tatarrus* can only be applied in very specific circumstances and in only a handful of circumstances. A number of conditions would first have to be met before a human shield could be killed, although the problem with his formula is that it was much too subjective. For example, he argued that fighters should first assess whether "the resulting advantages of targeting the hostages [are] certain and definite." He also argued that an attack should only be launched in cases where "fighting the enemy could not possibly be delayed, deferred or be allowed to benefit from extra surveillance."[112]

Conclusion

The practicality of waging jihad through terrorism or insurgency poses a number of significant challenges for fighters in the field. These problems start from the very basis on which war itself can be declared, requiring non-state groups to create sophistic arguments of causation that hold Western states primarily responsible for problems in the Muslim world. Viewed in this way, offensive attacks become defensive measures. Contemporary militant movements have needed to construct a malleable theological framework to achieve this, one that moulds classical opinions to fit the modern world. But there is more to the process than just pragmatism. As the discussion around *tatarrus* has shown, the exigencies of war have proved to be a driver and catalyst of theological change. This has given rise to revisionist theories which both develop and expand Islamic principles relating to *jus in bello*. As the subsequent chapters will demonstrate, following the 2003 invasion of Iraq it appeared as if al-Qaeda was prepared to develop its own understanding of the rules relating to jihad in such a way that they could license almost anything at all. It was not that they dismissed classical interpretations, but that they were pushed into adopting a modernising doctrine—albeit to achieve, ironically, ancient aims.

Such a process is invariably subjective, creating fissures in the debate between religious authorities over issues of legitimacy and authenticity. This does not just apply to Muslim critics of the contemporary jihad movement in general, but also to those within the Salafi tradition who regard militant interpretations as an aberration of Islamic law. Some of those differences have already been touched upon in this chapter, particularly over disagreements relating to the application of both *qiṣāṣ* and *tatarrus*. Notably, where fault lines do appear, they do so between theorists and those who are operationally active in the field—a feature of the debate that will present itself throughout this book.

TAKFĪR

4

ESTABLISHING DISBELIEF

The foundations of *takfir*

Just as the 2003 invasion of Iraq precipitated changes in the way Salafi-Jihadi militants constructed Islamic rules of war, the conflict also inspired a number of changes relating to the concept of *takfir* (excommunication). Its practice, and public awareness of the term, grew dramatically during this time when al-Qaeda in Iraq, led by Abu Musab al-Zarqawi, employed it liberally to license a fratricidal civil war against the Iraqi Shi'a community. *Takfir* can seem like an archaic concept because it draws a line against those deemed to have left the Islamic faith, either voluntarily or through an act. For the global jihad movement it has become a valuable tool for the protection of Islam, a means of expelling those from the faith who are thought to be subverting it from within. As such, in its current constructions, the concept is used to license intra-Muslim violence—particularly in highly sectarian environments. Ever since the 2003 invasion of Iraq, the use of *takfir* has become especially pronounced in the Levant, not least among fighters in the Syrian civil war. This chapter explains the origins and emergence of *takfir* as a concept within Islam, how it has been used to fuel sectarian violence, and the manner in which concerned parties have tried to limit its use.

In its most basic formulation *takfir* is the process of declaring another Muslim, or a group of Muslims, to be outside the fold of Islam.

The one who pronounces *takfir* on another is said to be performing *mukaffira*, a practice that is governed by a dense and distinct series of rules. In contemporary usage, however, practitioners of *takfir* are often simply referred to as *takfiris*. As an approximation, it can be thought of as being analogous to that of excommunication in the Catholic Church although there are some notable differences. The Islamic process is much less formal and far more subjective, meaning that pronouncements of *takfir* are frequently contested and ignored.

Its importance as a concept to the contemporary Salafi-Jihadi movement stems from the principal purpose of *takfir*: defining precisely what the Muslim community is and who its constituents are. In short, it concerns itself with the question of who is a Muslim. A natural consequence is that it also preoccupies itself with the conceptualisation of who is a disbeliever, or *kafir*. By doing so it explicitly delineates the boundaries of faith, creating an "in-group" of rightful adherents while also identifying an "out-group" of heretics. This matters to some Salafi theorists because *takfir* is seen as a mechanism for the protection of Islam itself, a means by which to expel errant Muslims from the faith whilst safeguarding its doctrinal purity for those who remain within its ranks. By linking belief in Islam to practice, the use of *takfir* can be seen as helping construct a view among Salafi-Jihadis of the religion as an active and living ideal. Faith is necessary but insufficient. It must be accompanied by acts. The Saudi cleric Safar al-Hawali explains:

> *Al-irjā'* [meaning to postpone; used here to refer to those who do not pronounce *takfir*] has become a conscious movement aiming at leaving out works or outward practices and *ta'ah* [following the *shari'a*]...so the *umma* has seen *al-ṣalāa* [prayer], *al-zakat* [alms giving], *al-ṣiyam* [fasting], and *al-hajj* [pilgrimage], simply as duties; they [also] need to practice the works.[1]

This underscores the dual concerns of those who practise *takfir*: firstly by protecting the faith through calls for homogeneity and secondly by ensuring that its adherents are active, rather than passive, agents. From here, it is not difficult to see how Salafi-Jihadi theorists have developed this doctrine into a coercive political mantra of communal conformity. Dissent, opposition, reform and scepticism are all heresies. Those who subscribe to them belong in the "out-group" and, by extension, fall out of the faith altogether. Viewed in this way, it becomes apparent how this construction of *takfir* among Salafi-Jihadi militants has been particularly effective in fuelling intra-Muslim violence.

Defining kufr

It is necessary to first appreciate the different categories of disbelief in order to understand the manner in which *takfir* operates. In a linguistic sense *kufr* simply means to cover and veil something. The *Qur'an* itself uses the term with reference to the pleasure of a farmer who sees his crops growing after rainfall.[2] The legal, *shari'a* definition, is more distinct. It means the absence of faith, or the belief in anything other than Islam. "It is the complete decrease in *īmān* [faith] and it is the opposite of *īmān*," says Abu Hamza al-Masri. "It is the unbelief in Allah, the mighty and majestic, and his favours."[3]

This explains what *kufr* is, but not its distinctions. On the one hand there are those who consciously reject Islam by choice, conviction, and deed. This is classified as *kufr al-inkār*. According to Muhammad ibn 'Abd al-Wahhab this is tantamount to *shirk* because it denies the oneness of Allah by ascribing the reality of creation to something other than him. Those who deny God have "committed a sin, the like of which there is no other."[4] This is neither contentious nor problematic as it applies to those who freely choose to identify as non-Muslim.

Judging by what is apparent

Those who self-identify as Muslim but fall short of its required standards are much harder to classify, with *takfir* and *kufr* becoming much more important in this context. For example, a believer may fall into disbelief by engaging in an act of *kufr akbar* (great sin)—a transgression so severe that it negates faith.[5] There are six broad types of sin that can constitute *kufr akbar*, although there are about 70 different acts which can constitute *kufr* in general.[6]

There are obvious difficulties here. Where *kufr akbar* is manifest through word or deed it can be determined easily enough. Yet, on a number of occasions it principally relates to matters of the heart or inner belief, rendering it impossible to know what an individual is thinking without some form of testimony or confession. *Takfir* would become a charter for constant adversarial inquisition if left like this. Normative Islamic theology addresses this by generally forbidding attempts to measure the sincerity of ordinary persons who profess and identify with the faith.[7] The underlying premise is what matters here. Rather than have a system predicated on distrust, the opposite applies. Muslims are therefore told to "judge by what is apparent," where the status of an individual is gauged by their everyday actions. This principle stems from an incident when the Prophet Muhammad chastised one of his companions for killing an enemy in battle who, as he was surrounded, quickly declared the Islamic testament of faith. Believing this to be an insincere attempt to save his life, the Prophet's companions killed their adversary. They were sternly rebuked. It is not for one man to judge what is in the heart of another. Man's role is only to measure what is apparent, with this safeguard supposedly designed to act as a barrier against the unchecked practice of *takfir* against other Muslims.

Salafi-Jihadis tend to accept this understanding but politicise it, thereby creating a far more subjective environment in which it operates. For example, Anwar al-Awlaki cites an incident where Abbas ibn 'Abd al-Muttalib, the Prophet Muhammad's paternal uncle, was captured and taken prisoner of war during the Battle of Badr.[8] Abbas claimed he should be freed because he was Muslim, but the Prophet replied, "What is apparent to us is that you were against us."[9] This type of incident is used to target anyone deemed to be opposing the global jihad movement and has, in contemporary environments, included attacks on Muslim soldiers, policemen and civil servants in countries like Iraq, Syria, Afghanistan and Egypt. What is in their hearts is irrelevant. God will judge them on that. "We do not judge by what is in the heart," said Anwar al-Awlaki. "We judge by what is apparent."[10] The issue of subjectivity here comes when assessing the intention of the apparent act—which, although done openly, may still be subject to broad interpretation.

Barriers to takfir

There are numerous injunctions, in both the *Qur'an* and *ḥadīth*, that warn against the reckless proclamation of *takfir*, making it clear that the matter is a serious one. Those who declare *takfir* should do so with caution because, among other things, the Prophet Muhammad warned:

> If a person says to his brother, oh unbeliever! Then surely one of them is such.[11]

The implication is clear. Wrongly or falsely accusing another Muslim of disbelief is tantamount to committing one's own heresy. For this reason a number of leading Salafi-Jihadi theorists such as Abu Hamza al-Masri, Abu Muhammad al-Maqdisi, Omar 'Abd al-Rahman, and Abu Basir al-Tartusi have all written extensively about the need to exercise caution when pronouncing *takfīr*.[12] Maqdisi argues that while judging by what is apparent, if an individual is able to offer a straightforward explanation about their actions and the intentions behind it, then they should be given the benefit of the doubt. Even in cases where the act alone is sufficient to pronounce *takfīr*; he stresses the importance of allowing the accused to offer consideration for their actions. Maqdisi gives an example of someone who votes in the democratic process, arguing that, "taking part in legislative elections is an action of *kufr*, [but] we do not make general *takfīr* [on those who vote]."[13] What matters here is the intention of those who vote. People vote for a plethora of different reasons including desperation, coercion, and because they do not believe their representative will legislate in a manner that contradicts the *shari'a*. "We say he is a believer who is deficient in *īmān* or a believer with his *īmān* who is a corrupt one due to his major sin," says Maqdisi.[14] Ideas like this give rise to a series of strictures which aim to limit the wanton use of *takfīr*. Some other barriers to *takfīr* include stipulations such as confirming that the accused is sane, that they are performing an indisputable act of *kufr*, aware that what they are doing is wrong, and are undertaking the act freely, deliberately and consciously.

The emergence of *takfīr* as a tool for intra-Muslim violence

Islamic rules generally place a premium on stability within the community, discouraging rebellion and internecine strife even when confronted by oppressive rulers.[15] This view has persisted with an extensive body of literature, both ancient and contemporary, warning against rebellion or other forms of public dissent.[16] Yet, this prohibition is not absolute. Khaled Abou El Fadl has shown that in normative Islamic theology there are three circumstances in which an Islamic state can fight against its own people (and, by extension, when Muslims can fight other Muslims). These are cases when the following need to be confronted: apostates (*murtaddūn*); bandits (*muhāribūn*); and rebels (*bughāt*).[17]

Options are far more limited for private citizens of the state. They are only permitted to confront the government in cases where the ruler strays from the *shari'a*. Even then, if their deviation is relatively minor and represents only a small departure from the rules of Islam in an environment which otherwise generally implements the *shari'a*, then dissent should be limited to advice (*naṣīḥa*), or campaigning for reform (*iṣlāḥ*). Only in circumstances where the ruler engages in an act of unequivocal *kufr*, or where they deviate excessively from normative Islamic rules, does rebellion become mandated.

There are no objective criteria by which to assess when rebellion becomes obligated, exposing such decisions to the ambiguity of subjective reasoning. Problems in this regard arose almost immediately after the Prophet Muhammad's death, with political instability plaguing the period of the four rightly guided Caliphs who succeeded him—known as the *khulafā' rāshida*. The Prophet's first successor, Abu Bakr al-Siddiq, was immediately confronted by crisis after a series of tribes apostatised from Islam, requiring him to launch the apostasy wars, *ḥurūb ar-ridda*, in order to subdue them.[18] Yet, this should not be seen as the first instance of intra-Muslim violence. Those who broke away had already renounced their belief in Islam and were consequently treated as an alien and rebellious community.

More serious problems came with the last of the rightly guided Caliphs, 'Ali ibn Abi Talib, who took power after the assassination of his predecessor, Uthman ibn Affan. 'Ali's rule was overcome by a series of complex challenges that are important to consider here due to events they later precipitated.

Significant outcry followed the assassination of Uthman, not least because he was the second successive Caliph to have been killed. Pressure mounted on 'Ali to bring his killers to justice. The Prophet Muhammad's widow, Aisha, along with two of the *Ṣahāba*, Talha ibn Ubaidullah and Zubayr ibn al-Awam, eventually raised an army and marched it to Basra because it was felt that 'Ali was not doing enough to address this crisis.[19] Forces loyal to 'Ali were then moved from Kufa to Basra where they intercepted Aisha, Talha and Zubayr. All sides were under strict orders to find a negotiated settlement to the impasse, although confrontations broke out which resulted in the Battle of the Camel in 656. This has come to be known as the First Fitna, or the *fitnat maqtal Uthman* (*fitna* of Uthman's killing), and constitutes the first instance of intra-Muslim violence in Islamic history.[20] 'Ali was a reluctant adversary. When the conflict was over his soldiers were ordered to free all captives, not take any war booty, and to leave alone all of the retreating soldiers.[21] The important issue is how the confrontation was initially framed—and how the sequence of events it initiated then spiralled out of control. Gerald Hawting has convincingly shown that 'Ali's opponents were not concerned with rebellion per se, but were much more interested in reform, *iṣlāḥ*.[22] They did not pronounce *takfir* on him. When Aisha, Talha and Zubayr marched to Basra their primary aim was to establish justice, *iqāmat al-ḥudūd*, and the rule of Allah's book, *iqāmat kitāb Allah*. Regardless, an important psychological barrier had been crossed: Muslims had demonstrated their willingness to violently confront one another in response to political events.

The first takfiri *movement*

Even when the Battle of the Camel was settled, it resolved nothing. The governor of Damascus, Muawiyah ibn Abi Sufyan, still refused to recognise 'Ali and insisted that Uthman's killers must be brought to justice. Less than a year had passed but 'Ali sensed another battle was looming. He marched his army northwards from their base in Kufa and chanced upon Muawiyah's forces along the Euphrates where the Battle of Siffin (*waq'at Ṣafin*) broke out. Muawiyah's soldiers hoisted copies of the *Qur'an* in the air with their spears, appealing to 'Ali to resolve the dispute through arbitration.[23] 'Ali agreed to the initiative—and, in doing so, set in motion a sequence of events that would provide a turning point in the Islamic understanding of *takfir*.[24] Some of his men were deeply opposed to arbitration, arguing that both Muawiyah and his soldiers had committed apostasy by challenging 'Ali's authority and threatening the unity of the community, *jamā'a*. That was not the end of it. They also pronounced *takfir* on 'Ali, arguing that his decision to enter into arbitration negated Allah's right to pick a victor through battle. As such, 'Ali had usurped God's rights.

Those who broke away coalesced into a movement which came to be known as the *khawārij* (singular: *khārijī*), which literally means "those who went out."[25] The term has persisted in the Islamic lexicon and is today used pejoratively against terrorists, extremists and Muslim groups which otherwise condemn the broader community of Islam. As a label, the term *khawārij* is particularly loaded and invested with derisory religious significance. The renowned Salafi scholar of *ḥadīth*, Muhammad Nasir al-Din al-Albani, described them as "the dogs of hell," and "the worst of people, the worst of all creatures."[26]

The original *khawārij* applied the doctrine of *takfīr* liberally and argued that every major sin automatically constituted *kufr*. They consequently declared *takfīr* on nearly all of the notable *Ṣahāba* of their time, while some historical accounts suggest they made *takfīr* on them all.[27] They justified their actions with the slogan, "there is no rule, except for the rule of Allah."[28] Anyone deemed to have violated that rule instantly became a legitimate target of their *takfīr*. It was an important moment.

An independent movement had emerged which argued that its legitimacy was derived not through the established institutions of Islam—such as the Caliph or the Caliphate—but through scripture alone. Religious authority could instead exist without the state or its structures, residing instead in personal righteousness. Viewed in this way, a potent doctrine of personal and partisan empowerment had emerged. "The fact that ['Ali] was Muhammad's nephew[29] only confirmed them [the *khawārij*] in the militancy of their egalitarianism,"Tom Holland has argued, "that the true aristocracy was one of piety and not of blood."[30] Although 'Ali achieved a comprehensive victory over the *khawārij* in the Battle of Nahrawan in 658, the intellectual damage was already done: a process had been set in motion and its fallout would prove impossible to contain. In a footnote to this story which foreshadows the bloodshed which was to come later, the *khawārij* who survived the battle were able to regroup and subsequently assassinated 'Ali.

The postponers emerge

Takfīr emerged in the early Muslim world as a doctrine of empowered personal agency principally concerned with the preservation of God's rights. Its political applications had already proved disastrous, spawning the first episodes of intra-Muslim violence while subjecting the Caliphate to greater turbulence than it had ever encountered before. Little more than two decades had passed since the death of Prophet Muhammad and already it seemed as if his fraternity of the faithful were busying themselves with levels of fratricide which would rival Tudor England or Medici Florence. 'Ali's grandson, Hassan bin Muhammad bin al-Hanafiyya, eventually responded to the growing instability from groups such as the *khawārij* by theorising the first major work of the *murji'a* in *Kitāb al-Irjā'*. When it finally appeared in 694, more than thirty years had passed since the assassination of 'Ali.[31] The term *irjā'* literally means to defer or postpone, and those who came to adopt this practice are known as the *murji'a*. Deferral is precisely what the *irjā'* did because, although they had not participated in the *fitna*, they were deeply concerned by its implications.

The *murji'a* reasoned that the maintenance of communal unity and avoidance of civil war took precedence over declarations of *takfir*. As a result, they argued that it was better to defer judgement on the key issues which led to the *fitna*, such as the validity of the decisions taken by 'Ali or Muawiyah. Daniel Lav argues that the early *murji'a* were really just refusing to declare "which side they would have taken in the *fitna*—to whom they would have given their loyalty had they been present at the events."[32] His view is much too cynical and uncharitable, failing to appreciate the shock caused by the onset of the *fitna*. In *Kitāb al-irjā'* Hassan explained:

> Among our Imams we approve of Abu Bakr and Umar [the first two *khulafā' rāshida*]; we approve of their being obeyed, and are angered at their being disobeyed. We are enemies of their enemies. [But] we suspend judgment on those of them who first participated in the schism.[33]

Lav's revisionist scholarship of the *murji'a* argues that it was neither a quietist nor coherent soteriology.[34] While there is some evidence to support this, it can only be said to apply to the movement during its incipient phases. The whole point of *irjā'* was that it would be a doctrine to redress the balance. Demonstrating loyalty to the ruler was a serious matter for Muslims in early Islamic communities, a political act that was inherently bound up with notions of piety and salvation. The *murji'a* sought to remind their compatriots of this, stressing the virtues of communal unity over political intrigue.

Development of murji'a *soteriology*

Imam Abu Hanifa—who founded one of the four main schools of Islamic jurisprudence—developed what might be called the "*murji'a* philosophy" just over a century after *Kitāb al-Irjā'* was written. His work is far more theoretical and abstract than what his predecessors had produced and is less concerned with the heresiographical aspects of the circumstances relating to the assassinations of Uthman and 'Ali.[35] This is hardly surprising, given the passage of time. Shorn of any connection to the events which birthed the doctrine of *irjā'*, Abu Hanifa's work developed two important ideas in relation to it and, in the process, unintentionally fomented a school of thought on the theology of *īmān* too.

The first way that Abu Hanifa developed the doctrine of *irjā'* was that he said no sin—even major ones such as *kufr akbar*—automatically negate an individual's faith.[36] The second position followed on from this and argued that faith could be achieved by just two things: the ascension of the heart, *taṣdīq bi-l-qalb*, and affirmation of the tongue.[37] In practice this means that intellectual conviction and oral testimony are sufficient to establish *īmān*—there is no need for works. It is worth briefly exploring this because the nature of belief is highly disputed in Islam.[38] Abu Hanifa argued that religion, *dīn*, is something quite distinct and separate from faith. After all, according to Islam, all prophets throughout history had preached the same essential message of monotheism and obedience to God despite bringing their own legal codes. This demonstrated that religion and faith had to be different. To that end, Abu Hanifa even looked to the legal codes of previous prophets (*shara' man qablana*) as one of the sources of jurisprudence in his school of thought (although he only used it sparingly).[39]

Irjā' remains a key characteristic of quietist and introverted Salafis today. Within the contemporary tradition, the most important figure with whom it is typically associated is the Saudi scholar, Rabi' ibn Hadi 'Umayr al-Madkhali.[40] His followers represent a vociferous and ongoing *irjā'* movement within contemporary Salafism and are pejoratively known as *Madkhalis*.

Salafi-Jihadi theorists reject the very premise on which *irjā'* is established. They argue that conviction and testimony are necessary prerequisites of *īmān* but that these aspects of faith are meaningless unless they are accompanied by acts (*'amal*). The most important text for adherents of this view comes from Ibn Taymiyya in *Kitāb al-īmān* (the book of faith). Two chapters of his book are dedicated to the issue. Whereas Abu Hanifa separated *īmān* and *dīn*, Ibn Taymiyya argued that only the heart could bring an individual to *īmān*. That is, the heart makes one a believer. By contrast, religious devotion is dependent on actions because the whole notion of *dīn* is that it constitutes the outward and physical manifestation of inward belief. Ibn Taymiyya therefore insisted individuals should strive for *iḥsan*, the perfection of faith, once they have committed themselves to performing its acts (*'amal*).[41] This led him to conclude:

> *Īmān* has requirements and counter-requirements. It requires fulfilling the requirements and rejecting the counter-requirements, which requires affirming its requirements and negating its counter-requirements.[42]

Opponents of *irjā'* therefore regard the doctrine as dangerous and toxic, arguing that it undermines Islam by exposing it to sinners and inactive members. It is a charter for the secularisation of Islam, allowing for lazy, passive membership. The famous Austro-Hungarian convert to Islam, Muhammad Asad, who produced a celebrated translation of Sahih Bukhari, even argued that if the practice of *irjā'* became mainstream, "Islam would have rapidly assumed the role of present day Christianity, in which belief and worship are entirely dissociated from the realities of life."[43] The fear of Islam becoming like its forerunners—Judaism and Christianity—is pervasive and perennial in Muslim communities. Islam validates itself on the idea that previous religious communities broke their pact with God by introducing compromises and laxities into religious practice. That is why God shunned them and decreed alternative revelation. To do the same with Islam—the last testament and salvation—would be to decisively break mankind's pact with the divine, and to unravel the very grounds on which Islam legitimates its own existence. The issues of *irjā'* and *takfir* are therefore inextricably intertwined with highly emotional ideas about the protection and authenticity of Islam itself.

Conclusion

Takfir can seem like a confusing idea at first glance. While its function is straightforward enough—to excommunicate—the premium placed on it by Salafi-Jihadi movements appears bewildering. After all, why should they care about the personal and private faith of others? This includes not just alternative sectarian identities but also those deemed to be insufficiently pious and practising. It should be clear by now that *takfir* is more than a tool of devotional jockeying or a mechanism for one-upmanship among religious adherents. Its antecedents reach back to the earliest stages of Islam and were birthed by some of the first fault lines to emerge from exchanges between the pious and their politics. Whilst the doctrine quickly licensed intra-Muslim violence, this conflict was not being waged for its own sake. As the emergence of the *irjā'* doctrine has shown, the implications of *takfir* go right to the heart of questions about faith. These envelope expansive issues including the relationship between faith and action, and the maintenance of Islamic authenticity.

Once the *khawārij* began pronouncing *takfir* in the struggle against 'Ali they also set about recalibrating the balance of power within the Islamic community. Perhaps no other event has left as enduring or indelible a mark on Islamic history as this. By challenging 'Ali they were wresting power away from the established structures of the state and its institutions by arguing that true authenticity was derived from piety. It did not matter who was challenged—even if it were a family member of the Prophet himself. Of course, what becomes apparent is that *takfir* has always operated in political environments and tends to have political or social implications whenever pronounced, making it especially useful to the contemporary Salafi-Jihadi movement.

5

PRAXIS IN ACTION

The roots of modern *takfir*

The destructive implications of *takfir* are evident across the Muslim world today. From Indonesia to Pakistan, the Levant, the Arabian Peninsula, and across North Africa, militant groups have frequently invoked the doctrine to justify mass casualty attacks against ordinary Muslims—ironically, the very constituency in whose defence they often claim to act. The emergence and evolution of this idea as a tool of intra-Muslim agency, operated as a wedge between a supposedly righteous "in-group" and everyone else. It was in the 1980s and 1990s that militant Sunni groups first began developing the doctrine of *takfir* for the modern era, but it was only following the 2003 invasion of Iraq that it crystallised into a more coherent idea, along the lines we would recognise today. This was when al-Qaeda and their supporters from the broader ecosystem of Salafi-Jihadi thinking were forced to produce a dense and detailed body of work explaining the jurisprudential framework behind their understanding of *takfir*. The process was borne of necessity. When the United States and its partners first invaded Iraq, they did so against a backdrop of widespread opposition both in the Muslim world and beyond. Included in this were large numbers of Muslims who did not support Islamic militancy but who were otherwise deeply opposed to military intervention in Iraq. For al-Qaeda, this presented a unique opportunity. If this constituency could be won over to its way of thinking, then the group could claim greater legitimacy for its cause. Those hopes were quickly dashed.

The brutality of the Iraqi insurgency, stemming in large part from its liberal use of *takfir* to stoke a sectarian war with the Iraqi Shi'a, caused many to recoil from the group and its actions. In their attempt to carry Muslim public opinion, Salafi-Jihadi theorists who supported the Iraqi insurgency produced a wealth of books and other literature seeking to rationalise and explain their actions. For example, literature produced by al-Qaeda in Iraq during this time revealed how the group painted apostasy in the broadest of brushstrokes—whilst true believers existed only through narrow strictures. "We believe that all tenets of secularism—including nationalism, communism, and Baathism—are a blatant violation of Islam," the statement declared. "A person who believes in any of them is non-Muslim."[1] Documents such as this provide a goldmine of primary source material for those hoping to shed light on how the concept of *takfir* has been developed and used by the contemporary Salafi-Jihadi movement.

Ibn Taymiyya and the basis of modern takfīr

Although their opponents often label Salafi-Jihadis as *khawārij*, it is of course a marker they eschew—not least because the *khawārij* pronounced *takfir* against most of the *Ṣahāba*. When considering the issue of *takfir*, the contemporary movement looks principally towards the work of Ibn Taymiyya, who is cited and referenced extensively on this issue.

Taqi ad-Din Ahmad ibn Taymiyya (1263—1328) is perhaps the most highly regarded scholar of Islamic antiquity for the contemporary Salafi-Jihadi movement. Such is his enduring relevance that he is regularly referred to with the endearing appellation "shaykh al-Islam," or the shaykh of Islam. Born in Harran (located in modern day Turkey), Ibn Taymiyya was a citizen of the Mamluk Sultanate based in Cairo. It was a harried state. Mongol invaders had slowly encroached into Mamluk territory over a series of raids starting in 1260. By 1265 the Mongols had pushed so far into Mamluk terrain that Ibn Taymiyya was forced to leave his home in Mardin and moved to Damascus after issuing a seminal fatwa about the need to resist Mongol rule. This fatwa is often referred to as the "Mardin fatwa." When the Mongols pressed on and reached Damascus in 1300, he raised an army to fight them.[2]

Ibn Taymiyya's legacy is far from settled. For proponents of radical beliefs, his work is taken as authorising armed insurrection through applying *takfir* to those who fail to rule by an austere and narrow construction of the *shari'a*. They argue that Ibn Taymiyya had branded the Mongols as heretics despite them professing a belief in Islam. The source of their heresy came from the *yāsa* or *yāsiq* legal system, which had been devised by Genghis Khan, and married aspects of the Islamic legal code with others. This is held by a number of Salafi-Jihadi theorists (and by a number of political Islamists too) as providing evidence for the supposed heresy of contemporary rulers who are judged to fall short of implementing *shari'a* in its purest forms. Yet, as Yahya Michot has shown, Ibn Taymiyya's fatwa was actually far more nuanced and reasoned than is often thought. Michot explains that the fatwa has been misunderstood by radicals and is actually a "progressive and balanced" document.[3] He writes:

> Any wolf eager to pounce on Mardin will certainly have been disappointed... whether Mardin is or is not a domain of peace matters little in the end since, in any event—and this is fundamental—the Damascene sheikh refuses to accord to it the status of domain of war, the inhabitants of which would have to be unbelievers. His fatwa is thus quite the opposite of a green light to the unleashing of general hostilities.[4]

This leads to another issue concerning Salafi-Jihadis today, which is how Muslim lands should be classified. They do not, on the whole, consider any modern country to be *dār al-Islam* (Islamic lands) because none is subjected to *shari'a* in a construction they regard as appropriately faithful. The same applied to Ibn Taymiyya. He could no longer reside in Mardin because its *shari'a* system had been replaced with the *yāsa/ yāsiq* laws. As Michot has shown, however, he did not then designate Mardin as a land of war, *dār al-ḥarb*. Instead, Ibn Taymiyya argued for an entirely new classification altogether, writing:

> As for whether it is a land of war or peace, it is a composite situation. It is not an abode of peace where the legal rulings of Islam are applied and its armed forces are Muslim. Neither is it the same as an abode of war whose inhabitants are unbelievers. It is a third category. The Muslims living

therein should be treated according to their rights as Muslims, while the non-Muslims living there outside of the authority of Islamic Law should be fought as is their due.[5]

Ibn Taymiyya was articulating a novel approach by saying that the prevailing institutional, legal, and canonical codes within a society do not define it. Instead, what matters is the people who reside within a particular society. This led Baber Johansen to conclude that Ibn Taymiyya provides for "localised, non-universal forms of political rule."[6]

Revisionist scholars have consequently tried to dispute the meaning of the fatwa by arguing that some of its words have been misunderstood or mistranslated by radicals. For example, the word "fought" (*qatilū*) should actually be read as "treated" (*āmilū*).[7] An entire conference was even dedicated to "reclaiming" Ibn Taymiyya's legacy in 2010, led by notable Islamic scholars including shaykh 'Abdallah bin Bayah and shaykh Habib 'Ali al-Jifri. The precise contours of this debate extend beyond present purposes and it is enough to note that revisionist efforts have failed to disabuse militants of their misunderstanding. Anwar al-Awlaki responded to the Mardin conference by calling it "an attempt at justifying the new world order." He went on to argue, "if a ruler has committed disbelief then it is obligatory to revolt against him. This is a matter of consensus among the classical scholars."[8]

Early manifestations of takfir *in Egypt and Algeria*

There is perhaps no country more important to the development of contemporary *takfiri* thought than Egypt, where the Muslim Brotherhood (*al-Ikhwan al-Muslimun*) helped develop the idea into both a problematic and potent tool of social dissent. The antecedents of its evolution stem back to the 1952 revolution that was led by Muhammad Naguib and Gamal Abdel Nasser whom the Muslim Brotherhood had initially welcomed. Nasser seemed like a promising prospect and his Free Officers were lionised for having fought against Israel during the First Arab-Israeli War in 1948. Such was the proximity between the Brotherhood and the Free Officers that Lorenzo Vidino has suggested the former even helped plan the coup that overthrew King Farouk.[9]

The Brotherhood naturally expected to share in the rise of Nasser and lobbied him to introduce *shari'a* law into both Egyptian politics and public life. It was quickly apparent that Nasser intended to do no such thing and relations between the two parties soured before he outlawed the group in January 1954. Angered by this rejection, just nine months later a member of the Brotherhood unsuccessfully tried to assassinate Nasser. It was a dramatic moment. Public support for Nasser swelled as he seized the moment to launch a draconian crackdown against the country's Islamists. Members of the Muslim Brotherhood were arrested, tortured, subjected to hasty military trials (many of them grossly unfair), sent to concentration camps and ultimately executed.[10] The effects of this were transformative for the Brotherhood, whose members struggled to comprehend the brutality being perpetrated against them by other Muslims. It was during this period of intense repression that the movement's most celebrated son, Sayyid Qutb, also spent a decade in prison (1954–1964) and wrote his most influential book: *Ma'alim fi-l-Ṭarīq*, or *Milestones Along the Way*.

Qutb's central contention was that society had regressed to a state of ignorance associated with pre-Islamic times, a period known as *jāhiliyya*.[11] This is typically imagined to be the period of polytheism in Makkah which preceded the dawn of Islam, although the term is vague and ill-defined today. Sayed Khatab has offered one of the most comprehensive, yet simplistic, definitions of how Qutb intended the idea to mean "the opposite of Islam, or anything other than Islam."[12] By characterising society in this way Qutb fundamentally recalibrated the way Islamists understood their relationship with the state. The old categories simply no longer applied. They were not residing in *dār al-ḥarb* or *dār al-Islam*, but found themselves in an entirely novel situation: a regressed society which had unravelled so much that it slipped to levels of pre-Islamic distance from the monotheism of the *Qur'an*. Society was in need of complete overhaul. *Takfir* now became mainstreamed as an idea in radical circles to combat and confront the state. Yet there is an important point to note with regards to Qutb's scholarship on the matter: he does not cite Ibn Taymiyya anywhere in *Milestones*.[13] There is simply no mention of him, his work, or the Mardin fatwa in the text.

One of those who was deeply influenced by Qutb's work was Shukri Mustafa, a onetime member of the Muslim Brotherhood who was arrested in 1965 for distributing leaflets on behalf of the group.[14] He eventually broke with the movement over disputes about how *takfir* should be applied to society and created his own group, popularly known as Takfir wal Hijra. Although it was short lived and is largely considered a failure, the nature of Mustafa's disagreement with the Brotherhood is instructive. He argued that it was not just the government who were heretics, but the whole of Egyptian society. This explains the *hijra* aspect of his movement which, having deemed all of society as having fallen into disbelief, broke-away and secluded itself in rural areas of the Egyptian countryside. In many senses Mustafa had created a neo-*khawārij* movement which challenged everyone other than those who subscribed to the narrow strictures of its own worldview.[15] When they confronted the state by kidnapping and killing the former Minister of Religious Endowment, Muhammad al-Dhahabi, in July 1977, government forces had just the pretext they needed to move against the group. A swift crackdown resulted in 620 of its members being arrested along with Mustafa, who was executed after a short military trial. Takfir wal Hijra never recovered and the group withered away.[16]

Although the 1952 Egyptian revolt inspired the first *takfiri* movements of the modern era, it was in the Algerian civil war that such ideas found their most vociferous expression, particularly after Antar Zouabri became leader of the GIA in 1996. Zouabri radically altered the nature of the Algerian opposition, broadening the scope of its attacks and making it much more nihilistic. He believed in waging total war against Algerian society in order to overwhelm and subdue it, hoping this would create the conditions for the establishment of a Caliphate.[17] Under his leadership, the GIA became so liberal in its application of *takfir* that its slogan for those participating in national elections was "one vote, one bullet."[18] Quintan Wiktorowicz explains that Zouabri "shifted GIA operations away from the state and toward softer targets in society, eventually leading to widespread civilian massacres."[19] He notes that from 1992 to 1997 the number of civilian casualties rose from 10% to 87% when measured against the total number of casualties the group was inflicting—a staggering rise that did not go unnoticed in Salafi-Jihadi circles.[20]

Hassan Hattab, a former regional commander of the GIA, grew dismayed at Zouabri's tactics and could not accept his strategy of broadening out *takfir* to encompass civilians. He split from the GIA and established another movement, the *Groupe Salafiste pour la Prédication et le Combat* (Salafist Group for Call and Combat); GSPC.[21] This new movement limited its campaign to military and political targets. It maintained this policy until 2006 when it merged with al-Qaeda in a "blessed union," subsequently becoming part of al-Qaeda in the Islamic Maghreb (AQIM) the following year.[22] Further afield, Abu Qatada had been lending ideological support to the GIA from London and was also concerned by Zouabri's broad application of *takfir*.[23] The same was true for Atiyyatullah al-Libi, who had been advising the group through the Libyan Islamic Fighting Group (LIFG) before growing weary of the manner in which the GIA was using *takfir* to confront its enemies. It was a stark reminder of its destructive nature if left unchecked.

The tyrants (*ṭawāghīt*)

Most of the significant works on *takfir* from Salafi-Jihadi thinkers can be codified in a number of different ways to explain how the concept works in practice. To do this effectively it is possible to organise *takfir* into three distinct categories. This involves *takfir* being pronounced on: (1) tyrannical (*ṭawāghīt*) or apostate (*murtadd*) Muslim rulers; (2) criminal transgressors or oppressors (*mujrimūn* and *zalīmūn*), such as the intelligence or police services, and others who more generally enforce or support oppressive rulers; and (3) heretics (*mushrikūn* or *rawāfiḍ*) such as the Shi'a.[24] Each of these will be considered in turn here.

Ṭawāghīt

Just a few weeks before Anwar Sadat's favourite public holiday, featuring a military parade to celebrate Egypt's reclamation of the Sinai, a young Lieutenant named Khalid Islambouli learned he would be participating in the event. He was tasked with leading an independent detachment from the 333rd Artillery Brigade along the procession route.[25] It was just the opportunity he had been looking for. With hand grenades hidden in his helmet, Islambouli and three soldiers broke off from the procession and assassinated Sadat on October 6, 1981. "I have killed Pharaoh," Islambouli famously proclaimed in a statement that was loaded with ideological significance, referencing the tussle between Moses (Musa in Islamic scripture) and the Pharaoh of Egypt.[26] The ideological antecedents of Sadat's assassination can be traced to Muhammad 'Abd al-Salam Faraj, an electrical engineer based in Cairo. He had established himself as an important theorist around the same time as Takfir wal Hijra was imploding under state pressure in the late 1970s. Faraj shared Shukri Mustafa's views regarding the decadence of the political establishment but disagreed with his generalised views about the decline of Muslim society as a whole. Moreover, whereas Mustafa believed in withdrawing from society through *hijra*, Faraj wanted to confront it through jihad—something he believed was a forgotten obligation among the Muslim *umma*.

His views were published in a hugely influential tract, *Jihad: The Absent Obligation*, which quickly found a receptive audience in radical circles. The environment in which it was conceived naturally contributed to its success too. Not only had domestic opposition been intensifying towards Sadat ever since he launched a crackdown against the Islamists, but grievances against him accelerated after the Camp David Accords were signed in 1978. Even Sadat's assassin was partly motivated by personal feelings of vengeance after his brother, Muhammad Islambouli, had been rounded up as part of Sadat's campaign of mass arrests at the start of 1981. A febrile atmosphere swept across Egyptian universities, transforming them into hotbeds of radical dissent, with large numbers of Islamist students starting to gather under a new umbrella movement, al-Jama'a al-Islamiyya, which coordinated their activities across the country.

Confirming the rulers as ṭāghūt

Faraj developed two principal arguments with regards to tyrannical Muslim rulers (*ṭāghūt*). The first was that they have fallen into disbelief by failing to rule by the *shari'a*. This was not a particularly unique innovation, although Faraj was responsible for reviving and popularising it to a broader audience in the modern era. The second argument was more novel and suggested that contemporary rulers had become *khawārij* by "rebelling" against the rule of Allah. This view adopts an esoteric approach towards the meaning of *khawārij*, but asserts that when those in authority fail to uphold the laws of God they become renegades from the community. Either way, the corrective prescription was always the same—that errant rulers should be fought and removed. Faraj was much more explicit than his predecessors, such as Sayyid Qutb, in calling for open insurrection against the state. Unlike Qutb, he also invoked the work of Ibn Taymiyya and, in particular, cited the Mardin fatwa in support of his beliefs.

The use of Ibn Taymiyya's work by Faraj was not uncritical. He disagreed with the Damascene scholar over precisely which characteristics should define a state. "Do we live in an Islamic state?" Faraj asked his readers.[27] He reasoned that Egypt was not an Islamic state because it did not implement the *shari'a* and Muslims had therefore "lost their safety."[28] There were two reasons for this. The first related to Israel, which Faraj believed posed an existential threat to its Arab and Islamic neighbours. He was dismayed that Egypt had abandoned armed confrontation against its Zionist neighbour. The second issue related to the state's policy of rounding up Islamists and crushing their movements. Both factors confirmed the malignant decay of Egyptian society to Faraj's mind: "When Islamic laws govern the state it is *dār al-Islam*, and when the laws of *kufr* govern, it is *dār al-kufr*."[29] This was sharply at odds with Ibn Taymiyya's work which held that the prevailing laws and institutions of a state do not define its nature. Instead, he looked to the inhabitants of the state in question. Another point of difference between Ibn Taymiyya and Faraj came from the latter's invocation of *Qur'an* 5:44 which states:

> And whoever does not judge by what Allah has revealed—then it is those who are the disbelievers.[30]

Two subsequent verses (5:45 and 5:47) replace the word "disbelievers," with *zalīmūn*, meaning oppressors or tyrants; and *fasiqūn*, meaning wicked, or someone who openly flouts the laws of God with blithe indifference. These verses are now ubiquitous in the writings of Salafi theorists who criticise Muslim rulers, but are not found in Ibn Taymiyya's work when discussing Mongol implementation of the *yāsa/ yāsiq* laws.

This leaves room for ambiguity. How is an errant Muslim ruler to be judged, exactly? Is he a *kāfir*, *zālim*, or *fāsiq*? The best exposition on how to distinguish between these categories comes from an example given by Abu Hamza al-Masri in a short tract condemning human legislation.[31] Hamza gives the fictitious example of a Muslim judge who presides over a case of adultery. If the judge simply denies the *hadd* (plural, *ḥudūd*) by claiming that it does not exist, is irrelevant, or that he knows better, then he has committed an act of *kufr*. However, if he substitutes the *hadd* with another law while acknowledging (even just quietly within his heart) what the *hadd* stipulates, then he is a *zalim*. Meanwhile if he recognises the *hadd* but thwarts its implementation by, for example, acquitting the accused on a technicality in order to prevent the *hadd* from being implemented, then it is an act of *fisq* (the act carried out by a *fasiq*).

Most Salafi scholars tend to regard errant Muslim rulers as falling into the categories of *zulm* or *fisq*, rather than *kufr*.[32] Jihadi clerics are less charitable, arguing that the head of state should be judged by higher standards than ordinary people. In their case, "it is actually *kufr* just to fail to rule by it [the *shari'a*]," according to Abu Hamza.[33] That view was echoed by 'Ali ibn Khudair al-Khudair in an essay considering whether a Muslim ruler should be regarded as a disbeliever in every case where they fail to implement the *shari'a*. "Rulers who rule with other than what Allah has revealed, ruling instead with man-made laws, or with habits and traditions, they are [always] *kuffār mushrikūn* [polytheistic disbelievers]," he replied.[34]

Reconfiguring the relationship with ṭawāghīt

Omar 'Abd al-Rahman, the so-called "blind shaykh" who led al-Jama'a al-Islamiyya until his conviction for the 1993 World Trade Center bombings, has produced important work seeking to establish an appropriate relationship between Muslim citizens and *ṭaghūt* rulers. He argued that nothing is owed to Muslim rulers who fail to implement the *shari'a*, citing Islamic rules on rebellion (*aḥkām al-būghat*) as evidence for this. "Who[ever] does such a thing has rejected both religion and justice, and must be deposed," he argued.[35] By contrast, an unjust and tyrannical ruler who nonetheless implemented Islam would require obedience. He explained:

> It is not permitted to rebel against the Caliph merely because of oppression or corruption so long as they do not change any part of the *shari'a*.[36]

Rebellion is triggered only by the absence or abrogation of *shari'a* while tyranny and injustice "is not sufficient to warrant [rebellion]."[37] This chimed with Faraj's belief that Sadat was a disbeliever because of his failure to implement the *shari'a*. "The present rulers have apostatised from Islam," he declared.[38] Views like this ensured widespread support for Sadat's assassination among Egyptian militants, many of whom had studied and disseminated Faraj's work. In fact, his arguments had become so persuasive within radical groupings that Islambouli had only been associated with the Egyptian Islamic Jihad group for a matter of months before carrying out his attack.[39]

When Islambouli finally shot Sadat it was the most dramatic pronouncement of *takfir* in the modern age. The act was invested with huge religious and ideological significance. Muslim rulers were suddenly legitimate targets and could no longer automatically expect obedience by virtue of their office alone. Rebellion against them was sanctioned, and their murder justified. It was a remarkable but inevitable development, borne of the fissiparous Egyptian environment where Islamists and the state found themselves locked in a perpetually combative relationship.

Claiming Ibn Taymiyya's legacy

The legacy of Ibn Taymiyya's encounter with the Mongols continues to loom large in Salafi-Jihadi circles. Sayyid Imam al-Sharif argued that contemporary Muslim rulers were even worse than the adversaries Ibn Taymiyya encountered because the Mongol legal system had at least been dualistic. In practice this meant that the *yāsa/yāsiq* laws were only applied to non-Muslims while Muslims were still governed by the *shari'a*. This still amounted to *kufr* because they had failed to implement the *shari'a* in its totality but it nonetheless made them better than contemporary rulers who judge Muslims by alien legal standards. In this regard they had surpassed the Mongols by way of defiance and disobedience towards God. Sharif told his readers:

> Today's rulers who are imposing the laws of *kufr* on the Muslims are greater in *kufr* and deviance than the Tatars [referring to the ethnic identity of the Mongol invaders].[40]

Faraj adopted a slightly different approach but arrived at the same conclusion. He argued that the *yāsa/yāsiq* laws were partly informed by

Islam and partly by other monotheistic legal systems derived from Judaism and Christianity. This made them less dangerous than wholly secular laws because they were at least partially grounded in some form of divine scripture. "There is no doubt that it [*yāsa/yāsiq*] is less criminal than the laws laid down by the West, which have nothing to do with Islam or any religious laws," wrote Faraj.[41] All of this built quite deliberately on Ibn Taymiyya's experience with the Mongols. The importance of Ibn Taymiyya to Salafis as a whole makes this kind of comparison particularly loaded. Muslim rulers alone are to blame for not implementing God's laws and their failure to do so is an unparalleled transgression. The corollary is clear: the absence of *shari'a* constitutes *kufr* and necessitates rebellion. This takes the legacy of Ibn Taymiyya and applies it in a unique way, using the lessons of Mardin to license popular unrest and intra-Muslim violence even during times of political stability.

Criminal transgressors and oppressors (*mujrimūn* and *zalīmūn*)

The decision to confront errant Muslim rulers was not particularly contentious in Salafi-Jihadi circles. Although their reasoning found its roots in the scholarship of Ibn Taymiyya, his Mardin fatwa was not always easily applied to the situation in which modern theorists found themselves. The Mongols represented a belligerent invading force which threatened the security of residents living under the Mamluk Sultanate, and everyone assisting their efforts was an equal partner in their enterprise. For contemporary theorists hoping to incite rebellion against their own governments, they would also have to justify confrontation against its agents: everyday policemen, intelligence officers, and soldiers. This required making the case for killing one's neighbour and fellow citizen-stranger, with whom a common citizenship, civic identity, and ethnic affiliations were often shared. Put simply, they could not just be dismissed as hostile aliens.

Organs of the state therefore had to be delegitimised. Whereas Islambouli was able to attack Sadat directly, confrontations between Islamists and the state typically involved clashing with members of law enforcement or the intelligence agencies. It is precisely these symbols of state power that continue to be attacked by militant Salafis, not least in Egypt, Libya and Saudi Arabia today.[42] This section will explore Salafi-Jihadi thinking with regards to those who directly support the state, barriers to *takfir* against those individuals, and the ways in which the Salafi-Jihadi movement has overcome such impediments.

The general rule about those who support the state

The principal argument used against those working for the state is that they are directly engaged in supporting tyranny (*anṣār al-ṭawāghīt*). That relational connection might seem straightforward enough, but a number of Salafi-Jihadi theorists have conceived of it in very broad terms. Abu Hamza argued that anyone who participates in the democratic process of the state, for example by voting, has committed heresy because they are supporting *kufr* and have entered into a social contract with elected officials to legislate on their behalf.[43] Abu Basir al-Tartusi echoed those sentiments with regards to supporters of the Saudi government:

> Everyone who supports, protects, and defends this regime from among the kings, princes and other than them from their associates who carry out their will, they are all *kuffār* and apostates... And what we say regarding the Saudi regime, we likewise say the same regarding its oppressive army, for it is an army just like any of the other Arab armies, put together for the sole purpose of aiding the *ṭawāghīt* and defending their thrones and their interests. So it is an army that turns along with the desires of the ruling *ṭāghūt*.[44]

This establishes a general theoretical principle: that those who aid oppressive and tyrannical rulers, the *anṣār al-ṭawāghīt*, become *kafir* themselves. Almost identical views are expressed by a number of other theorists including Omar 'Abd al-Rahman, Abu Muhammad al-Maqdisi, and Abu Hamza.[45] Despite the consensus, opposition to the *anṣār al-ṭawāghīt* appears to be somewhat of a new development within Salafi-Jihadi thought. Classical texts from antiquity do not seem to have considered the issue in any meaningful way (beyond some broader discussions about treason), and it is notable that in all of the contemporary works addressing this issue, that scholars such as Ibn Taymiyya are not cited.

It was nonetheless held that Muslims should refrain from any action that might lend support or legitimacy to the functions of a non-Islamic state. Those who do not are apostates. Militant organisations have used this reasoning to validate attacks against government buildings and institutions in circumstances where the casualties are invariably Muslim themselves. This line of thinking was prominently on display in a video produced by al-Qaeda in Saudi Arabia featuring an attack on the al-Muhaya housing complex in November 2003. One of the suicide bombers, 'Ali bin Hamid al-Harbi, warns police officers and security personnel to abandon their positions because their actions support the House of al-Sa'ūd. He also asks them to consider what they are seeking. Are they striving for the sake of God or a monthly salary and pension plan? The message concludes by warning state employees that while they remain in their posts, they are legitimate targets for attack. They are the ones, after all, who are directly supporting the rule of a government "that is very far from Islam."[46]

A number of similar attacks occurred in the years after 9/11 affecting Muslim countries across the world, from Morocco to Pakistan. Ayman al-Zawahiri was asked about the religious validity of these attacks during a virtual town hall meeting in 2007 when users of two jihadi internet forums—*al-Ikhlāṣ* and *al-Ḥisba*—were invited to quiz him about the global jihad movement. Several hundred questions were asked, of which a number focused on *takfir*. When Zawahiri eventually responded he only did so to a handful of questions but chose to answer one about the permissibility of killing Egyptian policemen. He argued:

> I believe that the officers of the State Security—Anti-Religious Activities Branch—who investigate Islamic causes and torture the Muslims are infidels, each and every one of them... And it is permissible to kill the officers of State Security and the rest of the personnel of the police.[47]

While there is broad consensus within the Salafi-Jihadi movement about the apostasy of those who support the state, the issue of killing them simply because of their association with a particular group or profession is much more controversial. There is an important difference of degree here. An individual may have fallen into apostasy for any number of reasons—not all of which would merit their death. For example, is a traffic warden in a Muslim country directly contributing towards the rule of an oppressor or tyrant? Are they guilty of "waging war" on Islam by carrying out their duties? Indeed, are they even conscious and cognisant of the serious charges being levelled against them by *takfiri* practitioners?

Barriers to general takfīr *against those supporting the state*

The issue of attacking employees of the state for heresy once again reveals a fault line in the Salafi-Jihadi tradition between theorists and practitioners. The former tend to be much more cautious and reticent about making generalised *takfīr* on everyone solely based on their affiliation with a particular institution. This is an important issue because it involves potentially licensing attacks against innocent Muslims. Abu Muhammad al-Maqdisi explains, "the blood of a Muslim is dear, and its sanctity is great, and the violation of Muslim blood is a great danger."[48] Theorists have consequently articulated a more nuanced approach. While it may well be the case that working in some positions constitutes *kufr*, it is necessary to first ascertain the understanding and intention of each individual with regards to the issue at hand before pronouncing *takfīr* on them. Abu Basir al-Tartusi explained:

> The foregoing ruling on the regime is a general one, and it does not imply by necessity the *kufr* of everyone who argues on behalf of the regime or enters into its supporters...[because] many of those who argue on behalf of this regime are unaware of [its] realities.[49]

This affords protection to those who are, for example, misguided or ignorant. Tartusi argued that people should be excused from *takfīr* for all kinds of reasons. They may, for example, be well meaning and simply unaware that their actions constitute *kufr*. He also argued that while some people understood the issues, they may have been misguided either because of the ostensibly Islamic character of the government—particularly in places like Saudi Arabia—or because of fatwas from government scholars. Tatrousi insisted these were all factors that could serve as barriers to *takfīr*, arguing that it is forbidden to make generalised pronouncements of *takfīr* over entire classes of people. "We have to declare them disbelievers individually, *takfīr bi'l mu'ayyan*," he wrote.[50] This means that while the police are institutionally condemned and joining the force is prohibited, those who work within it are nonetheless protected from generalised *takfīr* until their personal understanding of the issues has been ascertained. "We have to look at the *mawani'* [obstacles] and *shurūṭ* [conditions] of *takfir*, before we declare one of these individuals as disbelievers,"Tartusi wrote.[51] Both Tartusi and Abu Hamza al-Masri produced detailed studies exploring the various *mawani'* and *shurūṭ* that exist as barriers to *takfir*, with Abu Hamza warning against "the evil of excessive and exaggerated *takfir*."[52]

Tartusi was also keen to stress that generalised *takfir* should only be used sparingly and favoured a more detailed study of the issue at hand. For example, while it would be forbidden to work in those parts of the police service tasked with curbing Islamist activities, this would not mean that every function of a policeman is prohibited. Tartusi therefore refused to condemn traffic wardens because "there is a benefit in it, for the entire humanity."[53] This underscored the need to exercise *takfir* carefully, with due consideration first being given to an individual's personal circumstances and beliefs. It marked a serious point of rupture between fighters and theorists within the Salafi-Jihadi tradition, where the former regarded these nuances as intellectual luxuries born of abstraction. Their practical consequence would be to render jihad unworkable. What they needed were binary distinctions—and this is what they would act upon.

The approach of militant Salafis has led to accusations of zealotry and misunderstanding. The main criticism is that they pronounce *takfir* on the basis of *kufr dūna kufr* (disbelief less than full disbelief), which refers to those who commit major sins but nonetheless remain within the faith. This has exposed groups like al-Qaeda, al-Shabaab and Islamic State to accusations of being neo-*khawārij* movements because they are quick to make *takfir* on Muslims who, even if they are guilty of serious sins, cannot be dismissed as disbelievers.[54] Declaring *takfir* solely on the basis of major sins "shows the lack of fearfulness and piety" by those making the pronouncement according to Saudi cleric Jamal bin Farihan al-Harithi: "And this is the methodology of the *khawārij*, in that they perform *takfir* on account of major sins."[55]

Harithi also argued that contemporary practitioners of *takfir* confused two important issues. The first is that everyone is a sinner, and there is nothing exceptional about an individual who commits particular sins per se. The second is that there are individuals who declare forbidden acts to be lawful under Islam (*kufr istiḥlāl*), which is an act of *kufr akbar*. In each case, there is a duty to assess the understanding and intention of an individual before pronouncing *takfir*. "Everyone who commits a sin, whether a major or minor sin, then he did not commit it except after considering it to be minor and having belittled it," Harithi argued. "The one who [commits] sin is not the same as the one who [performs *istiḥlāl*]."[56]

The proclivity of Salafi-Jihadis for pronouncing *takfir* on their enemies has resulted in a number of establishment clerics declaring them *khawārij*. Shaykh Salih al-Fawzan, for example, argued that "they broke away from the scholars, broke away from the Muslim leaders, and the believers...so, they have become outcasts in Muslim societies. They are *khawārij*, no doubt."[57] Similar opinions are expressed by other quietist clerics including 'Abd al-Muhsin al-'Ubaykan and Muhammad Nasir al-Din al-Albani.[58] 'Ubaykan even published an op-ed in the London-based *Asharq Al-Awsat* criticising Abu Musab al-Zarqawi and al-Qaeda in Iraq, accusing them of propagating a "deviant *kharajite* ideology... [which] spread unspeakable evils."[59]

Overcoming the barriers to general takfir

Late in the evening on December 29, 2004, an al-Qaeda cell in Saudi Arabia known as the Muqrin Squadron (*sariyat al-muqrin*) launched a double car bomb attack against government agencies.[60] The first of these exploded outside the Ministry of Interior followed by a second outside a training facility of the General Security Emergency Forces (*Quwāt al-Ṭuwāri'*).[61] Twelve guards were wounded in the blasts. Attacks of this kind would be impossible, of course, if the qualifications on general *takfir* had been observed. Establishing the personal belief of each individual in those locations, from the support and administrative staff to the guards and soldiers themselves, is clearly impossible. Groups like al-Qaeda therefore need a way to overcome the obstacles, *mawani'*, to general *takfir* if they are to prosecute their war in Muslim states.

This has given rise to a body of jurisprudential work from those who fight in the field, to rebut and challenge the opinions of Salafi-Jihadi theorists who are not engaged in operational activities. There are two issues they need to confront. The first is overcoming the barriers to generalised *takfir* against people simply based on their affiliation to a particular group or institution. The second concerns the validity of taking ordinary Muslim life whenever such attacks are launched. Scholars such as Maqdisi, Tartusi, and Abu Hamza have very little to say on this second point, leaving it to groups like al-Qaeda to extend and develop the theology almost exclusively in their own image.

Crucially, al-Qaeda does not reflexively dismiss those who caution against the unfettered use of *takfir*. They accept that individuals have personal circumstances and that these are worth consideration. That issue was explicitly addressed in a short booklet published by al-Qaeda in Iraq, along with a denial that the group pronounces *takfir* on the basis of *kufr dūna kufr* (disbelief less than full disbelief) alone. It states:

> We do not excommunicate monotheists or those who pray toward the *Ka'ba* [house of God in Makkah] if they commit such sins as adultery, drinking alcohol, or theft [*kufr dūna kufr*] unless they declare these sins permissible [*istiḥlāl*]... every person, including an unbeliever, has individual circumstances.[62]

Arguments relating to *kufr dūna kufr* are actually misleading in this respect. Although al-Qaeda takes a harsh view on those who commit major sins, there is no evidence to suggest its members make *takfir* on this basis alone. In fact, they articulate two completely different arguments to overcome the *mawani'* to *takfir* which have nothing to do with this.

The first argument is that, in practical terms, enemy institutions need to be fought as a whole because it is the institution that is the oppressive element. Thus, the General Security Emergency Forces in Saudi Arabia are targeted because they have responsibility for counter-terrorism operations. This leads to the second argument which states that the jurisprudence of balances, *fiqh al-muwāzanāt*, overrules the barriers to *takfir*. This position states that when two competing obligations conflict, priority should be given to the more important one. In this case, the issues which must be weighed up are the necessity of jihad against a tyrant ruler, versus the prohibition on shedding innocent Muslim blood. Al-Qaeda in Iraq explained that it would prioritise jihad because "next to faith, there is nothing more important than repulsing an assailant enemy who ruins the religion and the world."[63] The conclusion is clear: Islam would wither and die without jihad, making its preservation the overriding and most critical issue. Ayman al-Zawahiri explained:

> Whether we declare them unbelievers individually or declare them unbelievers in general, if that is in the framework of a combat campaign which

> makes targeting them a method of harming them in the interest of the jihad—because the apostate refraining party is fought as one—it is [even] permitted to kill the one of them who flees and [to] put their injured to death… the obligatory defensive jihad is not suspended in order to determine their status.[64]

Zawahiri rejected the idea that al-Qaeda was responsible for deciphering the personal circumstances of everyone housed inside the institutions they attacked. "Clarification of status is in regard to the one under our control only," he argued.[65] This is not to say that al-Qaeda is entirely averse to considering barriers to *takfir*. Several years after the 2003 invasion of Iraq, al-Qaeda was keen to demonstrate that it was exercising caution. At one point the group claimed to have launched 2000 attacks aimed at stopping Sunni Muslims from participating in the Iraqi parliamentary elections in March 2010.[66] In the days prior to the election the group warned Sunnis against voting because of the "polytheism of democracy"—and, by extension, the polytheism of anyone who engaged with it. Abu Hamza al-Baghdadi, who led the group in Iraq at the time, also warned his men against launching indiscriminate attacks on polling day.[67] "What was wanted was to prevent Sunnis from participating in the elections," he explained. "The order was clear: stop them, do not kill them."[68] In this respect he claimed success and declared, "we did not deliberately kill a single Sunni. All those who were killed were of the rejectionist religion [referring to the Iraqi Shi'a]." This was an almost implicit recognition that al-Qaeda's *takfiri manhaj* had, at times, gone too far and resulted in the death of innocent Muslims.

Heretics (*mushrikūn* and *rawāfiḍ*)

Opposition to heretics is perhaps the least contentious category in which *takfir* operates. Although there are a broad number of people judged to have fallen into heresy, there are two types which must be considered with regards to the Salafi-Jihadi understanding of this concept. The first relates to spies and the second is in relation to the Shi'a. Both are singled out for particular disdain. Heretics tend to be singled out for attack much more frequently than those in the previous two categories—although this is probably due to circumstance and opportunity more than anything else.

The ruling on spies

Spying is classified as a major sin in normative Islam and is linked to the idea of backbiting (*ghība*) which is expressly prohibited in the *Qur'an* and is compared to eating the flesh of a dead sibling.[69] Within this category of sin there is a related concept of *namīma* which means to engage in malicious gossip and is the category under which prohibitions against spying are usually listed. The idea is that spying causes discord by spreading suspicion and strife (*fitna*). Spies also present unique challenges for militants and therefore this aspect of their jurisprudence receives particular attention. The issue of spies is discussed in an exhaustive study by Abu Yahya al-Libi titled, *Guidance on the Ruling of the Muslim Spy*.[70] He explained that spies—and, by extension, other members of the security apparatus—form "important fronts on which the infidels rely in their war on Islam and Muslims."[71] He concluded:

> Spying on the Muslims is non-belief and apostasy from God Almighty's religion…Every person who takes on this vile profession is an aid to the non-believers against the believers and fights against God Almighty's religion to which he claims to belong. He who does that has rid himself of Islam and has become an apostate from Islam and a non-believer…One should know that this ruling is not specific to those who spy for the original non-believers, which include Jews [and] Christians…[those] who spy for the apostates also fall under this ruling. There is no difference in the ruling between them.[72]

Spying is therefore always equated with both apostasy and inherent hostility towards Islam. It is worth bearing in mind that the definition of spy in this context is not limited to employees of intelligence agencies, but applies to anyone gathering information surreptitiously on behalf of another party. This is because the rulings on spies are derived from the concepts of *ghība* and *namīma*.

General Salafi *hostility towards the* Shi'a

Belligerent Salafi attitudes towards the Shi'a crystallised in the aftermath of the 2003 invasion of Iraq. This is not to suggest that attitudes towards them were favourable before—they were not—but the war allowed a state of open hostility towards them which has since intensified in the region as a result of the Syrian civil war. Hostility towards

Shi'a beliefs exists across the spectrum of Salafi opinion, including among quietists. This is hardly surprising given the emphasis placed on purification of the *'aqīda* by Salafis—the very issue over which their disputes with the Shi'a principally arise. They also deride the Shi'a for their hostility towards the *Ṣahāba*, the community whom the contemporary Salafi movement aims to emulate.

Quietists have traditionally viewed the Shi'a with suspicion and regard them as having adopted sinful beliefs into their *'aqīda*. "The Shi'a contain many sects," explained the former Grand Mufti of Saudi Arabia, 'Abd al-'Aziz bin Baz, "and every sect has forms of *bid'a*."[73] Quietists generally view the Shi'a as Muslim but regard them as misguided and sinful. Nonetheless they remain a sect within the faith. This is clear from the collected volumes of Bin Baz's fatwas where he accepts questions from the Shi'a while also imploring them to embrace Sunni beliefs. For example, after answering a question on marriage from a Shi'a, Bin Baz concludes by saying:

> I advise you and your like to stop following the doctrine of al-Baharah [a Shi'a sect] or any other sects of Shi'a, because they contradict the Islamic way called by the Prophet Muhammad (peace be upon him) in many aspects. Therefore, you must renounce them and follow the way of *ahl al-sunna wa-l-jamā'a*.[74]

Hostilities towards the Shi'a intensified following the Iranian revolution which delivered the first empowered and self-assured Shi'a political authority of the modern age. A brilliant essay by Nibras Kazimi shows that the antecedents of this hostility reach back to a book titled *Wa ja'a dawr al-majus* (Then came the turn of the *majus*), authored by 'Abdallah Muhammad al-Gharib.[75] This is a *nom de guerre* and the actual author is unknown, although Kazimi speculates that it is most likely a Syrian member of the Muslim Brotherhood named Muhammad Suroor Zein al-A'bidin.[76] The cynicism of the author is apparent from the title of his book. *Majus* is a catchall Arabic term referring to Persian Zoroastrianism from which the Shi'a are disparagingly said to originate.[77] The book's main argument was that the Iranian revolution was only partly about the revival of Shi'a Islam while the rest was about restoring Zoroastrian principles which threaten both Islamic and Arabic culture.[78] Leading members of the Saudi *ṣaḥwa* movement, such as Salman al-'Awda, echoed similar views in the early 1990s. Meanwhile, at official levels, the Council of the Senior Scholars (*Majlis Hay'at Kibar al-'Ulama'*) had commissioned a study on the Iranian revolution and its impact on Shi'a communities living inside the kingdom in the 1980s.[79] The Shi'a have therefore been viewed with both continuous suspicion and distrust within Salafi circles—a factor that would burnish militant attitudes towards them.

Al-Qaeda and the rāfiḍī

The merger of doctrinal disputes with political intrigue has produced a particularly toxic attitude towards the Shi'a, which has intensified sectarian difference in modern times beyond anything that preceded it over the last two centuries. The origins of this difference lie in Shi'a hostility towards the Prophet's wife, Aisha, because she raised an army against 'Ali and because the Shi'a also pronounce *takfir* on Abu Bakr and Umar ibn al-Khattab, two important *Ṣahāba* who succeeded the Prophet as Caliphs. This has earned them the pejorative appellation of '*rāfiḍa*' meaning 'rejecters.' Even quietists are harshly arrayed against the *rāfiḍa*. Bin Baz described them as the "most dangerous" sect of Shi'a Islam who are guilty of "major *shirk*."[80] He also counselled against marrying them or even interacting with them in social settings, expressing views that were echoed by numerous other clerics from quietist Salafi traditions including Saleh al-Fawzan and Rabi' al-Madkhali.

Militant Salafis have tended to regard all Shi'a as *rāfiḍa* and have exploited political unrest in the Levant over the last fifteen years to initiate a sectarian war against them. "The *rāfiḍa* are an evil sect that left the fold of Islam and fight the *ahl al-sunna wa-l-jamā'a*," Abu Musab al-Zarqawi concluded. Such views come from historical conspiracies about the Shi'a being created as a schismatic sect within Islam by Jews, in order to undermine the religion. "The *rāfiḍa* have never made enemies with anyone except the people of Islam," Zarqawi argued. "They did not fight the Jews or the Christians. How could they hate them when the founder of their *madhhab* [school of thought] was a Jew?"[81]

The obsessional hatred of Shi'as was a constant feature of al-Qaeda material following the 2003 invasion of Iraq. Zarqawi outlined a litany of grievances, many of them echoing the themes found in al-A'bidin's work, although his most serious charge was that Shi'as were working with the United States to undermine both Iraq and its Sunni population. This evoked memories of Ibn al-ʿAlqemi, the Shiʿa minister who had helped the Mongols overrun Baghdad in the thirteenth century. It was a theme Zarqawi regularly touched upon.[82] "*Al-rāfiḍa* liked the Tatars [Mongols] and their state," he said in a message to Iraqi Sunnis in April 2004. "Whenever Muslims triumphed over Christians and infidels, *al-rāfiḍa* became depressed."[83]

Just as Bin Laden had believed the United States was using corrupt Muslim rulers to control Islam and the Middle East during the 1990s, Zarqawi arrived at the same conclusion about Shiʿas during the Iraq War. They had invited the Americans into Iraq and were now conspiring with them to consolidate power. Zarqawi explained:

> The United States has started to hide in the background, pushing these supporters to the frontlines to replace it in fighting the mujahideen. Our enemy now and the impending threat to the jihad are these *al-rāfiḍa* along with the dregs of the Sunnis.[84]

Kazimi has shown that an unknown author who published under the *nom de plume* Imad ʿAli Abdul-Sami Hussein heavily influenced Zarqawi's analysis.[85] He was the first to draw parallels between ʿAlqami and the American invasion of Iraq in a booklet published in early 2003, describing the Shiʿa as "aggressors" for assisting "Crusader occupiers."[86] He argued they were actually serving the interests of both Iran and the United States simultaneously, operating as "paws used to strike at Muslims in Iraq."[87] Suspicions about Shiʿa collaboration intensified in June 2004 when Grand Ayatollah ʿAli al-Sistani convinced the radical Shiʿa cleric Moqtada al-Sadr to enact a ceasefire in Najaf and Kufa. Until then his Mehdi Army had been confronting Western coalition forces with vigour before Sadr eventually agreed to a truce. "There is no better ally for the Jews and Christians than the obscured *rawafids*," Zarqawi concluded. "Their Satan Sistani ordered his followers from the *rawafid* not to fight the Americans. After that, they became spies for the Jewish oppressors and an ally for the Christian criminals."[88]

The supposed treachery of the Shiʿa is what makes them candidates for *takfir* in this instance. Zarqawi always insisted that he had not wanted to fight them originally and that he was not doing so on account of their sectarian identity. His hand was forced when they began aiding the United States and its allies, crossing into a category of heresy that necessitated confrontation. "The *rāfiḍa* near us are more dangerous than the Americans," Zarqawi surmised. "They are more abhorrent and oppress the people more. They have come with a plan that does not have any other aim except suppressing *ahl al-sunna*."[89] The bitter and fratricidal sectarian conflict that followed was so brutal that even Ayman al-Zawahiri admonished Zarqawi for the manner in which he had launched such a frontal assault against the Shi'a.[90] Zawahiri did not have substantive theological disputes with Zarqawi's approach—instead his concerns were more tactical. He affirmed the righteousness of attacking the Shi'a, but warned that al-Qaeda's approach in Iraq was alienating potential supporters in the wider Muslim world. In order to carry public opinion he urged Zarqawi to desist from fomenting a sectarian war, although his pleas would ultimately fall on deaf ears.

Conclusion

That is the real point about *takfīr*. For all the discussion about the dangers of its excesses, the concept has become an intrinsic and essential feature of the contemporary Salafi-Jihadi movement. For al-Qaeda in Iraq and the movement it later birthed, Islamic State, *takfīr* has been particularly important. Their struggle since 2003 has been imbued with historical significance, given that much of their fighting takes place in many of the same places where 'Ali confronted his enemies. Moreover, to wrestle control from the demographically superior number of Shi'a in Iraq, Salafi-Jihadis in the region need this doctrine to fuel what is otherwise a straightforward struggle for power. They cannot abide the thought of Shi'a Muslims holding the reins of political authority in a land of such central importance to Sunni Islam.

This chapter has also shown how the medieval scholarship of Ibn Taymiyya relating to Mardin was instrumental for modern theorists wanting to legitimise violence against the state. If the Mongols were infidels for failing to implement the *shari'a*, then the same rules would have to apply today. Various Salafi-Jihadis have constructed a number of different rules for declaring *takfīr* against someone, ranging from outright heresy to the major sins of oppression and tyranny. Even theorists who urge caution such as Abu Hamza al-Masri have nonetheless insisted that the practice of *takfīr* is a necessity. Those who oppose it altogether have "come with their mouths open to drink from the curdled milk of *shirk* that is being fed to them by the wet nurses of democracy," he concluded.[91] Perhaps this lukewarm effort to check its worst excesses explains why it has proved so difficult to control the nihilistic tendencies for fratricide inspired by *takfīr*.

AL-WALĀ' WA-L-BARĀ'

6

THE MAKING OF LOVE AND HATE

Al-walā' wa-l-barā'

Al-walā' wa-l-barā' is a vague and slippery idea, one that is difficult to define both linguistically and conceptually. In its most basic construction the doctrine means "loyalty and disavowal" for the sake of Allah. The term is hotly contested by scholars. In traditional and normative Islamic theology the issue has generally concerned itself with the personal conduct of Muslims, counselling them to distinguish their manners—greetings, clothing, festivals and appearance—from that of non-Muslims. The concept was therefore a highly personalised one, which originally acquired political dimensions during the early nineteenth century when the first Saudi state faced collapse and ruin.

In its political and military contexts, the concept of *al-walā' wa-l-barā'* operates in a similar fashion to *takfir*, as a tool of "in-group" control which draws a line against those deemed to be outsiders. It forms a distinct delineation between the Salafi-Jihadi constructions of Islam and everything else, forming a protective carapace around the faith which guards against impurity and inauthenticity. Put this way, *al-walā' wa-l-barā'* is integral to the protection of Islam itself, just as *takfir* is also used as a protective tool. This chapter demonstrates how *al-walā' wa-l-barā'* was originally cultivated as a distinctly political idea in the last two centuries and has continued to operate as such. As has already been seen with the previous two concepts, the development of this idea comes about principally as a response to war and crisis. These events also reveal the origins of the idea as something which both protects the Muslim community—by preaching exclusivity and loyalty to it—while also licensing attacks on its enemies—by advocating violent disavowal from them. As it stands, *al-walā' wa-l-barā'* is therefore a concept of huge importance to the Salafi-Jihadi movement, helping perpetuate its Manichean worldview. The world is divided between loyalty and disavowal (*al-walā' wa-l-barā'*); truth and falsehood (*hāqq wa bātil*); faith and disbelief (*īmān wa kufr*).

While there is a dense body of work exploring *al-walā' wa-l-barā'* in general, only Joas Wagemakers has produced serious and insightful analysis of it with regards to the Salafi-Jihadi movement.[1] This chapter does not reproduce or emulate his work but distinguishes itself from it, because much of Wagemakers' focus relates to the approach, ideology, and influence of Abu Muhammad al-Maqdisi. Therefore, when Wagemakers considers *al-walā' wa-l-barā'* he usually does so from this perspective—measuring Maqdisi's interaction with the idea, the extent to which he shaped it, and the manner in which he used it. The discussion presented here is more concerned with the concept of *al-walā' wa-l-barā'* within the broader context of Salafi-Jihadi discourse. It therefore considers how the movement as a whole—not just Maqdisi—developed the idea, and how it empowered it in terms of licensing political dissent, sedition, and direct confrontation.[2]

Understanding *al-walā' wa-l-barā'* and its linguistic dimensions

The term *al-walā' wa-l-barā'* is linguistically ambiguous, resulting, unsurprisingly, in conceptual ambiguities too. It is commonly held that the term defies precise English translation although its general meaning or sentiment can be imputed. To do this it is worth first considering what the individual terms mean. *Al-walā'* derives from the root of *muwālah*, meaning "love" or "friendship" (although, in this case, it refers to friendship of a more emotionally proximate and intimate nature than that experienced by mere acquaintances).[3] It is also similar to terms like *wilāyah*, meaning "loyalty" or "devotion," and is linked to the word *tawallī* which appears in the *Qur'an* in the context of "obedience," such as in verse 60:100 which uses the term in the following phrase: "*yatawallawnahu*" with regards to those who obey Satan or those who doubt the oneness of Allah.[4] *Al-barā'*—along with associated words like *tabarrā'*—means "severance" or to "be free of."[5] Verse 9:1 of the *Qur'an*, for example, uses the word *barātun* to denote dissociation.

As with a number of Islamic concepts, some scholars argue that there is a distinct legal meaning which applies alongside the purely semantic interpretation. This is best demonstrated by the work of Muhammad Saeed al-Qahtani, a Saudi scholar who has produced one of the most important and exhaustive studies on the Salafi understanding of *al-walā' wa-l-barā'*.[6] This work formed the basis of his doctoral thesis under the supervision of Muhammad Qutb, the brother of Sayyid Qutb. Qahtani was also among a group of outspoken Saudi scholars who opposed their government's decision to ally itself with the United States in the early 1990s, giving his work both relevance and resonance among anti-state Salafi groupings such as the *ṣaḥwa* and jihadis.

His work illustrated the legal elasticity of the concept by explaining that *al-walā'* applies to all situations in which one is required "to help, to love, to honour, to respect something, and to stand next to like minded people both outwardly and inwardly."[7] By contrast, *al-barā'* applies to those situations in which one is required "to take heed of a warning, to disassociate oneself from something, avoiding it totally and showing enmity towards it."[8]

The concept is succinctly defined as love and hate, or loyalty and disavowal, for the sake of God. Moreover, the two should be thought of as occupying opposing ends of a spectrum where, by definition, the closer an individual draws to one end, the further they move away from the other. As a result, Salafi-Jihadi adherents of the principle adopt an uncompromising approach regarding the practice of *al-walā' wa-l-barā'*, viewing it as a zero-sum game. Wagemakers correctly identifies the idea as providing a tool to "steer Salafis away from *bid'a*, *kufr*, and *shirk*."[9] It is a powerful and preservationist idea, drawing a line against anything that might be termed "non-Islam," whether it be thought, action, individual, or institution. It also simultaneously brings together the "in-group" of Muslims by protecting them against the "other" and its dangers, explaining why this idea is given such prominence among Salafis. Bernard Lewis argues:

> Islam is still the basic criterion of group identity and loyalty. It is Islam that distinguishes between self and other, between in and out, between brother and stranger…there is a recurring tendency, in times of emergency, for Muslims to find their basic identity and loyalty in the religious community—that is to say, in an entity defined by Islam rather than by ethnic or territorial criteria.[10]

Lewis perhaps overstates the case but he touches upon some of the important outgrows which stem from the concept of *al-walā' wa-l-barā'*. The concept gives rise to, and interacts with, a number of broader concepts for the Salafi-Jihadi movement such as the idea of transnational brotherhood defined through confessional identity—and, by extension, giving primacy to the very notion of the *umma* itself. Loyalty is for the believer: any believer, regardless of sex, colour, or ethnic origin. What matters is faith alone. Islam thus becomes the sole basis of citizenship, identification, loyalty, and allegiance, where identity is defined solely through this fraternity of the faithful alone. This has become a powerful mobilising idea which resonates not just with Salafi-Jihadis but with political Islamists too.

The emergence and development of *al-walā' wa-l-barā'* as a political concept in the first and second Saudi states

The development of *al-walā' wa-l-barā'* as a political concept was principally shaped by events in nineteenth century Arabia, following the collapse of the first and second Saudi states.[11] As each state rose and fell, it sought to generate support and legitimacy for itself by appealing for reinforcements using arguments based on the principle of *al-walā' wa-l-barā'*. Understanding the background and geography to these developments is of particular importance.

The rise and fall of the first Saudi state

Early nineteenth century Arabia was a canvas of competing fiefdoms with each vying for political dominion over the rest. Muhammad ibn Sa'ūd, who created the first Saudi state (1744–1818) had initially found opportunities for expansion weighted against him.[12] His new statelet was officially known as the Emirate of Diriyah and was based in the

Najd hinterland, an elevated upland in the centre of the Arabian Peninsula. This divorced him from the traditional centres of Arabian power which, at the time, were based in the Hijaz, a sliver of land along the western coast of the peninsula where both of Islam's most holy sites are housed—the *Ka'ba* in Makkah which Muslims face for prayer, and the Masjid al-Nabawi, the Prophet's mosque (which also houses his tomb) in Medina.

Fortune would soon shine on al-Sa'ūd. In the unremarkable Emirate of Diriyah, he met an equally unremarkable scholar, Muhammad ibn 'Abd al-Wahhab, who was living a semi-nomadic existence at the time. A wanderer-scholar, he toured the Arabian Peninsula and grew increasingly worried by what he perceived as the proliferation of errant Islamic practices. As he saw it, the most pressing issue for Muslims concerned the way in which Islam was being practised. These fears stemmed from ritualistic impurities related to the rise of mystical Sufi practices in Makkah and Medina which Wahhab associated with four centuries of Ottoman suzerainty over Islam's most holy sites.[13] These concerns were shared by al-Sa'ūd who also regarded the proliferation of these practices as threatening both the authenticity and purity of Arabian Islam.

Al-Sa'ūd proposed a union. He would join with 'Abd al-Wahhab in a symbiotic relationship that would inspire the renewal and moral reform of Islamic practices within the *Jazirat al-Arab* (Arabian Peninsula). It was a deal that would forever transform the political landscape of the Gulf—and, arguably, of global Islam too. Wahhab was to provide religious validation for al-Sa'ūd's reign and would sanction his wars of conquest against neighbouring tribes in uniquely confessional terms. In return, his family—the Al ash-Shaykh—would be allowed to enforce Wahhab's particular brand of religious conservatism within al-Sa'ūd's dominion. This laid the basis for a division of power between these two families which has continued to define the Saudi state into the present day: with the al-Sa'ūds running political, economic and administrative affairs, while the Al ash-Shaykh control social affairs, public morality, and education.

This exchange reveals how ascetic scholars from the Al ash-Shaykh family became involved with al-Sa'ūd's otherwise wholly political programme. When their state came under attack—which it did frequently in its early stages—they developed the concept of *al-walā' wa-l-barā'* as a tool to repel aggressors. The first significant attack came in 1811 after the Ottoman Empire decided to wrestle back power from al-Sa'ūd who had managed to capture Makkah and Medina a few years earlier. These were holy sites on which Ottoman rulers had validated their claims to the Caliphate, prompting them to urge the Khedive, or *walī* of Egypt, Muhammad 'Ali Pasha, to reclaim the Hijaz for them.[14]

An important religious current underwrote the entire confrontation. Wahhab's doctrine revived the literalist Hanbali school of interpretation which is at odds with the more rationalist approach of the Hanafi school—whose jurisprudential approach was favoured by the Ottomans. In its most basic terms the conflict can be viewed as a battle for control over the future trajectory of Islam in the Arabian Peninsula, prompting Wahhab to develop *al-walā' wa-l-barā'* as a concept of political mobilisation in order to win the loyalty of wavering Hijazi tribes by appealing to them in distinctly confessional terms.

One of the most important early tracts in this respect came from Sulayman ibn Muhammad ibn 'Abd al-Wahhab (1785–1818), one of 'Abd al-Wahhab's grandsons.[15] The book, *Al-Dalā'il fī Ḥukm Muwālāt ahl al-Ishrāk* (The evidences for the ruling regarding alliances with the infidels), strongly warned Hijazi tribes against Ottoman attempts to secure their loyalty. They portrayed the Ottomans as *mushrikūn*, polytheists, due to their endorsement of spiritual and mystical practices associated with some adherents of the Hanafi school. Sulayman ibn 'Abd al-Wahhab wrote:

> If a person displays *muwāfaqah* [compliance/agreement] with the *mushrikūn*—out of *khawf* [fear] from them, *mudārāh* [friendship/lenience] towards them, or *mudāhanah* [compromise/deceit] to repel their evil: then verily, he is a *kafir* just like them.[16]

This is an emphatic statement, but it is important to unpack the broader points raised in Sulayman's work. He appears to have aimed his message at tribes, as distinct communities or collective units, when warning them against supporting "soldiers of *shirk* [ascribing partners to God] and *qibāb* [domes found on tombs—a reference, in this case, to the mystical practices of some Ottomans]."[17]

The significance of this is that it creates collective responsibilities and obligations on the tribes as communal entities while leaving it unclear what is required of individuals in their private or personal capacity. Sulayman does not tell his readers, for example, that they must disavow their tribe if it betrays the principles of *al-walā' wa-l-barā'* by making a deal with the Ottomans. There is no sense of them being held vicariously liable, incurring vicarious sin, or experiencing the creation of vicarious obligations arising from the decisions of their tribal leaders. That was just as well given that Sulayman's views had little impact beyond his inner circle and a number of tribes did end up supporting Muhammad 'Ali Pasha. When his forces eventually triumphed and overran the first Saudi state, Sulayman was executed for his troubles.[18] Despite his personal misfortunes his work reveals the first serious attempt to engineer political loyalty and support in wartime through arguments based on *al-walā' wa-l-barā'*.

The rise and fall of the second Saudi state

The second Saudi state encountered many of the problems which brought down the first. Almost immediately after Egyptian forces occupied Diriyah in 1818, Turki ibn 'Abdallah al-Sa'ūd began trying to reassert the dominance of the al-Sa'ūd tribe. The pushback was so fissiparous and chaotic that scholars are divided over precisely when the second state officially came into being. Both Tim Niblock and Joas Wagemakers argue that Turki revived the rule of the al-Sa'ūds by 1824.[19] Yet, Pascal Ménoret has shown that despite such claims, Egypt maintained strong and direct control over Diriyah by maintaining garrisons there, having responsibility for negotiating treaties between different tribes, and managing prisoners until as late as 1843. This was when Turki's son, Faisal bin Turki al-Sa'ūd, came to power (for the second time) and finally rid Diriyah of all Egyptian influence.[20]

Turki's reign as "Imam"—the title by which rulers of the first and second state were known—was extremely turbulent and, again, the concept of *al-walā' wa-l-barā'* was deployed as a tool for establishing social stability. Both Turki and his son 'Abdallah, who succeeded him, faced a series of competing challenges from rival family members for the Imamate. In fact, 'Abdallah's greatest challenge came from his own brother, Sa'ūd, who instigated a bitter civil war that stunted the second state and prevented it from enjoying the same territorial expansion as the first.[21] The brothers fought for almost two decades and as 'Abdallah tried to find new ways of decisively overcoming Sa'ūd he eventually enlisted the Ottomans' support, allowing them to dock their naval forces in Ras Tanura so that the eastern province of Qatif could be secured.[22] It was in this context that another highly influential work on *al-walā' wa-l-barā'* emerged: *Sabīl an-Najā wa-l-Fikāk min Muwālāt al-Murtadīn wa ahl al-Ishrāk* (the way of cutting relations off from the polytheist and apostate). Its author, Hamad ibn 'Atiq (1812–1883), was every bit as important to the second Saudi state as Sulayman had been to the first.[23]

Most contemporary scholars of the second Saudi state tend to neglect Ibn 'Atiq's work, although it contains a number of instructive points. Wagemakers notes that 'Abdallah was the focus of Ibn 'Atiq's work and that he was "strongly against 'Abdallah's call to the Ottomans for help, and he wrote this book [*Sabīl*] specifically to condemn it."[24] In fact, Ibn 'Atiq was condemning both 'Abdallah and Sa'ūd because the latter was also in a military alliance with British forces at the time.[25] This is evident from the broader discussions Ibn 'Atiq presented in his work. "Anyone who befriends a *mūshrik* [polytheist] is a *mūshrik*; anyone who befriends a *kafir* is a *kafir*, whether they are from the *ahl al-kitāb* [people of the book; monotheistic Jews and Christians] or not" he wrote.[26]

The rise and fall of the first two Saudi states provides important context for understanding the early politicisation of *al-walā' wa-l-barā'* as a concept in Salafi thought. Sulayman created a set of collective obligations and responsibilities, demanding tribal leaders give their loyalty to Muhammad ibn Sa'ūd in his confrontation with Muhammad 'Ali Pasha and the Ottomans. He therefore established the notion of *al-walā'* as being a collective endeavour where one Muslim community must support another. Ibn 'Atiq was different in the sense that, unlike Sulayman, he was criticising his own ruler by counselling 'Abdallah against seeking Ottoman support. This established the idea that even for a beleaguered Muslim ruler who was being unfairly attacked, the rules of *al-walā' wa-l-barā'* still prohibited him from seeking the assistance of apostates, polytheists, and disbelievers. Yet, much as Sulayman had done, Ibn 'Atiq's work focused on decisions being made by the state and did not make demands on individuals. To that extent, despite condemning 'Abdallah for working with the Ottomans, Ibn 'Atiq did not declare *barā'* from him.

When taken together both texts set the tone for theorising the manner in which Muslims should avoid collaboration with non-Muslims in political settings. The foundations laid by these texts have endured and their relevance continues to reverberate today. One of the main producers of contemporary Salafi-Jihadi material, Tibyān Publications, continues to describe these works as "the main books regarding the topic of collaboration written by the *salaf*."[27]

The development of *al-walā' wa-l-barā'* as a theoretical doctrine of dissent

The concept of *al-walā' wa-l-barā'* was less important after the unification of Saudi Arabia, when the modern state emerged in 1932. Domestic Salafism was now able to grow uncontested and in a quietist fashion, where stability and social unity were prioritised over everything else. This was important for two reasons. The first was that normative Islamic theology had long stressed political stability where the *'ulama'* were subordinate to political authorities. This was an accepted principle ever since the time of the rightly guided Caliphs and can only be negated in circumstances where the *amīr* fails to implement God's laws. Bin Baz captured this sentiment perfectly in a book explaining the relationship between Muslim rulers and their people:

> It is not from the *manhaj* [method] of the *salaf* to publicise the faults of the rulers and to mention such things from the pulpit because that leads to confusion, disorder and the absence of hearing and obeying the ruler in what is good... The followed path with the *salaf*, however, is to give *naṣīḥa* (advice) with respect to the matters which are between themselves and the leader, writing to him or by reaching him through the scholars who keep in touch with him (to advise him) until the ruler is directed towards the good.[28]

This led to the second reason why the *'ulama'* were keen to ensure social stability. Social unrest had led to the collapse of the first two Saudi states and, in the process, undermined their ability to create an ideal Islamic society. Roel Meijer explains, "For Salafism politics for its own sake is not important, but rather it is doctrinal purity that is the basis for political involvement."[29] Without a stable and organising central authority it was clear the Salafi social agenda would never be realised. With the emergence of a unified Saudi state, the *'ulama'* finally had a chance to embrace the opportunity that was being offered to them by the House of al-Sa'ūd. The *'ulama'* were now free to oversee social provision and public morality while the Sa'ūds organised the state, ensured security, and were left to run both the economy and foreign diplomatic relations. This delicate but nonetheless enduring dynamic has produced extraordinary stability in an otherwise febrile and fissiparous region.

It was a model that would not be left uncontested for long. Salafi-Jihadi theorists have argued that the rules of *al-walā' wa-l-barā'* necessitate active resistance against errant rulers. The approach currently adopted in Saudi Arabia by the Al ash-Shaykh family is to offer subtle and discreet advice behind closed doors. One of the most important texts rejecting this approach comes from Abu Muhammad al-Maqdisi in *Millat Ibrahim* (the way of Abraham), which was published in 1984. At least part of it was written during Maqdisi's stay in Afghanistan and Pakistan, when the Arab *mujahideen* were fighting against the Soviet Union.[30]

Millat Ibrahim is one of Maqdisi's most famous works. Almost three decades after its publication it enjoys a sustained readership within radical circles. By his own testimony it quickly became a cornerstone of "jihadi ideology" and a "thorn in the throats, and a pain in the chests, and an ulcer in the guts" of his enemies.[31] Some radical Salafi groups in Britain and Germany have even called themselves "Millat Ibrahim," with at least one mosque operating under this name in Solingen, before German authorities closed it in 2012.[32] The example of Ibrahim is an important one within Islam. After all, why would a Muslim cleric, particularly a conservative Salafi, write a treatise on lessons from the life of Ibrahim rather than the Prophet Muhammad? The answer comes from the manner in which Salafi clerics have interpreted the life of Ibrahim, reducing all of his experiences to a struggle of *al-walā' wa-l-barā'*. Maqdisi also saw it in this way, describing the concept as "the essence of the path of Ibrahim, and his *milla*."[33]

Islamic theology holds that although Adam built the original *Ka'ba* (also known as *bayt al-ḥaram*) in Makkah, it was destroyed during the

Great Flood that afflicted Noah. Ibrahim was then tasked with both its reconstruction—reviving the physical manifestation of *tawḥīd* on the earth—along with spreading the message of monotheism to a deeply polytheistic Arabian society.[34] These acts of devotion and loyalty represent Ibrahim's *al-walā'* to God. Yet, Ibrahim did not stop there and is also said to have destroyed a number of idols which surrounded the *Ka'ba* at the time, thereby demonstrating his *barā'* from them.[35] The same lessons are present in the life of Muhammad who was, according to Maqdisi, required to "make *tawḥīd* known [with] open enmity and disavowal towards *shirk*."[36]

It was this politicised understanding of the Prophets' lives that drove Maqdisi to an understanding of *al-walā' wa-l-barā'*, which was entirely different from the earlier works of Sulayman ibn 'Abd al-Wahhab and Hamad ibn 'Atiq. Under their construction of the idea, it was an essentially passive doctrine that counselled tribes and rulers against seeking the help of non-Muslims. An omission or refusal to act in a particular way was enough to satisfy the conditions of *al-walā' wa-l-barā'*, as they conceived of it. Maqdisi now transformed it into a concept that created a series of obligations requiring positive and affirmative acts. Consider how it relates to *barā'*. This otherwise passive doctrine was now transformed into a muscular and aggressive one, requiring an offensive approach. It was no longer enough to make *barā'* from something simply through omission. An act would be required. Therefore, when faced with an unjust Muslim ruler it was insufficient to just shun them. In order to realise the full meaning of *barā'* the ruler would need to be confronted and challenged directly. Maqdisi explained:

> The Muslim has not openly declared his religion until he opposes every assembly in whatever disbelief it is famous for, while clearly declaring his enmity towards it and his disavowal (*barā'*) from it.[37]

Maqdisi's most significant contribution to the development of *al-walā' wa-l-barā'* emerged from this understanding, with the creation of an extra series of obligations and responsibilities that were tied to it. Thus, whenever an expression of *al-walā'* was declared, it would have to be accompanied by an act of *barā'*. Sayyid Imam al-Sharif echoed similar sentiments in a treatise he wrote on the *Fundamental Concepts Regarding al-Jihad*.[38] He argued that the requirement to establish loyalty to Islam and Muslims while dissociating from everything else is a unique and specific challenge presented to Muslims alone. He argued that enmity from disbelievers towards Muslims was divinely decreed, innate, and ordained by God himself. It was therefore instinctive to them. Put another way, disbelievers are naturally inclined to establish their own *al-walāʾ* towards *kufr* and *shirk* while manifesting *barāʾ* from Islam. "Allah [has] empowered the disbelievers over the believers through a decreed empowerment," wrote Sharif.[39] He went on to explain:

> The disbeliever (*kafir*) takes the believer as an enemy due to his belief. And the more the faith (*īmān*) of the slave [of God] increases, then the more his share of the enmity of the disbelievers will increase… and the more his faith (*īmān*) decreases, then the more their enmity towards him decreases.[40]

Sharif advanced a deeply conspiratorial worldview, but it was one that further underscored the idea of *al-walāʾ wa-l-barāʾ* as a confrontational and militaristic doctrine. Disbelievers were "empowered" by God to have natural enmity and hostility towards Islam. Meanwhile, there is no comparable predisposition towards *al-walāʾ wa-l-barāʾ* within Muslims. Realising its goals is therefore a challenge that Muslims must actively embrace and strive for. The requirement to make *al-walāʾ* towards Islam and Muslims, and *barāʾ* from everything else is consequently viewed as a legislative command. Muslims are being tested to prove themselves capable of "repelling the disbelievers."[41] This happens in stages, according to Sharif. Disbelievers should first be invited to Islam and then, if they refuse, should be fully disavowed, "alive or dead."[42] Much like Maqdisi's construction of *al-walāʾ wa-l-barāʾ*, Sharif envisioned a doctrine of active dissent and rebellion. It is one that requires positive actions to realise its full meaning and becomes most relevant at times of conflict or strife.

Conclusion

The concept of *al-walāʾ wa-l-barāʾ* traditionally existed as an idea which related solely to matters of personal conduct and behaviour. It operated as a marker of identity in many respects, distinguishing believers from the rest, and aspired to create distinct cultural bonds within devotional communities. Yet, of all the ideas discussed in this book, *al-walāʾ wa-l-barāʾ* is perhaps the most opaque and ambiguous. It is also the concept about which least is known in Muslim circles, and has little reach in social groups beyond those already attracted to reactionary or millenarian interpretations of Islam. This pathology allowed it to adopt political overtures during the last two centuries when emergent rulers first began using it as a tool for popular mobilisation, particularly during times of crisis.

Its evolution in this regard appears to have come in stages: applying first to communal groups as a whole and then, later, to individuals. It does not seem as if *al-walā' wa-l-barā'* yielded many dividends for those who initially deployed it when the first Saudi two states collapsed, despite making demands for loyalty based on the concept. As the third Saudi state consolidated itself and moved towards a period of stability, the political evolution of *al-walā' wa-l-barā'* appears to have slowed down until Arab fighters began gathering in Afghanistan to fight the Soviet Union during the 1980s. What emerges thereafter, principally from the work of Abu Muhammad al-Maqdisi, is a more assertive and robust doctrine that aims to licence social dissent. The implications are profound. Whereas the political application of *al-walā' wa-l-barā'* had previously been used by those in authority and then only in order to rally support against external belligerent forces, Maqdisi and others were now fashioning it into a tool for popular use against established power structures. This turned it into an instrument of domestic dissent, allowing for groups and individuals to mobilise others against their own governments. The next chapter examines how Salafi-Jihadi theorists have done this over the last two decades.

7

AL-WALĀ' WA-L-BARĀ' AS SOCIAL EMPOWERMENT

Manifestations of *al-walā' wa-l-barā'* as a means of rebellion, separation and confrontation

The political environment immediately after the conclusion of the Afghan-Soviet war was near perfect for the development of *al-walā' wa-l-barā'* by non-state actors who suddenly found themselves in a state of flux. Their world was changing fast, with old boundaries shifting in response to political and military developments. Buoyed by an improbable victory in the mountains of the Hindu Kush, they found a climate of domestic repression in their home countries. Algeria was busy cancelling the electoral gains of Islamist parties, Egypt was cracking down on returning militants, and Saudi Arabia was entering into military alliances with the United States to repel Saddam Hussein from Kuwait. This chapter explores how the idea of *al-walā' wa-l-barā'* was used to oppose the institutions of state power and how it evolved into an absolutist doctrine demanding complete loyalty. Over time it has evolved into a doctrine concerned with issues of Muslim identity, exclusivity and difference, and been used by reactionaries to distinguish themselves from the strictures of modernity.

Early Salafi-Jihadi debates around isti'āna bi-l-kuffār

As had been the case with the first and second Saudi states, it was once again the exigencies of war—this time in Afghanistan—that would drive the way in which *al-walā' wa-l-barā'* manifested itself. One aspect of this doctrine focuses specifically on the issue of seeking or taking help from non-Muslims: *isti'āna bi-l-kuffār*. First discussed by Hamad ibn 'Atiq with regards to the conflict between 'Abdallah and Sa'ūd in the nineteenth century, the topic was revisited by 'Abdallah 'Azzam in his fatwa regarding the *Defence of Muslim Lands*. He wrote:

> Some people believe in seeking help from America and Western states for jihad in Afghanistan, and seeking help from Russia against Jews in Palestine. This type of assistance is *ḥarām*.[1]

Rejecting the assistance of non-Muslims, or as 'Azzam termed them *mūshrikūn*, in this context would "forfeit the ultimate aim of jihad."[2] This is because he linked the cause of jihad to achieving the supremacy of Islam, something he felt would be impossible with non-Muslim involvement. 'Azzam did not, however, regard this prohibition as being absolute and argued that there were certain instances when *isti'āna bi-l-kuffār* would be acceptable. These applied in cases where the following conditions were met:

1. The rule of Islam must have the upper hand, that is to say, the Muslims must be stronger than the combined group of the *mushrikūn* from whom they are seeking help as well as the *mushrikūn* they are fighting.
2. The *kuffār* must have a good opinion of the Muslims, and the Muslims must feel safe from their treachery and this is estimated from their behaviour.
3. The Muslims must be in need of the *kafir* or the *kuffār* they ask help from.[3]

The conditions in which 'Azzam imagined *isti'āna bi-l-kuffār* as being permissible were so narrow that it was impossible to implement them in practical terms. His conditions were far too abstract, with later theorists who worked on this issue simply arguing that such alliances are always prohibited.

Debates on isti'āna bi-l-kuffār *in the contemporary Saudi state*

One of Saudi Arabia's most important and influential state-sanctioned clerics in this period was 'Abd al-'Aziz bin Baz, who was not unfamiliar with controversies relating to the idea of *isti'āna bi-l-kuffār*.[4] Just nine years after the unification of Saudi Arabia in 1941 Bin Baz was appointed to the judiciary in the conservative province of al-Kharj, a stronghold of traditional Wahhabi teachings based 30 miles south-east of the capital, Riyadh.[5] The House of al-Sa'ūd had issued permits for American contractors to enter al-Kharj that year in order to offer expertise on three different projects: overseeing food production at local farms, assisting the California-Arabian Standard Oil Company (CASOC),[6] and helping the Saudi Arabian Mining Syndicate.[7] Bin Baz immediately rejected their arrival as a violation of *isti'āna bi-l-kuffār* and condemned the king for letting Americans use Saudi soil "as if it was not the Muslims' territory."[8]

Bin Baz was summoned to the royal court to explain himself in one of the first major confrontations between the unified Saudi state and the official clerical establishment.[9] The House of al-Sa'ūd insisted that the prohibition on seeking the help of non-Muslims is not absolute and that derogations are permitted in certain circumstances. After all, even the Prophet Muhammad had employed non-Muslims to work for him. How could it be wrong, then, for the king to emulate this Prophetic practice? In much the same way as 'Azzam had understood the concept, it was stressed that the American contractors were in al-Kharj only to serve the king as his guests and that their presence was transient.[10] Bin Baz found this persuasive and changed his opinions on the matter. He later stated:

> Non-Muslims may be recruited to take jobs or professions that Muslims cannot do. Upon completing such tasks, they are to be returned to their countries. The Prophet permitted the Jews to stay in Khaybar when there was a need for that. Then they were expelled by Umar [ibn al-Khattab] when their presence was no longer justified.[11]

This arrangement suited both parties. The royal family was keen to protect its image as the legitimate custodian of Islam's most holy sites, a desire that was galvanised and given greater urgency by the Iranian revolution in 1979 which marked the ascent of Shi'a Islam in the modern age.

In return, Bin Baz and his colleagues were given licence to promote Wahhabi doctrine both within the Kingdom and beyond through international proselytising arms such as the Muslim World League and the World Assembly of Muslim Youth.[12] Religious universities across the country were also generously funded, ensuring that by the early 1990s one in four Saudi students was attending a religious college.[13]

The accommodation that had been reached lasted for almost half a century before being severely tested in the early hours of August 2, 1990, when Saddam Hussein's elite Republican Guard invaded Kuwait. King Fahd immediately sought Western military support—led by the Americans—to defend Saudi Arabia against the prospect of Iraqi aggression. The issue of *isti'āna bi-l-kuffār* roared back into public life, giving rise to the first cases of significant social dissent in Saudi Arabia. Bin Baz led the pushback on behalf of the House of al-Sa'ūd. He issued a fatwa titled *Shari'a stance on the Iraqi invasion of Kuwait*, in which he sanctioned the presence of American troops in the Kingdom.[14] "It is obligatory on all Muslim and non-Muslim countries, as well as all Muslims, to deny and denounce such actions and explain how sinful aggression and oppression are," he wrote.[15] Iraq's invasion of Kuwait was presented as an urgent and unprecedented crisis. "This aggression is one of ugliest types of oppressions," Bin Baz wrote, "and the whole world unanimously agreed on denouncing it."[16] When it came to the specific issue of seeking help from non-Muslims, he advanced the following arguments:

> As for the measures which the Saudi Arabian government has taken as a result of these actions of aggression of the president of Iraq, such as seeking the help of multi-forces from different nationalities including Muslims and others to stop the aggression and defend the country, this is permissible. It is rather obligatory to do so and the Kingdom must play its role in defending Islam and Muslims as well as the sanctity of this country and its people. The kingdom is free of guilt and thanked for its initiation in order to protect the country against evil and its doers and to defend the country against expected aggression which the President of Iraq may wage because he is not to be trusted after what he has done in Kuwait and his betrayal is expected.
>
> It is thus necessary and mandatory to take caution and seek the help of multi-forces from different nations to protect the country and its people, preserve security and protect the country and people from all evil.[17]

The jurisprudential sleights employed by Bin Baz are important here. He was essentially arguing that the prohibitions of *isti'āna bi-l-kuffār* were trumped by the principles of *akhaff al-ḍararayn*, which is the principle of choosing between the lesser of two evils.

Akhaff al-ḍararayn as a means of derogation from the prohibition of *isti'āna bi-l-kuffār*

Akhaff al-ḍararayn is used in Islamic theology when choosing between the lesser of two evils and is a branch of a broader jurisprudential concept known as *maṣlaḥa al-mūrsalā*, which means to act in the overall public good, or public interest.[18] Acting in the public interest in this context, because it is a religious concept, means to do so in a way that promotes the overall aims and objectives of the *shari'a* which are known as the *maqāṣid al-shari'a*.[19] These aims are normatively held to encompass the belief that, in its most basic construction, the *shari'a* came to promote or protect five things: religion, life, honour, intellect, and property. When the *Qur'an* then implores believers to "enjoin what is right" and "forbid what is wrong," it is these overarching aims that are first supposed to be given consideration. In his essay justifying military cooperation between Saudi Arabia and the United States, Bin Baz cited Ibn Taymiyya as an authority on *akhaff al-ḍararayn*. He argued:

> Ibn Taymiyya said in his book, *al-Muharar fi al-Fiqh* (vol. 2, p. 171): "It is not permissible to seek the help of the *mushrikūn* unless it is necessary. If the Muslim army will increase in strength by joining the *mushrik* army and they will both form a powerful front against the enemy, and they [the *mushrikūn*] hold good opinions about Islam, it will be permissible; otherwise it is not.[20]

Ibn Taymiyya gave a fuller understanding of this idea in his book *Enjoining Right and Forbidding Wrong*:

> Enjoining right and forbidding wrong, being one of the greatest obligations or commendable acts in Islam, it is essential that the benefit therein outweigh [any] negative consequences. This is the general spirit of the messages of the prophets and the revealed books, and Allah does not like chaos and corruption.[21]

This is the point on which the issue turns. The extent to which utilitarianism should apply within the *shari'a* is contested between different sects and marks the point of divergence between different types of Salafis on the issue. In this context, "benefit" (*maṣlaḥa*) and "harm" (*mafsada*) are both interpreted through the prism of achieving the goals of the *shari'a*.[22] Ibn Taymiyya explained this as doing whatever secures the will of God:

> If the good involved is greater, then they must be enjoined to do it, even if that necessitates the evil which is of lesser degree, and they are not to be forbidden the evil involved which would mean the loss of the good which is greater than it. In fact such a forbiddance in such a situation would be part of blocking the path of Allah and would be striving for the eradication of obedience to Allah and to His Prophet and toward the elimination of the doing of good.[23]

It becomes apparent that *maṣlaḥa al-mūrsalā* is therefore a theological concept which provides tremendous room for interpretation and debate when context and other considerations are factored into the equation. All of this exposes it to contention. The concept must necessarily engage the subjective—weighing up the relative merits of one political decision against another—making it unsurprising that different scholars have held wildly different views over its suitability and application in different circumstances.

Bin Baz faced an uphill battle when trying to convince Saudis about the merits of *akhaff al-ḍararayn* and *maṣlaḥa al-mūrsalā*. Many remained sceptical of its application, particularly if it was supposed to trump prohibitions on *isti'āna bi-l-kuffār* by allowing Western military bases to be established on the *Jazirat al-Arab*. The innate subjectivity of these concepts and their interaction with the prevailing political climate prompted something quite remarkable in the otherwise inert Saudi kingdom. A popular social movement expressing dissent began emerging for the first time in its history, ultimately manifesting itself in a movement known as the *ṣaḥwa* or awakening.[24]

Resistance to *akhaff al-ḍararayn* and the rise of popular dissent

The *ṣaḥwa* was a reformist group of university-educated Saudi clerics who combined aspects of conservative Salafi theory with careful and cautious political activism. It was the first time Saudis began to mobilise themselves in this way, a watershed moment in the kingdom's history precipitated by the Iraqi invasion of Kuwait. This is not to suggest Saudis had not been exposed to political activism before, but that it was never their own citizens who had been at the forefront of such movements—or that those movements were turning their attention to domestic events. Most of the country's activists prior to this had been immigrants from the wider Arab world, usually exiled members of the Muslim Brotherhood such as 'Abdallah 'Azzam and Muhammad Qutb. Another big source of migration had been Syria, following the Hama uprising in 1982 when scores of Islamists were expelled from the country. They often enjoyed good relations with the kingdom and directed little, if any, criticism at its structures.

The emergence of the *ṣaḥwa* was therefore a pivotal moment, representing the first grouping of Saudi public intellectuals, who created the most sophisticated Islamist movement in the country's history. Having come together informally in the 1980s, the *ṣaḥwa* came of age when they found themselves leading the opposition to the establishment of American military bases in Saudi Arabia. The movement was clear: allying with the United States and other Western countries represented *al-walā'* towards them, even if they were only coming to repel Saddam Hussein.

One of the movement's most important and erudite figureheads was Safar bin 'Abd al-Rahman al-Hawali. Having written his doctoral thesis on secularism (*al-'ilmaniyya*), he was deeply suspicious of the West's political and cultural mores, which he associated with the decline of spirituality and godliness in Europe.[25] These ideas were dangerous and threatened the Muslim community, requiring *barā'* to be made from them. That much is clear from Hawali's influential work, *Wa'd Kissinger* (Kissinger's Promise), which revealed his concerns about American influence in the region:

> The Crusader invasion of the Arab Peninsula has already undermined the honour...of every Muslim. It will not be long until your blood is shed with impunity or you declare your abandonment of your belief in God.[26]

This not only epitomised the dangers of failing to make *barā'* from the West, but was also a direct result of cooperating with it. Hawali therefore warned King Fahd:

> Your regime has committed the forbidden things in Islam which nullify its validity before God....by pledging your allegiance [*al-walā'*] and support to the infidels against the Muslims, you have committed many of the things which are contrary to the teachings of Islam and which demand that you be revolted against and removed.[27]

Hawali and many of the *ṣaḥwa's* leaders had essentially begun using *al-walā' wa-l-barā'* as a mechanism for both mobilising and licensing social dissent. This was unprecedented. Their invocations to rebellion and sedition represented the political manifestation of theoretical arguments first advocated by scholars such as Maqdisi, Qahtani and Sharif who had originally argued that *al-walā' wa-l-barā'* required affirmative action.

Moreover, not only were the *ṣaḥwa* leaders now applying that theoretical approach in a practical setting, but they also enjoyed a fair degree of support for their agenda. The movement was built around Safar al-Hawali and another *ṣaḥwa* leader, Salman bin Fahd al-'Awda. As their campaign against the American-Saudi military alliance intensified, the *ṣaḥwa* produced two historic documents that shocked the House of al-Sa'ūd: the *khiṭāb al-'ulama'* (letter of the scholars), and the *mudhakkirat al-naṣīḥa* (memorandum of advice).

Ṣaḥwa *arguments prove hard to refute*

Bin Baz attempted to address these concerns in a speech held in one of Riyadh's most important Islamic centres, the King Khalid Mosque. The Grand Mufti gave his most forthright assessment of the situation to date, addressing all the issues of *maqāṣid al-shari'a, maṣlaḥa al-mūrsalā*, and *isti'āna bi-l-kuffār* in a long and exhaustive speech.[28] He told the congregation:

> Due to this critical situation, the Kingdom of Saudi Arabia had to seek help of the Muslim and non-Muslim countries. It had to defend the country and its people and escape the evil of this irreligious criminal [Saddam]... [Western] soldiers have one purpose which is driving out the oppressing troops from Kuwait. Neglecting this matter and being indifferent to it is a great danger because the oppressor has a great and well-trained army that was engaged in war for 8 years with their neighbouring country Iran.[29]

This established the case of necessity. Bin Baz further argued that the Prophet Muhammad had also relied on non-Muslim support to occasionally overcome more powerful adversaries. "When the Prophet (peace be upon him) needed a guide to show him the way to Medina, he hired one of the pagans to guide him," he explained.[30] "There is nothing wrong with seeking the help of the enemy when the latter is in favour of us against our enemies."[31]

Bin Baz also gave examples from the Prophet's life where he had worked with non-Muslims, hoping this might allay concerns about the legitimacy of King Fahd's decision. "The obligation is to use whatever means to remove harm and evil," he explained, "even if this means the aid and assistance of some of the *mushrikūn* with respect to repelling aggression and injustice."[32] As a result, he assured the congregation:

> The Council of Senior Scholars, therefore, examined this event thoroughly and decided that there is no harm concerning the government seeking help of non-Muslim countries. The government did so out of necessity and to avoid the great danger threatening the country if this oppressor continued in his transgression and ruined the country.[33]

Another fatwa followed shortly after this speech, which focused much more specifically on scholarly opinions surrounding the issue of *isti'āna bi-l-kuffār*.[34] It was published under the title *Ruling on seeking the help of the disbelievers in fighting against other disbelievers*. Bin Baz essentially reiterated his already stated positions: yes, there exists a general prohibition against seeking help from disbelievers, but this general ruling could be derogated from in specific circumstances. "Seeking the help of *mushrikūn* was initially prohibited but this prohibition was later lifted by a concession; [and] this opinion is the closest to correctness," he argued.[35] "According to *ijmā'* [consensus of the scholars], it is permissible to seek the help of the hypocrites for the Prophet (peace be upon him) sought the help of [equivalent] people."[36]

None of this was new and public opinion remained sharply divided—more so than it had ever done before. The *ṣaḥwa* were responsible for that, having popularised arguments which rejected both *akhaff al-ḍararayn* and *maṣlaḥa al-mūrsalā* as valid reasons to derogate from the prohibition on *isti'āna bi-l-kuffār*. In doing so they inadvertently birthed the first social movement based on the principle of *al-walā' wa-l-barā'* as an idea requiring affirmative actions.

Contemporary Salafi-Jihadi interpretations of *al-walā' wa-l-barā'*

Saudi unease about a military alliance with the United States persisted, although an uneasy calm descended when most turned a Nelsonian eye to the issue after Operation Desert Storm finally started. A number of important points should be noted about the manner in which the *ṣaḥwa* used the idea of *al-walā' wa-l-barā'*. They did not break with the government by declaring *barā'* from it, but were instead advising and lobbying the House of al-Sa'ūd to remember its duties under this principle. The nature of their campaign was therefore one of *naṣīḥa*, attempting to correct the misguidedness of their leaders. What the *ṣaḥwa* were doing largely mirrored the approach taken by Sulayman ibn 'Abd al-Wahhab and Hamad ibn 'Atiq. It was in the aftermath of 9/11 that *al-walā' wa-l-barā'* would once again undergo significant ideational developments as al-Qaeda tried to recast it as a principle to suggest that all Muslims owed it *al-walā'* in its fight against the United States.

Al-Qaeda demands al-walā'

Afghanistan was a paragon of Islamic virtue to the radical mind. This was demonstrated most dramatically when Taliban rulers demonstrated their commitment to the principles of *al-walā' wa-l-barā'* by refusing to hand over Osama bin Laden to the United States in 2001. It was perhaps the most significant demonstration of dedication to this idea in the modern era, a commitment the Taliban embraced regardless of consequence—sacrificing their administration in the process. Mustafa Abu al-Yazid (also known as Saeed al-Masri), who served as al-Qaeda's "chief financial manager" according to the 9/11 Commission Report, thanked the Taliban for their unwavering support.[37] He expressed al-Qaeda's joy at Mulla Omar's decision to reject American appeals, and explained how this demonstrated their commitment to *al-walā' wa-l-barā'*. Yazid argued:

> He [Mulla Omar] insisted on making supreme the meaning of *īmān* [faith], the loyalty [*al-walā'*] to the believers and [*al-barā'*] against the unbelievers, so may Allah reward him in the best way… He refused to back down, and refused to bargain over the believers [meaning Osama

bin Laden and the rest of al-Qaeda]. He took the stance of heroism, courage, dignity and defiance.[38]

In all of the previous cases of *al-walā' wa-l-barā'* examined here, the discussion focused on relationships between governments, or what duty individual Muslim citizens owed their governments. This was the first time, however, that a group or sub-state actor had demanded the government owed it *al-walā'*—rather than it being the other way around. Abu Zubair al-Abab, a member of al-Qaeda in the Arabian Peninsula's *Shari'a* Committee, explained that the principles of *al-walā' wa-l-barā'* should mean giving loyalty to every Muslim in all circumstances.[39] This applied even in cases where individual Muslims might legitimately disagree with one another over issues relating to belief, ideology, or method. Differences of opinion, after all, are valid and accepted within normative Islam provided each party has based their reasoning on scripture.[40] Abab consequently advised his readers to "not take difference as a reason to throw ourselves into the embrace of the secularists and unite with them against the *mujahideen*."[41] He went on to ask:

> Which is the greater disagreement? Is it the one who disagrees with you on an issue of *ijtihād*[42]...or is it the democratic, secular ruler who is loyal to the crusaders, domesticated by Israel, and who appeals to *kufr*, contrary to the principles of the religion?[43]

The corollary was clear: even if Muslims disagreed with al-Qaeda's reasoning they still owed it their loyalty because of the obligations the principle of *al-walā'* placed on them. Mere differences of opinion would not be enough to negate this.

The 'Shu'aybi school' supports al-Qaeda's calls for al-walā'

That message resonated among some Salafi-Jihadis who, despite their radical inclinations, were not members of al-Qaeda. The Saudi cleric Nasir bin Hamad al-Fahd, for example, argued that even if the Taliban and al-Qaeda committed a crime by perpetrating 9/11, the rules of *al-walā' wa-l-barā'* still prohibited Muslims from cooperating with the United States against them. In a fatwa offering an "exposition regarding the disbelief of the one that assists the Americans," he explained:

> What is obligatory in the likes of this situation is that they are judged by the Islamic *Shari'a*, not according to the standards of the *kuffār*! ... Even if the Muslim is an oppressor, his *wilaa* [loyalty] remains because of what is with him of Islam and it is not permissible to assist the *kuffār* against him.[44]

Fahd was one of several radical Saudi clerics who vehemently opposed the assistance being offered by Muslim countries to the United States in the aftermath of 9/11. Much of this group can be pooled together in what Thomas Hegghammer calls "the 'al-Shu'aybi school," named after its key theorist, Hamud al-Uqla al-Shu'aybi from Burayda.[45] Shu'aybi's popularity partly stemmed from the fact he was unaligned with the clerical establishment and he drifted further from the possibility of any official position after parting ways with the Imam University where he had taught until 1994.[46] Factors beyond his control would also contribute to his growing influence during this time. A government crackdown against *ṣaḥwa* leaders in the mid 1990s resulted in the arrest of prominent figureheads such as Salman al-'Awda and Safar al-Hawali, allowing Shu'aybi to fill the space created by their absence. Moreover, the state's trusted clerical bulwarks who would have ordinarily guarded against Shu'aybi's more vituperative statements all passed away within a relatively short period of time. Bin Baz (d. 13 May 1999), Muhammad Nasir al-Din al-Albani (d. 1 October 1999), and Muhammad bin Salih al-'Uthaymin (d. 10 January 2001) all died in close succession, removing a triumvirate of charismatic and well-regarded clerical authorities. Hegghammer has described their absence as creating a "theological power vacuum" inside the country.[47]

Shu'aybi filled the void and became increasingly influential by cultivating a following among several important rejectionist scholars including Fahd, Sulayman ibn Nasir al-'Ulwan, and 'Ali ibn Khudair al-Khudair.[48] These men were collectively among the first and most persuasive theorists to use the ideas of *al-walā' wa-l-barā'* to urge other Salafi-Jihadis to lend both the Taliban and al-Qaeda their support after 9/11. It was a natural move for this grouping of scholars. Shu'aybi had admired the Taliban and believed they represented true Islamic authority. "It is the only country in the world in which there are no man made laws and legislations," he argued. "It is the only country in the world which is striving for women's rights according to the *shari'a* and not according to the ways of the secularists who encourage the women to display their beauty, cast off their hijabs, mix freely with men, drive cars alone and other things like that."[49]

When the United States then prepared to invade Afghanistan in retaliation for the 9/11 attacks, members of the Shu'aybi school rallied in its defence using the principles of *al-walā' wa-l-barā'*. Nasir al-Fahd consequently declared that helping the United States "is one of the nullifiers of Islam."[50] This echoed Ayman al-Zawahiri's view that anyone failing to live by the teachings of *al-walā' wa-l-barā'* is guilty of heresy. It is important to note the manner in which these clerics appealed for Muslims to support al-Qaeda and the Taliban. It was not because the principle of *isti'āna bi-l-kuffār* had been violated. That issue relates to seeking the help of non-Muslims, which was not the case here. Rather than a Muslim seeking the help of a disbeliever, the issue now related to helping a non-Muslim prosecute a war against other Muslims. In this context, they argued that it was emphatically prohibited for any Muslim to support the United States which, according to Fahd, was "the central base of corruption and moral decay; it is the land of shame, crime, vile filth, and evil."[51]

This statement gave rise to an important theological development regarding Salafi-Jihadi thinking on *al-walā' wa-l-barā'*. It has already been seen how Maqdisi and Sharif previously advanced the idea that obligations arising from the concept of *barā'* required affirmative acts. Omissions alone would not be sufficient. The same approach would now be developed towards *al-walā'* too, this time by Nasir al-Fahd and 'Ali ibn Khudair. They argued that any failure to demonstrate loyalty and allegiance to other Muslims, or any displays of loyalty towards disbelievers, would automatically amount to apostasy in almost every case.

To underscore their point they explained how the idea of *al-walā'* can be divided into a series of categories known as *muwālāt* and *tawallī*.[52] The latter relates to matters of the heart, where an individual is emotionally attached to a disbeliever. In these cases, Khudair argued, "*tawallī* is *kufr* within itself, it does not matter what the person believes."[53] By contrast, he explained that *muwālāt* is divided into two subsections where only one negates the faith. Minor *muwālāts* do not fall into apostasy and consist of actions towards non-Muslims that are cordial but not empowering. Khudair argues this constitutes a major sin but does not amount to outright disbelief.[54] The corollary of this is that loyalty to other Muslims—whether as states, groups or individuals—is always a mandated article of faith.

Not all Salafi-Jihadis accept this categorisation of actions, with Sayyid Imam al-Sharif, for example, believing them to be unnecessary. Ironically, it appears as if the concepts of *tawallī* and *muwālāt* are better established in Shi'a Islam than in Sunni thought.[55]

Vicarious liability arising from al-walā' wa-l-barā'*: attempts to undermine Muslim governments and state sanctioned scholars*

Ayman al-Zawahiri published an important book on *al-walā' wa-l-barā'* in which he suggested that whenever the prohibition on *isti'āna bi-l-kuffār* is violated, then *takfir* and jihad become obligatory.[56] It follows on from the idea that *barā'* is a concept requiring actions, in this case of excommunicating and physically confronting those who have offended God by disobeying him. Although this builds on ideas first advanced by Maqdisi and Sharif, there are no such injunctions for *takfir* or violence in any of the earlier works produced by Sulayman, Ibn 'Atiq, or 'Azzam, despite all of them counselling against alliances with disbelievers or errant Muslims. Yet, Zawahiri was adamant. He argued that confrontation is not just mandated in these circumstances but is also "one of the greatest and most individually binding jihads in this day and age," because those who work with disbelievers must always be "governing without the *shari'a* [and are] friends of the Jews and Christians."[57]

Zawahiri's text is divided into two parts with the first assembling a mass of opinions from scholarly and textual sources to support his view. He writes very little in this section, merely providing short passages of text in order to transition from one quote to another. The text he does write often aims to frame the presented quotes in a way that fits the modern world and situation in which Zawahiri found himself. Thus, when discussing *isti'āna bi-l-kuffār* he argued:

> What would [scholars of Islamic antiquity whom he is quoting] say if they were witnesses to American planes taking off from Pakistan in order to kill Muslims in Afghanistan? And what would they say if they witnessed American and Western ships and planes, stocking up on fuel, provisions, and ammunition from Gulf states, Yemen, and Egypt, on their way to lay siege to Iraq?[58]

This view is illuminated much better in the second part of Zawahiri's thesis where he attributes most of the Islamic world's contemporary stagnation to the abandonment of *al-walā' wa-l-barā'*. Much of his analysis is predictable and hackneyed, focusing on well-known grievances: Western troops in the *Jazirat al-Arab*, the Egyptian peace treaty with Israel, sanctions on Iraq and the isolation of Afghanistan. All of these have only been made possible because Muslims abandoned the principles of *al-walā' wa-l-barā'*.

Zawahiri did not limit his anger to the supposed betrayal of Muslim governments. He also held wider society responsible, naming the civil service, journalists, academics and *'ulama'* as being equally to blame. Their complicity is derived from their proximity to the state, which bestows legitimacy upon it. This idea has been seen before in relation to *takfir*, but was now used here in relation to *al-walā' wa-l-barā'*. Zawahiri argued:

> The grand mufti of Egypt is an official employee of the Egyptian government who receives his salary from it in order to render his service, which is to confer legitimacy onto the secular regime, which oppresses Muslims and befriends Jews.[59]

Osama bin Laden employed similar arguments to justify and celebrate an al-Qaeda attack on the US consulate in Jeddah in 2004.[60] He argued that under the House of al-Sa'ūd, "absolute obedience and supremacy are given to the king and his laws, and not to God's religion." In those circumstances, "the governed, on God's orders, must cease to obey," while those who failed to do so would be complicit in their crimes.[61] This manifestation of *barā'* is a particularly powerful tool of mobilisation for sub-state actors looking to undermine established institutions of power. It demands a withdrawal of support from the government, delegitimises the judiciary and police, and undermines the legitimacy of state-sanctioned scholars.

This last group came under particular scrutiny from Osama bin Laden. Sixty American scholars made the moral case for a "War on Terror" shortly after the 9/11 attacks in an open letter titled "What we're fighting for."[62] More than 150 Saudi intellectuals responded three months later—among them Salman al-'Awda and Safar al-Hawali—with a letter titled "How we can coexist."[63] The apparent acquiescence of these clerics to the United States provoked a strong response from

Osama bin Laden who wrote a letter in response titled "Moderate Islam is a prostration to the West."[64] Their attempts to promote reconciliation and coexistence were a betrayal of *al-walā' wa-l-barā'* in his eyes. By extension, he also regarded them as having betrayed Islam itself. By promoting coexistence and failing to make *barā'* from the West, Bin Laden believed that these scholars had fallen victim to a civilisational plot to destroy Islam from within. "What the West desires is that we abandon *al-walā' wa-l-barā'* and jihad," he wrote.[65]

It was an approach that complimented the message spread by Ayman al-Zawahiri, that anyone failing to adhere to the principles of *al-walā' wa-l-barā'* should be excommunicated and fought. Not only have they fallen short of what is required of them, but they have undermined Islam from within by empowering its enemies. Both Zawahiri and Bin Laden were invoking an Islamic principle which states "there is no obedience in disobedience," to argue that clerics failing to practise *al-walā' wa-l-barā'* should be shunned.[66] What they wanted instead was to establish themselves as alternative sources of authority. Again, this mirrors what has already been seen with regards to *takfir*, where legitimacy in radical circles is derived not from rank or position, but through devotional piety. Abu Zubair al-Abab characterised the group's thinking most succinctly when he warned state-sanctioned scholars they would be violently opposed because "your efforts and your friendship have been used to benefit the Crusader campaign because of your abstention [from *barā'*] and loyalty to the lackeys."[67]

Conclusion

The concept of *al-walā' wa-l-barā'* has undergone a series of profound changes over the last three decades. Originally deployed as a tool of social dissent and rebellion by political actors in Saudi Arabia, its ability to create popular agitations around key issues quickly became apparent. During this time the idea was largely a xenophobic one—counselling against alliances with supposedly hostile and alien cultures. Instead it urged exclusivity among Muslims, where believers should rely on one another while shunning everyone else. The inherently political nature of *al-walā' wa-l-barā'* became apparent during this time revealing how Salafi-Jihadis, much like those from other religious traditions, occupy their time searching for authenticity in the space between scripture and meaning.

Contesting that space meant that sub-state groups like al-Qaeda began arguing that Muslims owed them *al-walā'*, suggesting the idea was not limited to states alone. They went even further by arguing that *al-walā'* requires its own affirmative actions, without which individuals would fall into heresy. All of this was ultimately shaped to create alternative structures of legitimacy and authority for Salafi-Jihadi actors who typically operate beyond the framework of the state. It allowed them to delegitimise their opponents for not having displayed adequate levels of *al-walā' wa-l-barā'*, while presenting themselves as the custodians of a pure, unadulterated form of Islam.

More than any of the other ideas already explored in this book it is clear that the evolution of *al-walā' wa-l-barā'* has been driven and shaped principally by conflict. It is an indelible characteristic, present at every turn and stage of its conceptual development. Having emerged as a tool of political mobilisation during the incipient phases of the modern Saudi state, whenever subjected to the stresses of political unrest and conflict it has mutated into an evermore doctrinaire and demanding idea.

TAWḤĪD

8

REALISING MONOTHEISM

Tawḥīd in Salafi thought

Tawḥīd is the central pillar of Islam. It is the doctrine of monotheism and the omnipotence of God, representing the single most important characteristic of the faith, which distinguishes Islam from the preceding era of polytheism known as *jāhiliyya*. Sayyid Abul Ala Maududi argues that *tawḥīd* is "the most fundamental and the most important teaching of Prophet Muhammad."[1] Trying to realise the *tawḥīd* of God is the central goal of every Muslim's life, with Salafis tending to prioritise its fulfilment more than others. They also conceive of it in particularly narrow terms as evidenced in the work of Muhammad ibn 'Abd al-Wahhab and his seminal text on the issue, *Kitāb al-Tawḥīd*. Wahhab's thinking on the matter was shaped by the environment in which it was conceived. Concerned by the growth of mystical practices in eighteenth century Islam, he focused excessively on the promotion of *tawḥīd* in order to steer people away from *shirk*. He obsessed over *tawḥīd* the way Qutb worried about *jāhiliyya*, although both pursued the same ultimate goal of trying to prevent society from slipping back into its pre-Islamic state. This meant the creation of a streamlined and barren understanding of Islam that focused almost exclusively on the preservation of doctrinal purity. This chapter explains the importance and centrality of *tawḥīd* in Salafi thought, its role in making Islam a living ideal where faith and action cannot be separated, and its application to political contexts.

At the most basic level there is nothing unique about the way in which Salafi-Jihadis think about *tawḥīd* compared with other Salafis. All of them place huge emphasis on the work of 'Abd al-Wahhab and his conception of the doctrine. This means there are no major collections of theory, or extensive treatises written by Salafi-Jihadi ideologues, which specifically discuss the concept of *tawḥīd*. That is not to say it does not appear in their books. It is frequently discussed and cited, but generally with reference to 'Abd al-Wahhab's scholarship.

The concept of *tawḥīd* is complex and was broken down by 'Abd al-Wahhab into three constituent parts, in order to help Muslims better understand it. He reasoned that if each aspect of *tawḥīd* could be identified distinctly, then believers would find it easier to ensure they were satisfying all of the varied ways in which God was owed devotion. Differences of interpretation about how each of these branches should be understood reveal areas of intra-Salafi dispute, illuminating some aspects of Salafi-Jihadi thinking that are unique to the movement when considering *tawḥīd*. Before exploring those differences, it is necessary to briefly consider the manner in which 'Abd al-Wahhab categorised the various branches of *tawḥīd*. 'Abd al-'Aziz bin Baz explained these clearly as follows:

- *Tawḥīd al-rubūbiyya* (Oneness of Lordship)
  - This means the exclusive belief in—and recognition of—Allah as the unique and omnipotent Lord of mankind who enjoys absolute command and control over all creation.
- *Tawḥīd al-ulūhiyya* (sometimes also known as *tawḥīd al-'ibāda*; Oneness of divinity, or worship)
  - The belief in Allah as a unique deity, who is alone—and without partners—in being deserving of worship.
- *Tawḥīd al-asmā' wa-l-ṣifāt* (Oneness of names, qualities, and attributes)
  - The exclusive belief in all of Allah's attributes and associating these with Allah. Muslims believe that Allah possesses 99 names, each of which describes a different attribute such as al-Khaliq, the creator; al-Qayyum, the sustainer; and ar-Rahman, the merciful.[2]

This understanding of *tawḥīd* comes from the first half of the Islamic testament of faith—*lā ilaha illā-Allah*—with the absolutist proclamation that there is no God, no deity, nor authority worthy of recognition or worship; before asserting the dialectic negation provided by reaffirmation—but God. The assertion that there is "no God, but God" therefore implies three things: there is no agent but Allah, there is no object of worship besides Allah, and there is no reality but Allah. "This beautiful phrase is the bedrock of Islam, its foundation and its essence," Maududi argued.[3]

Wahhab believed that *tawḥīd* was going unrealised because people only understood one or two aspects of it. The Sufi practice of intercession, for example, represented a failure to realise the meaning of *tawḥīd al-ulūhiyya* (oneness of worship) because calling on others for intercession (typically dead saints) established intermediaries between individual agents and Allah—in much the same way as pre-Islamic Makkan idolaters had believed their idols would intercede for them with a metaphysical deity. The pre-Islamic tribes of Makkah "used to affirm *tawḥīd al-rubūbiyya* (unity of lordship)," Wahhab explained. "But their *kufr* was due to their attachment to the angels, the prophets, and the pious friends of Allah (*awliyā'*) about whom they would say, 'These are our intercessors with Allah'."[4] None of this is contentious among Salafi-Jihadi scholars. For example, although Abu Muhammad al-Maqdisi explores *tawḥīd* in his book, *This is our 'aqīda*, he does not expand or develop the concept in any meaningful way. Maqdisi simply argues that Allah must be "singled out" and that everything besides him must be rejected based on the principles of *al-walā' wa-l-barā'*.[5]

Tawḥīd al-ulūhiyya: Islam as a living ideal

The kaleidoscopic nature of *tawḥīd* incorporates the unity of lordship (*tawḥīd al-rubūbiyya*), unity of divinity (*tawḥīd al-ulūhiyya*), and the unity of names, qualities, and attributes (*tawḥīd al-asmā' wa-l-ṣifāt*) giving Islam a particular view on the relationship between individual agents and God. All of the separate conditions of *tawḥīd* require satisfaction if a Muslim is to realise the *'aqīda* in its fullest sense. In this context, faith alone is a necessary but insufficient condition of both belief and membership in Islam. Faith must instead be coupled with action and vice versa. 'Abd al-Wahhab told his followers that if they simply stated their belief in Islam and recognised Allah as a unified and omnipotent deity, this would only satisfy the conditions of *tawḥīd al-rubūbiyya* and *tawḥīd al-asmā' wa-l-ṣifāt*. The other condition of *tawḥīd*, that of *al-ulūhiyya* (divinity) would remain unfulfilled because Allah was not being worshipped in the way he commanded. Thus, the idea of a passive or non-practising Muslim would be an aberration because the faith necessitates positive actions which represent the practical manifestation of worship.

'Abdallah 'Azzam went further by dividing the nature of faith (*īmān*) into two distinct branches: the theoretical and practical. It is possible that Sayyid Qutb may have influenced him in this regard, having made the same distinction in his extraordinary fifteen-volume commentary on the *Qur'an*, *In the shade of the Qur'an*, although 'Azzam does not acknowledge or reference him explicitly.[6] He argued that the *tawḥīd* of *al-rubūbiyya* and *al-asmā' wa-l-ṣifāt* are theoretical and therefore only require oral and intellectual affirmation. This is the only way they can be satisfied. 'Azzam told his readers that these aspects of *tawḥīd* "can be understood by attending a lecture or two."[7] This is because they represent abstract ideas relating to the essence of Allah—omnipotence, omnipresence, and absolute knowledge—matters which can only be learned through scripture and assented to via the heart. "Every one of us memorises it—you've memorised it, right?" asked 'Azzam. "This is the theoretical aspect of *īmān* which does not require action, it is a matter of knowing it and affirming it."[8] Maududi had expressed similar views, arguing that expressions of belief were one of the necessary components for realising the *tawḥīd* of Allah. He explained:

> It is the expression of this belief which differentiates a true Muslim from a *kafir*, a *mushrik*, or an atheist. The acceptance or denial of this phrase produces a world of difference between man and man.[9]

Yet, this alone is not enough. The commission of positive acts is also needed in order to appreciate and realise the final category of *tawḥīd*, that of *al-ulūhiyya*. 'Azzam explained that "the *tawḥīd* of action is: *tawḥīd al-ulūhiyya*, firm reliance upon Allah alone, fearing Allah alone, worshipping Allah alone."[10] He even argued that it was because of this category that God had chosen to send messengers and prophets to mankind. "The only reason [prophets] were sent was to establish *tawḥīd al-ulūhiyya*," he wrote.[11] "*Tawḥīd al-ulūhiyya* is only affirmed through stances taken in life."[12] Again, similar ideas are found in Maududi's work. "The difference which occurs between the believers and the unbelievers does not result from the mere chanting of a few words," he explained. "The real difference lies in the conscious acceptance of this doctrine and complete adherence to it in practical life. Mere repetition of the word 'food' cannot dull hunger; mere chanting of a medical prescription cannot heal the disease."[13] Within the Salafi tradition, 'Abd al-Wahhab affirmed that "what is required of the '*aqīda* is its meaning, not merely its utterance."[14] The net sum of all these views, of course, is that God requires affirmative acts to confirm belief and that this characteristic is what distinguishes a Muslim.

Tawḥīd *necessitates action*

Ulūhiyya is the part of *tawḥīd* that makes Islam a living ideal. The necessity of coupling action with belief is demonstrated by one of the earliest incidents in the history of creation. According to Islamic belief God started by creating three sentient agencies: angels (*malā'ika*), *jinn* (supernatural and metaphysical beings occupying a parallel world to mankind; created from fire), and man (created from clay). Only the angels lack free will while the others (*jinn* and man) have an option to choose between good and evil or obedience and disobedience. When Allah created the first man, Adam, he commanded the angels and *jinn* to prostrate before him because Adam was "the best of creation." One of the *jinn*, Iblis, refused and was subsequently banished from the gardens of paradise.

There are two lessons from this incident that are of particular relevance to the concept of *tawḥīd*. The first is that it demonstrates the relationship between belief and action, while the second is that it reveals how each aspect of *tawḥīd* should be isolated in order to be realised. Consider that prostration before anyone other than Allah would ordinarily constitute *shirk*, unless the concept of faith (inward belief) and action (the outward manifestation of belief) were linked. Muslim scholars therefore argue that when Allah commanded the angels and *jinns* to prostrate it was not as an act of worship, but as a mark of respect.[15] Although the physical act of prostration is the same, the fact that the angels and *jinn* did not attach any powers of lordship (*al-rubūbiyya*) to Adam negated any *shirk* in their act.

When Iblis refused to bow, it also revealed the implications of failing to carrying out physical acts of devotion. "Practical apostasy includes acts like abandoning *salah* (prayer)," argued 'Abd al-'Aziz bin Baz. "[Even] if a person abandons *salah* while they admit its obligation, but [they] still abandon it, this person will be a *murtadd* [apostate]."[16] Prayer is just one example. The general principle that Bin Baz explained in another fatwa was, "turning away from Allah's religion, not learning it or implementing it is an act of disbelief."[17] Failing to practise the faith therefore meant that an individual had failed to satisfy the first half of the Islamic testament of faith, the *shahada*, because they had not discharged the requirements of "*lā ilaha illā-Allah*." Bin Baz was asked about this very issue on his biweekly radio show, *Nūr ala al-darb* (light along the way) which used to broadcast on the *Nida' al-Islam* (call of Islam) station from Makkah. He told listeners:

> Sayings are not enough and if this were the case, hypocrites would be Muslims because they repeat it [the *shahada*] despite the fact that they are disbelievers... Thus, we must declare the phrase with certainty, knowledge and actions—not just words uttered by the tongue.[18]

To understand just how closely some scholars have linked the requirements of *tawḥīd al-ulūhiyya* to ongoing physical acts, consider that Ibn Taymiyya even suggested it could also be known as *tawḥīd al-'ibāda* (the *tawḥīd* of worship). "The *tawḥīd* of *al-ulūhiyya* is also called the *tawḥīd* of *al-'ibāda*," he wrote.[19] "So in reference to Allah, it is *tawḥīd al-ulūhiyya*, and in reference to the slave, it is *tawḥīd al-'ibāda*." This explains the manner in which it should be seen. God has exclusivity over divinity (*al-ulūhiyya*) while man owes him exclusivity in worship (*'ibāda*).

Redemption through works

That distinction may only represent a difference in degree, but it is one invested with profound implications. Unlike its Abrahamic counterparts, the connection between the *al-rubūbiyya* and *al-ulūhiyya* aspects of *tawḥīd* means that confessional membership in Islam is contingent on continuous works. Islam therefore links salvation to works rather than just faith alone—unlike many Protestant denominations, for whom belief in the crucifixion of Jesus is sufficient for salvation. The process of active agency is sharply focused within Salafi constructions of Islam. With regards to sin, for example, 'Abd al-'Aziz bin Baz explained:

> Anyone who commits a sin should hasten to repent, regret, give up the sin, and be truly determined not to return to this sin to show honour to Allah (Glorified be He), devote himself to Him, and fear His Punishment. Allah (Exalted be He) accepts the repentance of those who repent. When a servant observes sincere *tawba* (repentance to Allah), regrets what he did, and determines not to return to his sins for the sake of and for fear of Allah (Glorified and Exalted be He), He will forgive him and blot out his past sins, because of His favour and kindness.[20]

The *Qur'an* also discusses this principle at length, with numerous passages linking the concept of God's forgiveness to the works of a believer. For example, the *Qur'an* states, "But indeed, I am the perpetual forgiver of whoever repents and believes and does righteousness and then continues in guidance."[21] The concept of seeking active forgiveness is therefore an ongoing one: to "continue in guidance." This interconnectedness between faith and works has coloured Salafi understandings of the entire faith, with the vast majority of them regarding the absence of works as equalling the absence of belief itself.

It follows that Salafi thought does not generally allow for a *murji'a* approach, with the most significant exception to this view being the so-called Madkhalis, who follow the works of Rabi' ibn Hadi 'Umayr al-Madkhali. A onetime activist with the Muslim Brotherhood, he broke with the group in the 1980s and became a staunch critic of the movement while also declaring himself a loyalist of the government in Saudi Arabia. During the 1990s he was one of the first—along with Muhammad Aman al-Jami' (b. 1930)—to challenge the *ṣaḥwa* over their opposition to the House of al-Sa'ūd, arguing that the *īmān* of the ruler should not be questioned. Both Madkhali and Jami' have uncoupled works from faith by arguing that only Allah can decide and assess what is truly within an individual's heart, creating a small but ultraquietist movement within Salafism which practices *irjā'* today.

Political applications of *tawḥīd*

The dispute between Jami' and Madkhali with their Salafi counterparts demonstrates how *tawḥīd* can become politicised, when posited in wider debates about both society and international events. This was also the moment when Osama bin Laden first began voicing his concerns. Filling the vacuum left by the arrest of key *ṣaḥwa* figures, he denounced the House of al-Sa'ūd as "transgressing God's law," committing indiscretions that were not just an affront to Islam but which were also serious enough to negate *īmān*.[22] In a letter sent to King Fahd in 1995, Osama bin Laden declared, "your political and military support for the Yemeni Communists turned out to be the mortal blow that broke your political backbone and the razor that shaved away your credibility on the Islamic front."[23] This view of *tawḥīd* began informing almost every aspect of Bin Laden's political outlook. He repeatedly condemned the House of al-Sa'ūd for supporting the Yemeni Socialist Party (YSP), which was trying to cede southern Yemen from the north, whilst enjoying strong ties to communist parties in the former Soviet Bloc.[24] It was an object lesson in the hypocrisy of modern politics.

Whereas the Saudi government had vigorously opposed Soviet machinations in Afghanistan it was now turning a blind eye to growing communist influence in Yemen. This was a serious matter for Osama bin Laden, not just because it concerned his ancestral homeland, but also because a godless political system was enjoying increased power over parts of the Arabian Peninsula's holy soil. Exasperated with the king's apparent indifference, Bin Laden turned his attention to Bin Baz and questioned his commitment towards the principles of *tawḥīd*:

> Did you not previously give a fatwa that the communists are apostates and it is an obligation to fight them in Afghanistan? Or is there a difference between the communists in Yemen and the communists in Afghanistan? So how did you lose your understanding in the issues of *'aqīda* and the principles of *tawḥīd*, and confuse them to such an extent?[25]

The gravity of the charge was an extremely serious one: accusing Saudi Arabia's Grand Mufti of betraying both the *'aqīda* and *tawḥīd* of Islam—the twin pillars on which the modern Saudi state is based. For Bin Laden it was a turning point, confirmation of the extent to which Bin Baz had become completely obsequious before the political decadence of the House of al-Sa'ūd.

Political tawḥīd *after 9/11*

Although the politicisation of *tawḥīd* emerged as a topic of intra-Salafi debate during the early 1990s, it was revived in haste after 9/11. In one of his first public addresses after the attacks, Osama bin Laden explained that his understanding of *tawḥīd* mandated a conflict with the United States. "Distancing oneself from a tyrant is not just an optional action," he said, "but rather it is one of the two pillars of *tawḥīd*, and *īmān* that cannot be established in the absence of either of them."[26] The political realisation of *tawḥīd* is therefore intrinsically linked to the establishment of faith itself, a theme on which Bin Laden expanded when eulogising the 9/11 hijackers on the sixth anniversary of the attack. In the process he explained how al-Qaeda had come to view the relationship between *tawḥīd*, *īmān*, and the *'aqīda*:

> Disbelief in the *ṭāghūt* (tyrannical Muslim rulers) one of the pillars of *tawḥīd*, and if he [the ordinary Muslim] doesn't fulfil this pillar, he is not a *muwaḥḥid* (a Muslim monotheist), and *tawḥīd* is the basis of *īmān* and is a must for the suitability of actions, and without it they are invalid.[27]

What al-Qaeda's leader did was to tether the concepts of *tawḥīd* and *īmān* with political ideas in an altogether more explicit and unyielding fashion than had been done before. Ayman al-Zawahiri explained how this lay at the root of reviving Islam.[28] Only a "renewal of *tawḥīd*" could save Muslims from "living on the margins of the New World Order."[29] This linked the idea of *tawḥīd* to a broader system of revolutionary change which involves the implementation of *shari'a*, political authority for Islam, and an end to occupation. The dichotomy between *tawḥīd* and everything else was absolute. There could be no third way.

The practical outcome of this was the formation of a rigid doctrine of political absolutism. It was incapable of accepting compromise because doing so would bargain away the *tawḥīd* of Allah. This is why al-Qaeda criticised political initiatives such as the Hamas-Fatah Makkah Agreement that was signed in February 2007. It aimed to bring an end to infighting between the two groups in Gaza by forming a national unity government that would act in the best interests of the local population. Zawahiri explained that al-Qaeda opposed the plan because of verse 3:103 of the *Qur'an* which states: "And hold fast, altogether, to the rope of Allah and be not divided among yourselves."[30] On the face of it, this is a verse which seems to implore support for the initiative, although Zawahiri interpreted it differently. The reconciliation talks had been sponsored by Saudi Arabia and were endorsed by the United States, which in Zawahiri's opinion meant that both Hamas and Fatah were uniting around "the rope of secularism" or the "rope of America," or something other than "the rope of Islam." This is why al-Qaeda felt it could not lend its support to a move which otherwise aimed at bringing about greater Muslim unity. "We don't want a single [united] rank full of holes through which crusaders and Jews can come in," Zawahiri explained. "We want unity around the word of *tawḥīd*."[31] The metaphorical imagery of uniting around *tawḥīd* was one that al-Qaeda invoked repeatedly. Zawahiri delivered the same message to Iraqis in 2009, telling them to prioritise *tawḥīd* over peace initiatives being sponsored by the West. "It is your road to victory and control," he said. "Continue with that as much as you can and Allah will grace, guide and take care of you."[32] A year earlier he had used the same idea to incite global jihad, arguing:

> ...from the requirements of this word [*tawḥīd*] is that [you] work to help Islam by ruling by his [Allah's] *shari'a* and not making it equal to any other rule, and that [you] confront the invaders usurping the homelands of the Muslims and neither recognise nor respect any obligation or agreement which gives up even a hand span to them, and that [you] work to dethrone and remove the corrupt, corrupting, hireling rulers who dominate [your] homelands.[33]

In this way *tawḥīd* became a potent political idea of emancipation and empowerment. It is tied to revolutionary change with the emergence of a confident and self-assured Islamic movement which implements Islam in its totality.

Conclusion

Tawḥīd is an emotive issue because there is no other concept that is as closely related to the essence of God. Salafis prioritise its realisation above everything else and quickly distance themselves from anything that might lead to *shirk*—the opposite of *tawḥīd*. They have reduced *tawḥīd* to three categories of divinity in order to better understand how to worship God, of which *al-ulūhiyya* has lent itself to political application. This transforms Islam into a living ideal, something which must be physically manifest and given continuous expression through acts. Faith alone is insufficient to achieve the requirements of *tawḥīd* here. Ayman al-Zawahiri argued that Muslims are so poorly educated about their own faith that they no longer appreciate the role of politics in realising the overarching aims of *tawḥīd*. "This awareness must be spread amongst us, the awareness of changing from the falsehood of *shirk*...to the truth of *tawḥīd*," he explained.[34]

9

HOLY WAR AND THE ESSENCE OF MONOTHEISM

Jihad as the means of realising *tawḥīd*

Salafi-Jihadis tend to view the issue of *tawḥīd* in much the same way as their more mainstream Salafi counterparts. This is unsurprising given that all Salafis look to the scholarship of Muhammad ibn 'Abd al-Wahhab on this issue, who wrote one of the defining works on *tawḥīd*. What this chapter reveals, however, is the manner in which some jihadist ideologues have cultivated *tawḥīd* as a militaristic doctrine in relation to its most practical component: *tawḥīd al-ulūhiyya*. This draws on a number of interconnected theological issues including divine will and predestination (*al-qaḍā' wa-l-qadr*) and having both absolute trust in Allah and fearing him alone (*tawakkul* and *khawf*). The basic argument of Salafi-Jihadi theorists with regards to these ideas is that they are impossible to establish in everyday life without taking to the battlefield. How else could the belief in predestination and fate be physically manifest in a believer's life without them risking their life to prove they have fatalistic faith? By contrast, anyone who avoids jihad because they fear for their life does not understand the true meaning of this concept, and has consequently failed to realise *tawḥīd al-ulūhiyya*.

Sayyid Imam al-Sharif argued that jihad is a source of empowerment for *tawḥīd*, noting, "jihad is a means for the actualisation of the *tawḥīd*."[1] This has a practical and social meaning, namely that jihad is the tool by which monotheism is established and implemented as a political system over society. This is not unique. Jihad is seen as a necessary means of establishing monotheism by a number of different Salafi-Jihadi theorists. Abu Muhammad al-Maqdisi even acknowledged this as one of the reasons why he called his popular website *minbar al-tawḥīd wa-l-jihad* (the pulpit of monotheism and jihad). He wrote:

> The sign that distinguishes us from others is, in short, jihad to make the world of *tawḥīd* the highest. That's why we chose the name...*minbar al-tawḥīd wa-l-jihad*. And we chose to put the word *tawḥīd* before jihad in the name because *tawḥīd* is the first purpose and the basic of the fundamentals, while jihad is the true method to establish it on earth.[2]

The relationship between jihad and *tawḥīd* when constructed like this is not the primary focus of this chapter. The idea of jihad as a tool for the realisation of Islam has already been covered in the sections exploring Salafi attitudes towards jihad. This chapter instead aims to explore the relationship between jihad and an individual's personal realisation of *tawḥīd*. "Jihad was a way of life for the pious predecessors," 'Abdallah 'Azzam explained.[3] This is a lifestyle contemporary Salafis aspire to replicate, reviving jihad and strengthening their understanding of *tawḥīd*. "There were previous generations that succeeded the Muslims who neglected the rules of Allah. They forsook their Lord, so he forsook them. They deserted his rules, and so they were lost," 'Azzam wrote.[4]

Al-qaḍā' wa-l-qadr, tawḥīd and jihad

"While living in Afghanistan, I have realised that *tawḥīd* cannot penetrate into the soul of the human being, nor will it intensify and strengthen the way it does in the fields of jihad," 'Abdallah 'Azzam wrote.[5] The importance of *tawḥīd* had been impressed upon 'Azzam after he moved to Saudi Arabia in the 1970s and joined the faculty of the King 'Abd al-'Aziz University. Once in Afghanistan, he constructed the concept in uniquely militant terms, arguing that only those who fought jihad could truly appreciate the full dimensions of *tawḥīd al-ulūhiyya*. It was a bold idea, suggesting that any Muslim who refrained from jihad was suffering from deficiencies in their faith. This view was fuelled by 'Azzam's supposedly supernatural experiences in

Afghanistan which constantly seemed to defy the odds, galvanising his belief in the primacy of jihad and its relationship with *tawḥīd*. 'Azzam had long argued that miracles were taking place on the battlefields of Afghanistan everyday and even wrote a book dedicated to the topic.[6] The conclusion he drew was that only divine intervention could account for what was transpiring. It was the experience of shaykh Tamim al-Adnani, one of 'Azzam's closest friends, that convinced him only jihad could unlock the secrets of *tawḥīd al-ulūhiyya*. Both men had a lot in common: a shared Palestinian heritage, both were educators—Adnani was an English teacher by profession—and neither was capable of settling comfortably anywhere in the Middle East.

During the early phases of the Afghan-Soviet war Adnani found himself working as an *imam* at the Dhahran airbase in Saudi Arabia. He was eventually expelled for repeatedly espousing radical views about the country's secular culture and its usurious banking system.[7] Without a livelihood and alienated from the Saudi authorities, he dedicated himself to aiding the war effort in Afghanistan full time. 'Azzam was immediately struck by Adnani's almost childlike exuberance and zeal for the cause. He craved martyrdom constantly, sought it out, and wept when it wouldn't come.[8] Adnani was stout and rotund, but exerted himself in training sessions so much that 'Azzam worried about him. He frequently got carried away, quarrelling with his superiors while also challenging men half his age and size to physical contests. All of this was borne of his relentless quest for martyrdom, a personality quirk that made him notorious among the *mujahideen*. It was during his participation in the Battle of Jaji that 'Azzam finally had an epiphany about *tawḥīd al-ulūhiyya*.

The confrontation followed a massive Soviet push into Afghanistan in 1985, which aimed to decisively crush resistance forces by deploying Soviet Special Forces, the Spetsnaz. Their initial successes were impressive. Within months they had closed more than 60 per cent of Afghanistan's border with Pakistan, choking off a number of vital supply routes in the process.[9] Their most significant mission would come about eighteen months later in the Battle of Jaji, which took place during Ramadan 1987.[10] Jaji was a formative battle for everyone involved, providing Osama bin Laden with a remarkable victory that would forever establish his warrior credentials while also convincing

'Azzam about the primacy of jihad.[11] Despite being outnumbered and overpowered, a small number of *mujahideen* based at the *al-Masada* training camp somehow managed to stave off advancing Soviet troops. A ferocious fight ensued. "Even though we were on top of the mountain, it was shaking under our feet!" 'Azzam recalled. "The sky was raining bombs and the earth was erupting volcanoes."[12] Bin Laden was charged with leading the battle and instructed Adnani to man the control room—much to his annoyance.[13] He craved the frontline but was now forced to retreat. Adnani found a compromise by positioning himself just outside the control room under a nearby tree. He began reciting the *Qur'an* and supplicating to God, hoping to secure the martyrdom that had eluded him for so long. Given the intensity of the conflict, 'Azzam recalled just how foolhardy Adnani's actions might seem to an outsider:

> No one could believe that he was still alive under that tree while the planes were bombarding [us], and the enemy mortars and missiles were being fired in his direction.[14]

When the Arab *mujahideen* later withdrew from *al-Masada*, Adnani had to be dragged away, sobbing about his misfortune. Martyrdom had still not come.[15] The significance of this event stems from Adnani's apparently impossible survival, overcoming the odds in a battle that 'Azzam insisted had been so severe that it would "make you forget your own name."[16] He later wrote that it was the only battle he hoped would end quickly.[17] But Adnani would not find martyrdom on any battlefield. His jovial disposition and fluency in English made him a unique and valuable asset for the Afghan *mujahideen*, prompting 'Azzam to send him on the road. He was constantly touring the Middle East, Africa and United States to fundraise for their operations—and to raise awareness of their mission. He eventually died on one of these trips, while on a lecture tour in Florida. Before leaving for the United States, Adnani had reflected on the Battle of Jaji and told 'Azzam:

> After that day I realised there is no death. None can die except in that specific second pre-decreed by the lord of the worlds, period. And taking daunting risks does not bring the appointed time closer, nor does safety and security distance death.[18]

This statement would be invested with great significance for 'Azzam. It came to epitomise the highest and truest ideals of *tawḥīd al-ulūhiyya*.

After all, this is the dimension of *tawḥīd* that represents the unity of worship—something that requires manifestation through practical agency. It was one thing to demonstrate this with ritual actions like prayer, fasting, and giving to charity, but these merely represented conventional and safe ways of realising God.

The relationship between al-qaḍā' wa-l-qadr *and* tawḥīd al-ulūhiyya

Normative Islamic theory holds that there are six articles of faith in which a Muslim must profess belief in order to enter the faith. One of these is *al-qaḍā' wa-l-qadr*, which is the belief in fate and divine predestination. Shaykh Saleh al-Saleh, a prodigious student of the highly regarded scholar shaykh 'Uthaymin, explained the Salafi position on *al-qaḍā' wa-l-qadr* as follows: "that which Allah has eternally preordained (in due measure) pertaining to His creation."[19] This understanding is based on a *ḥadīth* which recounts an incident where the angel Jibrīl (Gabriel) came to the Prophet Muhammad and quizzed him about the different aspects of Islamic belief. When he asked the Prophet what constituted *īmān* (faith), Muhammad replied:

> That you affirm Allah, his angels, his books, his messengers, and the last day, and that you affirm the decree [*al-qaḍā' wa-l-qadr*], the good of it and the bad of it.[20]

It therefore becomes clear that *al-qaḍā' wa-l-qadr* is an integral and intrinsic part of the Islamic belief system. 'Abd al-Wahhab even suggested that anyone who failed to believe in it would be guilty of apostasy and *shirk*.[21] *Qadr* represents God's decree and consists of four components which include: Allah's absolute knowledge of all events before they occur; his record of them before creation was created; his omnipotent will which none of creation can defy or escape; and God's role as the origin of all creation.[22]

What mattered to 'Azzam was the second aspect of *qadr*—the idea that Allah has already recorded a divine decree from before creation was even created. The lifespan of an individual is therefore preordained and fixed. Nothing can delay or hasten it, but for Allah's will. Anyone who truly believed in this could not then refuse to participate in jihad because of fear. Living in security will not prevent or delay death, just as participating in the battlefields of jihad will not hasten it. ʻAzzam pointed to verses of the *Qur'an* which state, "no soul can ever die except by Allah's leave and at a term appointed."[23] Another states, "to every people is a term appointed: when their term is reached, not an hour can they cause delay, nor (an hour) can they advance (it in anticipation)."[24] These verses inform a number of important *ḥadīth* by the Prophet Muhammad on the issue of *al-qaḍā' wa-l-qadr*. The Prophet told his followers that the first thing Allah created was a pen and then a tablet. The pen was commanded to write but hesitated at the instruction. "My lord, what shall I write?" it asked. "Write down what has been ordained for all things until the establishment of the hour," God replied.[25] This story is affirmed by the *Qur'an* which states that the tablet on which God's decree for all of creation has been recorded is known as the *al-lawḥ al-maḥfooẓ* (the preserved tablet) and that it resides with him in heaven. Muslims consequently believe that Allah has already decreed a number of things for them, including their spouse, progeny, lifespan (*ajl*), and level of wealth (*rizq*).

This has profound implications when considering *tawḥīd al-ulūhiyya* in its fullest sense. Yes, a Muslim can demonstrate devotion to God through prayer, pilgrimage, and charity—but these only satisfy the ritualistic aspects of *al-ulūhiyya*. Those acts also stem from specific commands—such as the obligation to pray (*salah*)—but none of them employs the concept of *al-qaḍā' wa-l-qadr*. Given that it is one of the six articles of faith, ʻAzzam insisted that Muslims had to find a way of giving expression to it in their daily lives. This was how he had understood Adnani's statement about there being no death except at an "appointed time." It confirmed that only *mujahids* were able to demonstrate their belief in *al-qaḍā' wa-l-qadr*, by risking their lives in battle. How else could Adnani have repeatedly defied the odds? Outgunned and outmanned, the martyrdom he so desperately craved evaded him because Allah had not appointed his death at those moments. It did not matter how many shells exploded around him, death would only catch up with him in the air-conditioned comfort of a Florida convention centre.

The implications of this idea are simultaneously liberating and empowering. Muslim armies have traditionally used it to motivate advancing soldiers to launch themselves at the enemy, often by plunging behind enemy lines in manoeuvres known as *inghimas* attacks (plunging into the enemy). It is worth noting that this is not a modern development in Islamic theology and was even written about by Ibn Taymiyya, who endorsed the principle.[26] In battle it is therefore a charter for bold and brazen assaults, licensing the use of kamikaze tactics against the enemy. *Inghimasis* (those who conduct *inghimas* attacks) are able to decisively demonstrate their conviction in *al-qaḍā' wa-l-qadr* by resigning their fate to God and whatever is sealed within the mysteries of *al-lawḥ al-maḥfooẓ* when charging forwards. For 'Azzam it was an idea that liberated the human soul by inspiring man to "behave with the Lord of the worlds as if he is seeing him, behaving in response to the divine attributes of Allah."[27]

Tawakkul *and* khawf

The Saudi cleric shaykh Salih bin Fawzan al-Fawzan has described *tawakkul* as "entrusting one's affairs to [Allah] and relying on him in all matters. Entrusting one's affairs to Allah entails not turning to someone else for support."[28] This is also an issue closely related to the idea of *tawḥīd al-ulūhiyya* because *tawakkul* consists of three components: *īmān* (having faith in God), *halaat* (resigning oneself to God), and *amal* (working righteous deeds). The *Qur'an* states, "so put your trust (in Allah) if ye are indeed believers."[29] There are very specific and precise theological terms to this verse. Believers are rhetorically challenged to put their trust in Allah and to then demonstrate that belief. Saudi Arabia's highest clerical authority, the Permanent Committee for Islamic Research and Fatwas, understood this to mean that "relying upon Allah (*tawakkul*) is a condition for *īmān* (faith)."[30] The verse is also understood to mean that anyone failing to trust in Allah—or trusting in something besides Allah—is guilty of *shirk*. "Trust and dependence are forms of worship, and directing worship to [anyone] other than Allah is an act of *shirk*," argued 'Abd al-Wahhab in *Kitāb al-Tawḥīd*.[31] This underscores the significance of the idea among Salafi thinkers, although it is not limited to them alone.

The celebrated Sufi thinker Sahl al-Tustari argued, "the essential reality of *tawakkul* is the declaration of God's oneness."[32] This can take many forms, such as trusting in Allah's grace before embarking on a new business venture, choosing a spouse, or simply devoting oneself in ritualistic worship. "*Tawakkul* is the rejection of the body [by bending it] to servitude, the devotion of the heart to God's lordship, and ridding oneself of worldly power," Tustari argued.[33] *Tawakkul* consequently relates directly to the idea of divine omnipotence and is a necessary prerequisite for the belief in *al-qaḍā' wa-l-qadr*. These ideas are therefore interrelated and complementary. Shaykh Fawzan echoed similar sentiments in his work, demonstrating a broad consensus of opinion on the matter of *tawakkul* across a variety of Islamic traditions. He noted:

> ...relying upon Allah can be in religious matters as well as worldly matters. So you should rely on Allah in your Creed and your *tawḥīd*. And put your trust in Allah for fulfilling your needs even if your needs are of a worldly nature, such as eating, drinking, clothing and accomplishing some set goals. Put your reliance and trust in Allah for all matters.
>
> Reliance on Allah is not limited to just matters of creed and *tawḥīd*. Rather, it even applies to worldly matters and seeking provision. When it comes to fulfilling any goal, do not rely on anyone besides Allah. This is since all of the affairs are in the Hand of Allah.[34]

'Azzam constructed the entire principle of *tawakkul* through the narrow strictures of *al-qaḍā' wa-l-qadr*, arguing that its highest form could only be realised through jihad. "The most valuable thing which a human possesses is the soul (*rūḥ*)," 'Azzam wrote. "And when you place your soul upon your palm, begging Allah to take it, day and night... then after that, what could you ever fear other than Allah?"[35] The risks of jihad therefore make it the ultimate form of obedience to God because of the *tawakkul* required to surrender to him in such circumstances. This lends itself to the interconnected concept of *khawf* which 'Abd al-Wahhab defined as "the obligation to fear Allah, alone, sincerely," coupled with the recognition "that fear of Allah is a sign of faith."[36] This understanding is based on a verse of the *Qur'an* which states, "it is only the devil who would make (men) fear his partisans. Fear them not; fear me, if ye are true believers."[37] Like the earlier verses about having absolute trust in Allah (*tawakkul*), the ones relating to *khawf* stipulate similar caveats. In both cases God gives his command to either trust in him or fear him, followed by a rhetorical rejoinder: "if you are true believers," elevating these matters to ones of doctrinal importance. Unsurprisingly, this led Wahhab to conclude, "it is clear that fear is a form of worship and directing an act of worship to other than Allah is *shirk*."[38]

Fear in this context is defined as consisting of four forms: the fear that someone other than Allah will cause misfortune or harm; fear that results in the embrace of forbidden acts or the abandonment of obligatory ones; fear of God's punishment for bad acts (which is encouraged); and natural instinctive fear such as being startled when surprised by a threat (which is permissible).[39] The implications of this doctrine in the life of a true believer are significant, because Muslims believe that only Allah is to be feared. 'Azzam therefore warned his men not to let the fear of death, the Soviet Union, imprisonment or hardship deter them from jihad. After all, the only thing to be feared was God—and the battle in Afghanistan was a righteous struggle in his cause.[40] 'Azzam quoted a saying attributed to the Prophet Muhammad:

> Let not the fear of people stop anyone of you from saying what is true, or doing something important, because what you say or do will not keep you from your *rizq* (provision/sustenance), or keep you from your *ajl* (life span).[41]

The concepts of *tawakkul, khawf*, and *al-qaḍā' wa-l-qadr*, when combined, produce an almost Nietzschean *übermensch* in Islamic form: uninhibited, unencumbered, and emancipated. 'Azzam argued that when all these factors came together in a true believer they produced "a liberation of the human soul from fear of death and position."[42] Using a similar example to that of Adnani sitting under a tree during the Battle of Jaji, 'Azzam informed his readers of an incident where an Afghan man, Muhammad Umar, brought together all of these ideas to demonstrate his belief in the concept of *tawḥīd al-ulūhiyya*. A Soviet bomber loomed menacingly overhead, causing the Arab and Afghan *mujahideen* to scramble for cover. Umar refused. Instead, he raised his hands to the heavens and supplicated to God asking, "O lord! Who is greater, you or this plane? Who is more superior, you or this plane?"[43] Wartime experiences like this helped illuminate the fullest meaning of *tawḥīd*, giving 'Azzam and his men a much better understanding about Islamic scripture, soteriology and law. "You will not grasp [this religion]," 'Azzam argued in relation to chapters from the *Qur'an*, "except according to what you give for its sake."[44] *Sura al-Tawba* (the chapter of repentance and dispensation), for example, is the ninth chapter of the *Qur'an* and focuses heavily on military issues.[45] "How can you understand [it] without struggling for jihad?" 'Azzam asked.[46]

Conclusion

This chapter has shown one of the most unique and important Salafi-Jihadi innovations with regards to the concept of *tawḥīd*. 'Abdallah 'Azzam developed an understanding of *tawḥīd al-ulūhiyya* that is closely tethered with the idea of fighting for the sake of Allah. In order to fully realise that most important and basic article of faith—demonstrating belief in the oneness of God—he cultivated the Wahhabi notion of Islam as a living ideal in particularly jihadist terms. Yes, Muslims could demonstrate their belief in the concept of exclusive worship for Allah through purely ritualistic acts, but doing so overlooked doctrinal matters relating to *al-qaḍā' wa-l-qadr*, *tawakkul* and *khawf*. Conviction in those ideas could only be demonstrated through jihad where a believer's life and livelihood were necessarily imperilled. Muslims who refrain from jihad are therefore breaking their covenant with God and fall into misfortune. "Fear for wealth, status, and this life brings about humiliation and subjugation," 'Azzam warned. "Freeing oneself from these things bears the fruit of honour."[47] It was a remarkable development, coupling the idea of jihad with the very essence of Islam itself: realising the *tawḥīd* of Allah.

ḤĀKIMIYYA

10

THE DAWN OF MODERN POLITICAL ISLAM

The birth of an idea: from reform to governance

The issue of Islamic governance has received much attention from academics and the popular press in recent years, not least because of the revival of a purported Caliphate across large parts of Syria and Iraq. Political Islamists have also capitalised on unrest in other parts of the region, particularly in North Africa, where groups from the Ennahda Party and the Muslim Brotherhood, to Islamic State and Ansar Dine, have all jockeyed for position as the contours of power continue to be recast. All of these movements—and many others besides—conceive of Islamic political systems in very different ways, revealing that there are few areas on which there is any real consensus. The various movements reveal how the concept of political Islam is not limited to those of a Salafi persuasion but includes many others—with numerous actors who favour constitutional means over confrontational ones. This is understandable. The issue of establishing political authority for Islam has persisted since the dawn of the religion itself and remains very important to large numbers of Muslims. Yet, when considering how political Islamists conceive of the idea today, it is events from the last 150 years that have proved most significant in moulding this concept into the form in which we recognise it in the modern era. In its earliest incarnations this impulse began as an anti-colonial construct with revivalist thinkers like Jamal al-Din al-Afghani (1838–1897) and Muhammad 'Abduh (1849–1905) at al-Azhar University. The Muslim Brotherhood is later credited with popularising the idea on an wide scale across the Middle East after Sayyid Qutb began writing about the need for political reform and social renewal. This chapter explores how the agitation for Islamic governance has evolved over time, starting with reformist movements which ultimately gave way to more reactionary ones. It will also illustrate how modern figures have come to regard the concept of *ḥākimiyya*—the securing of political sovereignty for God—as providing both spiritual and temporal empowerment.

There are three important ways in which the concept of *ḥākimiyya* differs from the other ideas explored in this book. The first is that the real genesis of the contemporary Islamist debate regarding *ḥākimiyya* finds its roots in the Indian subcontinent—not in the Arab world. This makes the discussion of *ḥākimiyya* unique when contrasted against the other ideas explored thus far. Their development was almost entirely self-contained within the Arab world, particularly in Saudi Arabia and Egypt. This was not the case with *ḥākimiyya*. The most important theorist in this regard was Abul A'la Maududi (1903–1979) who initiated much of the modern thinking about what shape and form an Islamic State should take. Indeed, his work played a huge role in influencing Qutb's own thinking on the matter.

The second way in which the development of *ḥākimiyya* differs is that there is no significant input from al-Qaeda on the topic. There is no substantive work from any of its leading members which discusses the issue or theorises what an ideal Islamic State should look like. Reza Pankhurst confirms this in his survey of attitudes towards the Caliphate, in a chapter exploring al-Qaeda's thinking on the matter.[1] Pankhurst shows that al-Qaeda never gave serious consideration to the Caliphate and never provided a coherent blueprint for governance, were it ever to achieve statehood. This is not because al-Qaeda does not believe in an Islamic State. It has a strong attachment to the idea and frequently references it. However, as previous chapters on jihad, *takfir*, and *al-walā' wa-l-barā'* have demonstrated, al-Qaeda principally concerns itself with developing Salafi-Jihadi concepts relating to militaristic struggle. It does this to justify its actions to Muslim onlookers, hoping to carry public opinion while also inspiring new supporters to join their cause.

There is no need to do this with *ḥākimiyya*. A varied number of groups have already developed the idea over a number of years and have popularised it to a large constituency in both the Middle East and beyond. The idea of an Islamic State is therefore an established idea within the Muslim world. This differentiates it from the other ideas already examined in this book which, although they may be known to ordinary Muslims, are not as well understood.

The third difference is that whereas all of the other ideas already examined find their antecedents in Salafi traditions, principally emanating from the works of scholars such as Ibn Taymiyya or 'Abd al-Wahhab, this one does not. The primary thinkers behind the idea of *ḥākimiyya* are more classically Islamist activists such as Maududi or Qutb. They developed and cultivated the concept in the modern era long before Salafi-Jihadi theorists were writing about it. This is partly due to the fact that Salafi-Jihadism is a much more recent phenomenon than the political Islamism of the kind that Maududi or Qutb engaged in. Yet, the concept of *ḥākimiyya* should not be regarded as arriving *ex nihilo*. The celebrated Iraqi scholar, Imam Abu al-Hasan al-Mawardi wrote about it in the tenth century in *al-Aḥkām al-Sulṭāniyya* (the rules of Islamic governance). Commenting on the idea, he said:

> When we say *ḥākimiyya*, we mean to protect the right of Allah that we have been entrusted with against his enemies. That right is the right for legislation, judging, and executing the judgements.[2]

Scholars of both political Islam and Muslim societies have advanced a number of different explanations to account for why fundamentalists have rejected modern politics in favour of Islamist models. The earliest and most influential work of this kind comes from Daniel Lerner who argued that tradition—a practice he considered pervasive in the Middle East—was the antithesis of modernity.[3] Lerner imagined the problem through the very strictures he accused his subjects of succumbing to when he wrote about this in the 1950s. He argued that a bald choice faced Muslim societies: "Mecca or mechanisation."[4] Although his summation of the problem was overly simplistic, it does capture the issue as perceived by some Muslim theorists. More recent scholarship from Gilles Kepel and Olivier Roy also suggests that Islamist suspicions of contemporary politics stems from the breakdown of tradition.[5] Islam has become uncoupled from its cultural mores in modern societies where people live increasingly atomised lives, prompting them to seek supra-cultural, transnational identities within an imagined *umma*. Other scholarship, such as that from Robert Pape suggests that Islamist motives almost always stem from acutely political grievances, rather than religious ones.[6] Studies such as these have aimed to explain what has happened and why.[7] We shall now attempt to explain which ideational shifts have occurred in Islamic political thought, what pathologies they have followed, and what events have helped shape their trajectory.

Modern Arab reformists

The suspicion of modern politics is perhaps one of the most pervasive and enduring features of Islamic political thought today, much of which is likely to have been informed by Muslim experiences over the last 150 years. Tracing the development of contemporary ideas relating to *ḥākimiyya* almost always leads back to earlier theorists whose ideas were born of the uniquely colonial environment in which they were conceived. This is not to suggest a chain of causation or responsibility stretching back to imperialist intrigue, but it does identify the roots from which contemporary thinking finds its source. In rejecting their colonial experiences these thinkers were casting aside everything associated with Western political structures, which were viewed as godless, exploitative and decadent.

It was not just the ascendancy of the West that fuelled this sense of vulnerability among early theorists, but also the collapse of the Ottoman Caliphate. An already decayed institution throughout much of the nineteenth century, its office was finally abolished in March 1924, ending the ostensible manifestation of Allah's regency on earth. This would have a profound effect on Islamic theorists who began arguing for a return to those principles almost immediately and whose thoughts on the matter are best captured by the popular Islamist mantra, "*Islam dīn wa dawla*," meaning, Islam is a religion and a state.[8]

Much of the scholarship which addressed the pre-industrial world emerged from one of the most distinguished centres of Islamic learning in the Muslim world, al-Azhar, during the late eighteenth and early nineteenth centuries. Two theorists in particular, Muhammad 'Abduh and his mentor Jamal al-Din al-Afghani, began putting together broadly revivalist and progressive works.[9] They were deeply concerned about the political, cultural and intellectual stagnation of the Muslim world and argued for a return to rational reasoning in Islamic jurisprudence, bringing back a number of *mu'tazila* traditions—a school of thought that prioritises jurisprudential rationalism.[10] They essentially campaigned for what might be termed Islamic modernism, fusing Western scientific inquiry and material progress with Islamic principles, a process that is often credited with heralding the dawn of the Arab Renaissance, *'Aṣr al-Nahḍa*.[11] This was to be an organic, ongoing, and fluid process with 'Abduh arguing in one of his most important papers that "laws should change in accordance with the conditions of nations."[12] The modernist tradition created by 'Abduh and Afghani was marked and influential, reaching across much of the Middle East. A lot of this was done by one of 'Abduh's most famous students—and his biographer—Rashid Rida (1865–1935), who published a monthly magazine, *al-Manar* (The Beacon; published 1898–1935) which enjoyed a large subscription base in the region. Through Rida and *al-Manar* the ideas incubated by these al-Azhar intellectuals were propagated across the Arab world.

'Abduh was not arguing for a secular movement in his paper about updating Islamic laws, although a number of his students did later advocate secular positions. Instead, what he wanted was to build a reformist environment which posited Islam within, and reconciled it with, the foundation stones of post-renaissance culture: science, reason, and scepticism. This would produce something quite distinct from Western culture and civilization, both of which the al-Azhar scholars were deeply sceptical of. The best summation of their views comes in an article written by Rashid Rida in *al-Manar*: *Renewal, Renewing, and Renewers*.[13] It rejected the "heresy and promiscuity, laxity and profligacy," of Western civilisation.[14] This rejection was coupled with repeated calls for "independent renewal," producing something that was neither subordinate to, nor wholly dismissive of, Western culture. Only this would create a:

> ...dignified *umma* and a strong state, while preserving our nation's religion, culture, laws, and language, and its national character...we need this glorious renewal, one that combines the modern and the old.[15]

This illustrates how 'Abduh and Rida were reformists who embraced the ethos of modernity while also worrying about its ethical and temporal baggage. It was a malleable and flexible philosophy which could be constructed in different ways and even gave rise to some secular movements. 'Ali 'Abd al-Raziq (1888–1966), for example, wrote a seminal paper on the collapse of the Ottoman Caliphate, titled *Islam wa-uṣūl al-ḥukm* which means "Islam and the roots of government."[16] Raziq's basic argument was that no authoritative source of Islamic law mandated a Caliphate and that, rationally, there was no incentive to revive one either. He claimed that the Prophet Muhammad was a religious figurehead and not a politician, arguably making Raziq the first to try justifying secularism in modern Arab societies.[17] The neo-*mu'tazila* of al-Azhar and the nascent secularism of 'Abd al-Raziq dominated the debate within the Middle East at this time. Meanwhile, an altogether more aggressive, doctrinaire and hostile strain of Islamic political thought was developing in British India.

The fear of secularism

To understand why the Indian subcontinent gave birth to a strain of Islamic thought that was deeply hostile towards the West it is necessary to first consider the prevailing climate there. Muslims were a large and significant minority in British India who were able to safeguard their position by working closely with the British Empire. This was done through the Aligarh College, a university created by Sir Syed Ahmad Khan which produced a cadre of civil servants schooled in English and a number of Western subjects. This made them well placed to win prestigious jobs working in the administration of the Raj, where they could then work to secure their communal interests. In many senses, Khan was already implementing the vision espoused by 'Abduh and Rida.[18] Yet, there was pushback against his initiative by elements of the Muslim community who regarded the Aligarh College as producing submissive and unambitious Muslims who were content with simply serving the interests of the Raj. Maududi expressed this view most forcefully, challenging the secular outlook of Aligarh graduates, while dismissing all other non-Islamic forms of government. He argued:

> The reigns of power have been in the hands of those persons who not only did not have any elementary understanding of Islamic law and constitution, but [who also] had their education and training for the running of Godless secular states... they are incapable of thinking except in terms of the nature and pattern of a state of the Western secular type.[19]

Maududi was one of Pakistan's most important public intellectuals and remains a highly significant figure within the Islamist—though not necessarily Salafi-Jihadi—constellation. His work on religion and politics reached a broad audience, inspiring Islamic activism around the world, although it was in the Indian subcontinent where his influence was most acutely felt with the creation of Jamaat e-Islami (a South Asian equivalent of the Muslim Brotherhood).[20] Much of Maududi's success was due to his training in journalism which allowed him to use his populist writing style to win mass public support for his ideas. He was such a gifted writer that by the age of seventeen he was appointed editor of *Taj*, and a few years later went on to lead one of India's most popular Muslim newspapers, *al-Jamiat*.

When Maududi considered how to restore Muslim pride he was deeply influenced by the colonial experiences of British India. "Wherever you turn your eyes, you will find that one nation dominates another, or one class holds another in subjection," he wrote. "The root cause of all evil and mischief in the world is the domination of man over man, be it direct or indirect."[21] Maududi would abide this no longer and, along with his followers, decided that a new direction was needed. "The chains of political servitude have been broken," wrote one of his closest political associates and future leader of Jamaat e-Islami, Khurshid Ahmad. "Nearly eighteen Muslim countries have attained independence in the last two decades."[22] The newfound independence of those states necessitated a clearer vision for the future of Muslim India. "Islam is the very antithesis of secular Western democracy," Maududi explained.[23] Secularism was equated with numerous social problems of which the two most important were exploitation and moral decay. The erosion of artisan culture under the ebb and flow of greater mechanisation and mass production was regarded as another malignant consequence of Western influence.

Secularism as exploitation

Through his association with the Indian freedom movement, Maududi was exposed to a broad spectrum of revivalist thinking about the role of Muslims in the industrialised world. One of the most important activists he encountered was the celebrated philosopher and poet, Sir Muhammad Iqbal (1877–1938), who convinced Maududi to move from Hyderabad Deccan to the Punjab in 1938 to work on Islamic revival projects there. Iqbal's analysis was that any political system devoid of God would inevitably arc towards exploitation and oppression, echoing a view that was held by most Indian Muslim activists at the time. Only God could check man's natural destructiveness. This formed the cornerstone of Iqbal's early work, which in turn influenced Maududi's thinking. During this time poetry provided one of the principal mediums of political dissent, affording theorists the luxury of artistic licence to express themselves. Iqbal wrote about the inherent tensions between the East's ascetic spiritualism and the West's secular culture in terms of love (*ishq)* and rationalism (*'aql)*. Muslim societies, he reasoned, should not eschew the West's post-Enlightenment culture which had championed the primacy of *'aql* in public life, while insisting this had to be checked with *ishq*.[24] Iqbal's thinking was that both of these elements needed fusing together in order to produce the highest state of both man and polity.[25]

This was a theme Iqbal visited frequently during his early career. In *Asrar-e Khudi* (secrets of the self), for example, he challenged Nietzsche's concept of the godless *übermensch* by stating that only spirituality could tame the *übermensch* into a productive—rather than destructive—force. *'Aql* alone could not provide the realisation of selfhood. It was a metaphor for the predicament facing both the spiritual East and materialist West. Iqbal summed up his suspicion of godless politics in a poem depicting a dispute between man and God. Dismayed at man's secular intemperance, God tells him:

> I created this world from one same water and earth,
> You made Tartaria Nubia, and Iran;
> I forged from dust the iron's unsullied ore,
> You fashioned sword and arrowhead and gun;
> You shaped the axe to hew the garden tree,
> You wove the cage to hold the singing bird.[26]

These criticisms applied to the two dominant ideologies of the time—capitalism and communism—and were ascribed to their relegation of God from politics. A year after Maududi had moved to the Punjab at Iqbal's insistence, he attended a meeting of the Inter-Collegiate Muslim Brotherhood in Lahore and delivered a speech which echoed many of the themes found in Iqbal's poems. "Representatives come into power by the votes of the common people, [but] soon set themselves up as an independent authority," Maududi argued. "They often make laws not in the best interest of the people who raised them to power, but to further their own sectional and class interests...this situation besets people in England and America and in all those countries which claim to be a haven of secular democracy."[27]

Secularism as moral decline

The exploitative tendency of secularism was one problem, but another which concerned Muslim theorists even more was the perceived moral decline in public standards that accompanied secular political values. Maududi explained:

> As a divorce has been effected between politics and religion, and as a result of this secularisation, the society and particularly its politically active elements have ceased to attach much, or any, importance to morality and ethics.[28]

This accentuated fears over the supposedly pernicious role of secularism in modern society. The entire idea of separating church and state was associated with exploitation, corruption, and social degradation. Khurshid Ahmad warned:

> The experiments of Western countries with secularism are in no way encouraging...politics has become out-and-out Machiavellian and this state of affairs has greatly impaired the poise and tranquillity of life... [secularism] must draw upon the psychological forces of hate, suspicion and resentment which tend to impoverish the soul of man and close up his hidden sources of spiritual energy.[29]

As Ayesha Jalal argues, these views were pervasive across much of Muslim India.[30] Maududi's fears in this regard found ready amplification in the writings of the Egyptian activist, Sayyid Qutb.[31] As the

Muslim Brotherhood's most famous son, Qutb's work has inspired more than a generation of Islamists and informed the theoretical framework—in one form or another—for most of the Middle East's radical movements. Qutb's biographer, John Calvert, argues that between them, Maududi and Qutb formed "the theoretical bases of Islamism in the post-colonial Muslim world."[32] This is no overstatement.[33] Maududi is known to have deeply influenced his Egyptian counterpart, who then developed and popularised his ideas to an Arab-speaking audience. Maududi's books, published through the al-'Urubah House for Islamic Call in Pakistan, were frequently translated into Arabic. In particular, two of his most popular, *Islami Inqilab ka Minhaj* (The method of the Islamic revolution) and *Qur'an Ki Char Bunyadi Istilahen* (Four basic terms in the *Qur'an*), found large and receptive audiences in the Middle East.[34]

The primary source of the intellectual cross-fertilisation from Maududi to Qutb was the Indian cleric Abul Hasan 'Ali Hasani Nadwi, who translated most of Maududi's books into Arabic. Closely connected to the Free India movement, Nadwi remains one of the subcontinent's most underrated Muslim intellectuals of the late colonial period.[35] His influence is not to be understated. His role in transferring ideas from the subcontinent to Muslim revivalists in the Arab world was pronounced and had an enduring impact on the trajectory of Islamic political thought around the world. "No Islamist intellectual of the twentieth century better illustrates the ties between South Asia and the Arab Middle East than the Indian religious scholar Abul Hasan 'Ali Nadwi," wrote Euben and Zaman.[36]

Transposing Maududi's thought to the Arab world

Nadwi wrote in both Urdu and Arabic, although it was his first book in the latter which became his most important and influential, *Madha khasir al-'alam b-inḥiṭāṭ al-muslamīn* (What the world lost with the decline of Muslims).[37] Much like his counterparts, Nadwi was deeply concerned by the stagnation and decline of the Muslim world at a time when the West was enjoying its ascendancy. His book was published in 1950 in Cairo where Sayyid Qutb read it carefully. He was only just becoming interested in the more theoretical and political aspects of

Islam, having thus far predominantly published works concerned with literary criticism.[38] His only book of any Islamic relevance at this time, *al-'Adala al-Ijtima'iyya fi-l-Islam* (social justice in Islam), had gone to press the previous year when he was briefly residing in the United States.[39] Many of the defining features of Qutb's work are found in Nadwi's polemic on the delirious consequences of Islam's global decline. In turn, Nadwi was largely just echoing much of Iqbal and Maududi's work on the godless decadence of secular Western culture. Nadwi wrote:

> We will not speak now of the grievous material losses the Eastern countries have suffered since the rise of the West. We will speak only of the real—the moral and spiritual—losses of mankind as a whole... Questions relating to spiritual truths arose in Europe before the Renaissance, but as the innate character of its civilisation gradually unfolded and the West got lost in the adoration of its material achievements, they were disregarded.[40]

Arguments put forward for Islam's temporal failures were well rehearsed. Muslim societies had lost their way, momentarily misguided by the chimera of Western material progress. "The world of Islam will have to rediscover its spiritual roots," Nadwi concluded. "[Muslims] cannot brave the onslaught of the ungodly West by imitating its empty cultural forms, customs, and social concepts." The message was simultaneously isolationist and revivalist. Progress would only come through the creation of a distinctly Islamic civic polity. Nadwi did not blame the West for this state of affairs—but instead held Muslims culpable. They had allowed their societies to become "complacent and compromising."[41] It was here that Qutb was first introduced to the concept of *jāhiliyya*, the idea for which his work is now best known.[42] That much is confirmed in the foreword to Nadwi's book, which was written by Qutb:

> The age before Islam was steeped in *jāhiliyya* in which the mind and spirit of man had become benighted and high standards and values of life debased... the very roots of humanity were being corroded by a criminally luxurious and wasteful life on the one hand, and hopelessness and frustration and despair on the other.[43]

Qutb went on to argue that "Islam played a significant role in the reconstruction of humanity."[44] Islam became the sole basis of revival, progress and salvation. This was not an abstract moral philosophy but a deeply political one. Qutb began echoing a number of sentiments present in the works of South Asian revivalists, such as their concerns about the exploitative nature of secularism and its effects on moral decline. Maududi argued in *Tanqihat* (Inquiries) that America could not enforce Prohibition in the 1920s because it required people to accept human, rather than divine, reasoning for its proscription.[45] A near identical argument appeared in Qutb's *Milestones*. America had failed in its campaign to achieve Prohibition because people did not sufficiently respect human legislators. Divine legislation, by comparison, does not rely on temporal penalty. Escaping worldly authority might be one thing but celestial omnipotence is quite another. In any event, the righteous belief in God would be enough to make people abstain from sins through their devotion and submission to God's law. "When belief in '*lā ilaha illā-Allah*' penetrates into the deep recesses of the heart, it also penetrates through the whole system of life, which is a practical interpretation of this faith," Qutb wrote. "The spirit of submission is the first requirement of the faith." With the premise of submission to God established, it followed that moral and social renewal would then follow. Qutb explained:

> It can be said that Muhammad—peace be on him—was capable of starting a movement of moral reform for the establishment of moral standards, for the purification of the society, and for self-evaluation...But God Most High knew that this way is not the way. He knew that morality can only be built on faith, a faith which provides criteria, creates values, defines the authority from which these criteria and values are to be derived, and prescribes the reward of the one who accepts this authority and the punishment of those who deviate or oppose.[46]

A year after Nadwi's book first appeared, Qutb produced a pamphlet called *The America I have seen*, which is based on a series of discrete letters he wrote during his time in the United States. Whereas Nadwi and his contemporaries were writing about their experiences of colonial occupation under British rule, Qutb refashioned his ideas to frame them in opposition to America's cultural ascendancy. While the United States may not have been directly occupying foreign territories in the way Britain once did, its cultural project—and Qutb's experience of it—meant that it merited his attention. "I fear that a balance may not exist between America's material greatness and the quality of its people," he wrote.[47]

The material progress of the United States impressed Qutb, but despite marvelling at the country's technological advances he rejected the price at which they came. "In America, man was born with science, and thus believed in it alone," he wrote.[48] Again, Qutb echoed the work of Iqbal in this respect, mirroring his ideas about *'aql* and *ishq* while expressing concerns about the moral decline of society. He also reflected the preoccupation with social enterprise which dominated the thinking of South Asian Islamists. Qutb consequently wrote very little about *tawḥīd* or *shirk* in *Milestones*. Although these ideas make occasional appearances, they do so only fleetingly and are framed in the context of discussions about *jāhiliyya*.[49]

Arab discourse on *ḥākimiyya* shifts from inclusive to aggressive: the fight against domestic tyranny

The work of Maududi and his contemporaries can be characterised by their belief that greater division was needed between the Muslim and Western worlds—creating an environment of separation and confrontation. Qutb adopted this view. Islam would have to survive within its own silo: isolated, distinct, and diametrically estranged from anything other than Islam itself. In many respects it is this belief which forms the entire basis of Qutb's best known doctrine—that of *jāhiliyya*—which had of course first been inspired by Nadwi. Sayed Khatab, who has produced a valuable study on the role of *jāhiliyya* in Qutb's political thought, offers a neat and comprehensive definition of the idea: "*jāhiliyya* does not refer to a particular period or place, nor does it refer to a particular race," he wrote. "Rather, it is the opposite condition to Islam."[50] Qutb exposed Arabs to the idea of *jāhiliyya* in *Milestones* as an exclusivist one. This happened just months before his execution by the Egyptian state in 1966, although a broader recalibration of Islamist thought had already been taking place over the preceding decade, making people more receptive to it than they might otherwise have been. Following the rise of Gamal Abdel Nasser and his breakdown in relations with the Muslim Brotherhood, the period thereafter was characterised by draconian repression. Almost all political parties were banned and a massive crackdown against the Muslim Brotherhood ensued. Its members were rounded up, tortured, and consigned to concentration camps.[51] It was a disaster for the movement and many of its members were sent to the gallows or faced firing squads. Qutb became one of its many martyrs, another fallen hero whose persecution became emblematic of an unjust—and more importantly, *jāhil*—political culture.

This was the final point in an antagonistic process, which had not started off as inherently confrontational. The Muslim Brotherhood's founder, a school teacher from Mahmudiyya named Hasan al-Banna, had been open towards the West. "People may imagine that our Islamic way of life in this modern age disconnects us from the Western nations," he wrote. "Those nations which are suspicious of us will not be content with us whether we follow Islam or not… every nation is free to adopt whatever path it wishes within its own borders, provided it does not infringe on the rights of others."[52] This was a nationalist statement shorn of theocratic ambitions. It also chimed with the original aims of the Muslim Brotherhood, which had been to secure the social and moral purity of Egypt, with Banna making the preservation of Egyptian society his main priority. In its earliest phases this is precisely what the Muslim Brotherhood was all about: achieving justice; engaging in social welfare activism; and, more generally, seeking to fill the gaps created by the state's shortcomings.[53]

The clearest exposition of Banna's views came in May or June 1947 in a letter titled *Naḥwa al-Nūr* (Towards the Light).[54] This letter was addressed to King Farouk and his Prime Minister, Mustafa el-Nahhas Pasha, along with several other heads of state in the Muslim world. Anti-colonial in tone, it argued for an Islamic renaissance based on two principles. The first was the rediscovery of "lost independence and sovereignty," while the second was "progress towards social perfection."[55] Many of the anti-colonial themes expressed by Indian writers were present in this letter too, with Banna describing Western civilisation as "bankrupt and in decline."[56] He argued:

> Its foundations are crumbling and its institutions and guiding principles are falling apart.[57]

Banna's letter was wide-ranging and vague. Much like his Indian counterparts he wrote in broad brushstrokes about the need for Islamic revivalism based around the idea of national sovereignty. He concluded the letter by proposing fifty "steps towards practical reform."[58] Of these, only twenty relate to political, judicial, or economic matters.

The rest relate to social and educational reform—the twin pillars of the Muslim Brotherhood's early agenda. However, Banna died in 1949 shortly before Qutb began turning his attention to politics, and several years before Nasser's crackdown against the group. In his absence, Qutb would reframe the narrative of ideas on Islamic governance borrowed from the subcontinent into a more aggressive and confrontational domestic agenda based on the principle of *jāhiliyya*.

Ḥākimiyya as temporal empowerment

The most novel development which Muslim theorists created at this time was the idea of *ḥākimiyya* as a tool of temporal empowerment. To do this they looked at the *hijra* of the Prophet Muhammad as he moved from Makkah to Medina to create an Islamic state. His migration was accompanied by a reconfiguration of the social organisation in Islam, from one of personal agency to a period of much greater communal cooperation and exchange. Both the horizons of Islam and the Prophet's ambitions grew accordingly. Whereas Muhammad's mission had previously been confined to Makkah and the Quraysh tribe which lived there, the move to Medina now meant that Islam could be propagated on a global scale, with delegations dispatched to Persia, Egypt, and Byzantium.[59] For Maududi this was a uniquely empowering moment in the history of Islam, demonstrating both the potency and necessity of establishing *ḥākimiyya*. With the creation of an Islamic State, he explained,

> Islam was no longer a persecuted religion; it was able to obtain a firm foothold and was provided with the historic opportunity to establish an Islamic State and society. This constitutes the most important development of the post-*hijra* period. The leaders of Makkah, the defenders of the old order, did not miss the significance of this change. They realised that a new model was being set up, which would be a challenge to the way they were running their society. Now things were changing. Muslims were concentrating at one place and organising a new society with its own government.
>
> [...]
>
> Arabia had the most singular government of the time, based as it was on the principle of the sovereignty of God and the vicegerency [*sic*] of man. The law of the land was Islamic. The administration of the state lay in the hands of the honest and pious people. The country had no trace of vio-

> lence, oppression, injustice or immorality. Peace, justice, truth and honesty reigned supreme everywhere. Many of the people of the country had come to possess the highest moral attributes because they were honest in worshipping God and obeying Him.
>
> The Prophet Muhammad (peace be upon him) changed the character of Arabian life in a short period of only twenty-three years. He instilled in the people a spirit that helped to serve the cause of Islam. They set out with the great mission of spreading Islam throughout the whole world.[60]

This touched on all the themes that were important to Maududi: challenging the prevailing international order; achieving social and moral renewal; and realising political servitude to God. There was wider significance to the *hijra* too. Prior to the Prophet's migration from Makkah to Medina, the concept of jihad had not existed in Islam. Muslims believe that the *Qur'an* was revealed piecemeal over a period of 23 years and that the verses pertaining to jihad were only revealed in the post-migration era.[61] Verses revealed in Makkah tended to be much more abstract and focused on issues such as *tawḥīd*. The Medina verses are more socially oriented, focusing on public life, economy, laws of inheritance, and the rules of jihad.[62] Sayyid Qutb speculated about why God might have delayed the revelation of the jihadi verses until after *ḥākimiyya* was achieved:

> After the *hijra*, or emigration to Medina, however, the Muslims emerged as an independent community, prepared to face up to the Makkan leadership which was actively recruiting fighters and organizing military expeditions against it. The situation had changed; instead of individual persecutors targeting individual victims, a collective and deliberate campaign was being organised.
>
> To these reasons one may add the fact that the Muslims in Makkah were a dangerously exposed minority. Had they engaged the unbelievers in armed conflict as an organized group, they would have faced total annihilation. God's will was that they should first gather in a safe place before He granted them permission to go into battle. However, the rules governing fighting were issued gradually, as and when the need arose, and as dictated by the needs of the development of Islam, first within Arabia and later outside it as well.[63]

Anwar al-Awlaki was much more explicit in stating how *ḥākimiyya* had bestowed jihad on Islam. Writing for *Inspire* magazine, a once quarterly publication of al-Qaeda in the Arabian Peninsula, he argued:

> When the Messenger of Allah was giving *da'wa* [the call] in Makkah for thirteen years, only a few hundred became Muslim. When he made *hijra* to Medina, within ten years, over a hundred thousand became Muslim. So how come his *da'wa* in Medina was much more fruitful than his *da'wa* in Makkah? That was because he was using a superior form of *da'wa* in Medina and that is the *da'wa* of the sword.[64]

'Abdallah 'Azzam expressed similar ideas, arguing that the empowerment of Islam through jihad was the single most important aspect of the religion. "A religion which does not have jihad, cannot become established in any land, nor can it strengthen its frame," he wrote.[65] This reinforces the idea that *ḥākimiyya* is a tool of temporal empowerment, licensing jihad as a means to advance and expand the faith.

Conclusion

This chapter reveals how nineteenth-century Islamic political thought was profoundly shaped by the colonial experience. This occurred most pointedly in British India where Muslim theorists including Sayyid Abul A'la Maududi, Muhammad Iqbal and Abul Hasan 'Ali Nadwi began expressing concerns about secular and modern political systems while proposing an Islamic alternative. By contrast, the Middle East appeared to be experimenting with neo-revivalist ideas as propounded by Jamal al-Din al-Afghani, Muhammad 'Abduh and Rashid Rida, before the radical culture of South Asian political Islam was adopted by Arab theorists such as Sayyid Qutb. The cross-pollination of these ideas resulted in a philosophy that was deeply sceptical of the West and its associated political culture. Instead, theorists such as Maududi and Qutb reasoned that establishing the sovereignty of God in the political system—through *ḥākimiyya*—would not just secure God's rights, but would also provide temporal empowerment, because this was the stage at which the Prophet Muhammad's message was transformed and transmitted on a much larger scale than it had been before. This provided the theoretical basis from which Salafi-Jihadi theorists would later revive and develop the idea of *ḥākimiyya*.

11

SECURING GOD'S RIGHTS

The revival of *ḥākimiyya* discourse in Saudi Arabia

The First Gulf War and its aftermath had a transformative effect on Salafi discussions about the nature of *ḥākimiyya* in the modern world. Some of the biggest areas of conflict came from debates between *ṣaḥwa* Salafis and their jihadi counterparts, over issues relating to what shape and form an Islamic state should take.[1] The introduction of American military power into the Arabian Peninsula also had the effect of replicating Muslim fears from half a century earlier about the malignant influences of colonial rule. Saudi Salafis now found themselves harbouring many of the same anxieties as those that had once afflicted Egyptian and South Asian theorists. They were suddenly forced to confront the prospect of Western secularism being introduced into their country. In response to calls for greater separation between religion and the state, scholars began linking the idea of *ḥākimiyya* to that of *tawḥīd* (oneness of God), creating a new category in addition to those already identified by 'Abd al-Wahhab. This became known as *tawḥīd al-ḥākimiyya*.

The concerns of the ṣaḥwa

The reformist movement in Saudi Arabia which brought together political activists was known as the *ṣaḥwa* (awakening). One of its most important leaders was Safar al-Hawali who wrote his thesis on secularism (*al-'ilmaniyya*) at the Umm al-Qura university in 1981, exposing him to Western thinking on the issue almost a decade before American troops arrived in the Hijaz.[2] His familiarity with the topic and some its key thinkers is evident from his work which seamlessly moves between (almost exclusively negative) assessments of Henry Kissinger, Immanuel Kant, Francis Fukuyama, and Samuel Huntington.[3] Like many of his predecessors, Hawali viewed the West's post-enlightenment culture with great suspicion, associating it with the decline of spirituality and godliness in Europe.[4] "Democracy, freedom and the philosophy of evolution," he wrote, "have come and spread as infectious diseases invading the minds and hearts of those who misunderstand the meaning of … *lā ilaha illā-Allah*."[5] However, unlike Maududi or Qutb, Hawali also fused his fears of secularism with the principle of *irjā'* (previously discussed in the chapter on *takfir*), which formed the topic of his doctoral thesis, *Ẓahiratu al-irjā' fi al-Fikr al-Islami* (The phenomenon of postponement in Islamic thought). Hawali considered secularism as a form of *irjā'* where belief and action became divorced—anathema to those who insist that belief must be coupled with action.

Secular societies allow for individual agency and free will in a neutral public space, all of which encourages *irjā'* with regards to the observance or practice of Islamic commandments. Secularism is therefore not only inherently problematic because it introduces foreign ideas to Muslim societies—as Maududi and Qutb had already warned—but because it also restricts the capacity for social controls based on piety. Hawali explained:

> Through studying reasons for secular influence on contemporary Islamic life, I have seen that the reason for each deviation, humiliation, defeat and fragmentation in our life, is [a result of] living far from the *ahl al-sunna wa-l-jamā'a* [people of the prophetic tradition and (Islamic) community] in *'aqīda*, behaviour, and way of reform.[6]

Hawali was assisted in his leadership of the *ṣaḥwa* by two equally important scholars: Salman al-'Awda and Nasser al-Omar—both of whom were also deeply opposed to the Saudi-American alliance. They had been pushing back against postmodern culture since the early 1980s, after three alarming events for Sunni Islam had closed the previous decade: the siege of Makkah by Juhayman al-'Utaybi, the Iranian revolution, and the Soviet invasion of Afghanistan. These tumultuous events threw the world of Sunni Islam into a state of flux. In Mansoor Alshamsi's study on political reform in Saudi Arabia, he argued that Hawali, 'Awda, and Omar tried to achieve their aims through a process known as *al-mudafa'a*, or countering. "*Al-mudafa'a* is to convince people by argument and by nullifying an opponent's argument," Alshamsi writes.[7] In the Saudi context it was a "two dimensional policy of both countering and appeasing as applied to civic-civil strife for political change and reform."[8]

For its time and environment the movement was remarkably progressive. Unlike the mainstream Wahhabi establishment its members refused to dismiss new technology out of hand and were among the first to use audiotapes to spread their message to a mass audience.[9] The official clerical establishment, by contrast, dithered for months and held protracted debates about the permissibility of using tapes to disseminate the content of Islamic talks. Salman al-'Awda pushed back by dedicating an entire lecture to the topic, *al-Sharīṭ al-Islami* (the Islamic cassette) in which he defended its use.[10] It was initiatives like this and the early embrace of technology that gave the *ṣaḥwa* an advantage over government clerics.

Activist Salafis challenge the government

Hawali was most effective at harnessing this new medium and transformed himself into Saudi Arabia's first Islamist public intellectual, with a comparable status to that of his foreign contemporaries such as the Sudanese Hasan al-Turabi, the Tunisian Rashid Ghannouchi, or the Egyptian Yusuf al-Qaradawi. Hawali had the position to do it too. By 1988 he was dean of *'aqīda* in the Umm al-Qura University—arguably the most distinguished position in one of the country's most respected institutions and in its most holy city.[11] It was just the platform he needed when the *ṣaḥwa* began challenging the government in 1991. This was the moment they emerged as a public bloc after the House of al-Sa'ūd had invited the Americans to establish military bases in Saudi Arabia. Bin Laden was outraged and sent letters to King Fahd criticising "the overwhelming level of corruption" in Saudi Arabia "which reaches every aspect of life."[12] He regarded the banking system, which permits usurious transactions, as one of the regime's greatest crimes—a sign of its increasingly secular orientation. Similar concerns pervaded Hawali's thoughts, where he imagined that Western secularism as defined by its culture, customs, and commerce would slowly erode Saudi Arabia's Islamic identity.

Stringent Islamic rules about debt and finance ensured that economic reform became a central pillar of both activist- and Salafi-Jihadi differences with the government. Growing frustration with the House of al-Saʿūd was ultimately given expression through two historic documents which shocked the regime: the *khiṭāb al-ʿulama'* (letter of the scholars), and the *mudhakkirat al-naṣīḥa* (memorandum of advice). The *khiṭāb al-ʿulama'* signified the first time any unsanctioned political association—let alone an Islamist one—had come together to petition the modern Saudi state for civil reforms. Signed by more than 400 figures from the clergy, academia, and judiciary, it was distinctly Saudi in both its focus and character. The aim was not to upset the balance of power enjoyed by the House of al-Saʿūd, but to tilt it gently in favour of reform. The signatories had no interest in revolution per se and regarded themselves as loyal oppositionists, or friendly critics.

The *ṣaḥwa* was content with applying gentle pressure on the regime, outlining the need for political and social reform in general terms. Remarkably, even Bin Baz signed the *khiṭāb al-ʿulama'*, as did several other members of the clerical council in Saudi Arabia.[13] The letter demanded:

1. Establishing a consultative council to handle domestic and foreign policy according to Islam.
2. Bringing all the state's political, economic, and administrative laws in line with the *shariʿa*.
3. Appointing only qualified and ethical people for public office.
4. Establishing justice and equality, and ensuring individual rights.
5. Make all state officials accountable and equal before the law.
6. Achieving a more even and equitable distribution of public funds in line with the Islamic economic system.
7. Enact military reforms.
8. Ensure the media and press uphold the state's Islamic identity.
9. Creating a foreign policy that achieves the national interest and promotes Muslim causes around the world.
10. Develop and support proselytising missions.

11. Create an independent judiciary.
12. Remove all oppressive laws and ensure individual rights in accordance with the *shari'a*.[14]

The endorsement of the letter by establishment clerics momentarily threatened to unravel the understanding between the House of al-Sa'ūd and its religious scholars. Thus, while these were not revolutionary demands per se, they challenged the very foundations on which the modern Saudi state was based. The real significance of these demands lay in the fact that they called for economic reforms and a recalibration of the state's foreign policy in line with "promoting Muslim causes around the world."[15] This amounted to an attempt to reclaim the sovereignty of God in military, economic, and foreign policy matters—all of which were areas that had traditionally been under the control of the royal family alone. Viewed in this way, the *ṣaḥwa* was trying to erode the House of al-Sa'ūd's sphere of influence and extend the role played by *'ulama'* on issues that had nothing to do with social affairs or education.

From friendly critics to open challengers

When the House of al-Sa'ūd rejected the letter, its authors compiled a substantively more detailed and daring document, the memorandum of advice, which was published in July 1992. This was a markedly Islamist document, demanding a return to first principles for the Saudi state through a much more puritanical implementation of *shari'a*. It explicitly held the government responsible for the weakening of *aḥkām al-shari'a*, or *shari'a* rules inside the country.[16] It also took the dramatic step of directly criticising the House of al-Sa'ūd for allowing Western troops to enter the Arabian Peninsula, an unprecedented departure from the quietist style the movement had adopted thus far.[17] And the *ṣaḥwa* did not stop there. It listed a series of cases where the government had acted unjustly by appointing corrupt officials to public office and by violating human rights. This represented the natural culmination of the intellectual journey 'Awda, Hawali and Omar had made in reformulating Islam's civic role in the modern era. In a brazen move of direct activism that would have impressed even the Egyptian Muslim Brotherhood, the *ṣaḥwa's* members personally delivered the memorandum of advice directly to the king's office.

Not everyone was ready for this level of direct confrontation and the memorandum consequently suffered for want of support. Whereas the letter which preceded it had collected 400 signatories, the memorandum would attract only 111 because of its more daring approach. Bin Baz and his committee of scholars pointedly refused to endorse it and later passed a resolution condemning its authors.[18] The real significance, however, lay in the nature of Bin Baz's disagreement. He did not condemn the memorandum's contents but criticised its authors for publishing it as a public document. Bin Baz otherwise insisted that advising a Muslim ruler in private was an Islamic duty imposed on those with requisite knowledge.[19] The House of al-Sa'ūd disagreed and arrested the *ṣaḥwa's* leadership. For Osama bin Laden this apparent injustice underscored precisely why the time for private advice was over—and why challenges to the government now had to be made publicly. He explained:

> Our religious scholars have advised you to lay off those actions that have involved breaking rules and committing crimes that run against God's law. However, all you have done in response is mock us, stonewall us, and refuse to take appropriate action to remedy the situation. Your actions did not end at that—you have committed greater transgressions in the land of God and religion. Hence it is not possible to remain silent.[20]

The regime was betraying God by violating the principle of *ḥākimiyya* and could not therefore automatically expect the obedience of its citizens. This built upon the jurisprudential opinion that there was no obedience in the disobedience to God.

Intra-Salafi debates on obedience, jihad and *iṣlāḥ*

Salafi opinion is divided over precisely what effect sin has upon the legitimacy of a Muslim ruler, particularly one who fails to implement the *shari'a* in its totality (however that is defined). Most of the *ṣaḥwa's* leading figures argued that everyday sins do not remove a ruler from the fold of Islam. The rulers are ordinary individuals who, like everyone else, commit sin. This alone cannot then automatically invalidate their authority. A sinful ruler would still remain worthy of obedience and loyalty but should also be given scholarly advice, *naṣīḥa*, encouraging them towards reform, *iṣlāḥ*. This represents a novel third-way between servitude and violent confrontation. The approach advocated by Salman al-'Awda and his associates did not just argue for *iṣlāḥ*, but also gave more progressive and open-minded consideration to the nature of Islamic political systems. 'Awda rejected the basic philosophical premise of democracy as it is practised in liberal societies, with separation of church and state, and where legislation is passed with the consensus of elected representatives. He nonetheless recognised that democracy can take numerous forms with highly localised characteristics. What mattered to him was that the sovereignty of God was reflected through a system that also secured the rule of law, transparency, equality, justice and human rights. Throughout that process, however, the *shari'a* must remain the sole and guiding source of legislation.

Activist-Salafis should not, therefore, be confused for democrats. Canonical authority resides not in individuals but in scripture, the *Qur'an* and *sunna*. Differences arise over how these sources of scripture are best interpreted at the political level. Some Islamists argue this should be done through consultation (*shūrā*), while Salafi-Jihadis usually suggest that all executive authority must reside with the Caliph alone. This is significant because it diminishes the role of consultative bodies, leaving the head of state free to dismiss mainstream opinions on issues where they have adopted an alternative view. The alleged Caliphate currently operating in parts of Syria and Iraq is run in this way with its leader, Abu Bakr al-Baghdadi, adopting unilateral opinions which then bind his citizens.

Regardless of the form taken by an Islamic state, quietists take the view that Allah's sovereignty can only be realised through absolute obedience to the ruler because: (a) Allah has entrusted them with power; they are the rulers chosen by God, and it is therefore incumbent upon people to obey them even if they are oppressive; (b) they believe Allah doesn't change the condition of a people until they change what is within themselves. This is the mantra of personal purification (*al-taṣfiya wa-l-tarbīya*); and (c) they prioritise stability over everything else. Rebellion only causes problems and social strife.

Salafi-Jihadi frustrations with modern politics

Disillusionment with secular movements was not a wholly modern phenomenon for Salafi-Jihadis. 'Abdallah 'Azzam expressed his discontent with the idea right from the earliest stages of the Afghan campaign, reasoning that a collapse in Islamic political authority would result in the unravelling of faith because there was no arbiter to ensure religious observance. "Jihad is a necessity for the protection of the rituals," he wrote. "So enabling [political Islam] on earth is an imperative necessity and a needed obligation to protect worship."[21] His thinking on this matter was deeply influenced by the Arab-Israeli conflict which found popular expression through nationalist sentiments. The main Palestinian movements which emerged during 'Azzam's formative years were predominantly secular in their outlook. Their campaign against Israel was consequently framed through a narrative of national liberation and identity, despite bearing religious iconography and insignia.[22] This estranged 'Azzam irreconcilably from nationalist leaders, who told him, "the revolution has no religion behind it."[23] He later argued, "the leadership has been appropriated by a variety of people, of them sincere Muslims, communists, nationalists and modernist Muslims. Together they have hoisted the banner of a secular state."[24] That was not an agenda to which 'Azzam could subscribe. He came to regard the secular movement as betraying Palestine, robbing it of jihad as a vehicle for its liberation. It was only the formation of Hamas in 1988 that brought 'Azzam back, albeit nominally, within the orbit of Palestinian politics, after the group asked him to edit its charter and write an introduction to the document.[25]

It was not just Palestinian nationalism that disappointed 'Azzam. Attempts by Syria's Hafez al-Assad and Iraq's Saddam Hussein to offer a neo-Baathist model of socialism and pan-Arab nationalism also proved unworkable. "There are [a] handful of [secular] Officers, some of whom may think that it is possible for them to carry out a collective Muslim effort—this is a kind of fantasy or delusion reminiscent of the past," he wrote. "It will be no more than a repetition of the tragedy of Abdel Nasser."[26] Despite his reservations, 'Azzam's disillusionment must be viewed in context. He had not given the idea of Islamic governance any significant or meaningful thought, nor had his ideas been widely accepted by others within the Arab-Afghan jihadi network. 'Azzam even enjoyed cordial relations with the rulers of his time and was exceptionally close to the House of al-Sa'ūd who allowed him to preach about the Afghan jihad during the Hajj pilgrimage in 1984.

Events such as this convinced a number of Saudis to join the jihad in Afghanistan. When Osama bin Laden decided to go, he first sought the permission of King Fahd because he regarded him as *walī l-amr*. *The Oxford Dictionary of Islam* describes the *walī l-amr* as a "male legal guardian, usually the father."[27] In political terms it can also be used in reference to a legitimate head of state who has custodianship over the affairs of his people. Hudayfa 'Azzam, 'Abdallah's son, explained:

> When my father asked him [Osama bin Laden] to go to Afghanistan in 1985, he had replied that he would only do so if King Fahd personally granted permission. At that time Osama still referred to Fahd as *walī l-amr*.[28]

The process of Bin Laden's estrangement from the Saudi establishment was a slow one. Although scholars like Hawali, 'Awda, and Omar were openly challenging the government by 1992, Bin Laden was conspicuously absent from much of the initial debate. During the *ṣaḥwa's* early phases of agitation he said nothing, preferring to observe events rather than participate in them.

Activist-Salafi emphasis on iṣlāḥ *and social unity*

Activist Salafis do not believe in openly disobeying the government or engaging in acts of civil disobedience. Their challenges to the government were instead framed in the context of *naṣīḥa*, which is clear from the title of the memorandum of advice that was titled: *mudhakkirat al-naṣīḥa*. This has very specific connotations within Islam and is described as "morally corrective criticism," by Talal Asad.[29] Islamic injunctions to "enjoin good and forbid evil," stem from the *Qur'an* and obligate Muslims to offer *naṣīḥa* with humility and sincerity in a way that addresses the errant shortcomings of an individual or institution. Viewed in this way, *naṣīḥa* is not simply something to be encouraged, but is actually an obligation. It is a necessary first step in "enjoining good," by offering constructive criticism.[30]

The *ṣaḥwa's* model was therefore one of constructive engagement with the House of al-Sa'ūd. It established a method for delivering *naṣīḥa* while prioritising social unity over unrest. "We must obey the Muslim rulers in everything that does not entail disobedience to Allah," wrote Salman al-'Awda, "and we must refrain from rising up against them even if they fall short of what is expected from them."[31] 'Awda explained that a number of rules govern the issue of *naṣīḥa*, and that it can only be practised in very particular circumstances when the following conditions are met:

1. There has to be reason to believe that doing so will bring about a positive effect.
2. The act to be prevented has to be a clear act of wrongdoing.
3. That wrongdoing has to be actually going on at the time of taking action against it.
4. The benefit of preventing the wrongdoing has to be greater than any possible harm that might come of doing so.
5. The act of wrongdoing must be perpetrated in the open and in public.
6. The wrongness of the act must be something that is agreed upon; it must not be something wherein there exists a legitimate disagreement about its incorrectness.[32]

These considerations must be weighed up before giving *naṣīḥa* and, if they are not met, then it should not be offered. "If forbidding an act of wrongdoing will result in a greater wrong, then it is obligatory to refrain from forbidding it," 'Awda concluded.[33] This is an area where the activist Salafis overlap considerably with their quietist counterparts, placing a premium on the maintenance of social order even in extreme circumstances. "It is unlawful to rebel against the rulers even if they are oppressive as long as they do not exhibit outright unbelief," 'Awda explained.[34] The potential consequences of any action must first be weighed up based on the principle of the jurisprudence of scales (*fiqh al-muwāzanāt*). Before any action is embarked upon there must be a reasonable prospect of success, with the benefits of action outweighing potential downsides. The action being corrected must also be one that is universally considered wrong in Islamic jurisprudence, before *naṣīḥa* is offered. The process is an encumbered and cautious one.

This was a view which hardened over time. Following the Arab uprisings in 2011—popularly referred to as the Arab Spring—Salman al-'Awda reiterated his previous position. Regimes in the region had a duty to embrace reform and offer genuine rights to their people, while the people were obliged to refrain from causing unrest. The obligation of restraint, compromise and understanding therefore rested with both parties. In the aftermath of the 2011 uprisings, 'Awda offered the clearest exposition yet of the activist Salafi position, advocating a third-way between automatous obedience and bloody insurrection.

Surveying the evolution of Europe's political climate during the eighteenth and nineteenth centuries, 'Awda concluded that revolution on the continent had become inevitable. This view was informed by his reading of Karl Marx who argued that European unrest was the product of an angry and disenfranchised proletariat that had emerged after the industrial revolution. A similar fate awaited Arab governments now. The hyper-accelerated development of Gulf petro-states created not dissimilar conditions, prompting 'Awda to intensify his calls for Arab governments (and the House of al-Sa'ūd in particular) to initiate urgent reforms in order to ward off unrest. He argued that European leaders had only diffused rising tensions because they gave "the working classes many rights and entitlements."[35] They also "opened the doors to free expression, which allowed the people to articulate their grievances clearly and openly. In this way, those countries were able to bypass the revolutionary current that had been fomenting among the people."[36]

What makes 'Awda's thinking so unique and important here is the manner in which he maintains the validity of both parties—the rulers and the ruled. An errant ruler who fails to implement a narrow and draconian version of Islam does not immediately usurp the sovereignty of God. Indeed, provided there is legitimate difference of scholarly opinion with regards to the political system, 'Awda reasoned that the benefit of the doubt must be given to the ruler. "We should refrain from referring to legitimate differences of opinion as gross errors," he explained, "but focus on the merits and demerits of the various points of view."[37] Moreover, where the government does stray into error, reform is preferable to confrontation. Mistakes should therefore be noted "with fairness and compassion," whilst not overblowing or magnifying issues beyond proportion.[38] 'Awda later consolidated these ideas in an expansive book on the topic of revolutionary change, *Questions of Revolution* (*As'ilat al-Thawra*).[39] What made his work so important through much of 2012, is that he surveyed a broad range of

Western thinkers, experiences, and documents, from the Franco-Prussian War and Bolshevik revolution, to Alexis de Tocqueville and Karl Popper, to the Magna Carta.[40] At the heart of his understanding of *ḥākimiyya* is its ability to secure the aims of the *shari'a*. This can only be achieved, he reasoned, through a new social contract between private citizens and the state.

Ḥākimiyya *and the social contract*

'Awda did not negate the principle of *ḥākimiyya*. In his construction of the idea, authority is not vested in the masses, *al-jamahir*, as it might be in a secular state. Authority remains solely with Allah. "To permit what Allah has forbidden and prohibit what Allah has made lawful," he argued, "is impermissible in Islam. If we go further and believe that doing so is improving upon Islam, then we fall into unbelief."[41] There remains a role, however, for *shūrā* councils which merge both the principles of democracy and the sovereignty of God in a uniquely Islamic way. He explained:

> When we talk about democracy from the vantage point of Islamic Law, we must first define what we mean...[if] we mean to use a democratic approach merely as a system of governance that we employ within the context of Islamic Law, using it only for matters that are open to interpretation, juristic discretion, and human decision making, then there is nothing wrong with it.[42]

It is worth pointing out that the idea of an Islamic democratic model is not unique to activist Salafis. 'Abdallah Nasir al-Subayh argued for it as early as 2005. For 'Awda and Subayh the process is not about denying God's sovereignty—but one of reconciling it with individual rights. In many respects, what they are grappling with is a Salafi variance of Matthew 22:21—"Render therefore unto Caesar the things which are Caesar's; and unto God the things that are God's." They argue for an Islamic social contract that not only secures God's rights as *hakim* (ruler), but which also safeguards an individual's human rights, justice and security. It is a mantra for realising both the sanctity of man and the sovereignty of God, simultaneously. Subayh and 'Awda talked constantly of the need to safeguard individual rights. Subayh argued that "the true essence and spirit of democracy" is apparent with "the primacy of the constitution, transparency of government, independence of the judiciary, separation of powers, freedom of speech, respect for human dignity, and the preservation of human rights."[43] In this context, they wanted a discussion between individual Muslim agents and their rulers in order to achieve "a form of democracy that is compatible with our identity."[44]

The lack of an established clergy within Islam means that authority is not automatically invested in juristic institutions. It resides instead in textual sources: the *Qur'an* and *sunna*. The manner in which those sources are interpreted would then form the basis of an Islamic democracy where, according to Subayh, "the people are to be consulted, and they have the right to express their opinions and object to what they disagree with."[45] The principle of *ḥākimiyya* in this model is therefore achieved through a social contract which places the sanctity of individuals and their rights at the centre of the state.

Salafi-Jihadi support for a social contract

The idea of placing a social contract at the heart of an Islamic State even has some limited traction in Salafi-Jihadi circles. Shortly after the uprisings in Egypt and Libya, Abu Basir al-Tartusi issued a paper suggesting it is permissible for Muslim countries to adopt some of the principles that define democratic institutions. This includes "elections, voting, government turnover, freedom of speech and criticism, [and] public oversight of the leadership," He went on to warn, "whoever adopts this aspect of democracy alone is not a heretic."[46] Tartusi even encouraged his Egyptian followers to vote for Hazem Salah Abu Ismail, a Salafi presidential candidate from the Al-Raya party in the 2012 elections.[47] From Tartusi's perspective, the administrative aspects of democracy find their origins in Islam anyway. "Voting, elections, and asking people who they want as their leader are [ideas] anchored in Islam and in our Islamic history," he wrote. "They do not constitute a deviation from the Islamic *shari'a*."[48] Tartusi is clear, however, that aspects of democracy which place sovereignty in the hands of the people and which recognise them as the sources of legislation are categorically prohibited in Islam.

Tartusi's views on the social contract provoked a strong reaction within the Salafi-Jihadi community, which condemned him for even recognising democracy. Scholars such as Abu al-Mundhir al-Shinqiti, a prominent figure within Maqdisi's network, suggested Tartusi had called on his readers to "deliberately embrace polytheism," although such a view really misunderstands the essence of Tartusi's message.[49] Salafis arguing for the social contract are orthodox believers in the concept of *ḥākimiyya*. They believe that ruling by anything other than the *shari'a* is a sin, although it does not necessarily constitute apostasy, and the sovereignty of God must be established through the state. However, in this context, individual rights must also be guaranteed by bringing to bear many of the mechanical and procedural functions of the modern democratic state. This involves allowing citizens the right to have a say in how the *shari'a* is interpreted and implemented through a consultative body, or *majlis al-shūrā*.

Tawḥīd al-ḥākimiyya as a Salafi-Jihadi neologism

Debate surrounding authentic or legitimate Islamic authority intensified in Salafi circles at the start of the 1990s. One of the most important Salafi-Jihadi interjections during this time came from Abu Hamza who published an important work in 1999 regarding *Allah's Governance on Earth*.[50] In what is a long and erudite book Abu Hamza surveys centuries of Islamic history, juxtaposing this alongside esoteric jurisprudence that strongly links the idea of governance with the *tawḥīd* of Allah. "*Ḥākimiyya* is directly associated with *tawḥīd*," he wrote.[51] This leads to the idea that *tawḥīd* should have an additional category, beyond the three already identified by 'Abd al-Wahhab, known as *tawḥīd al-ḥākimiyya*.

This has been a highly contentious matter in Salafi debate. For quietist Salafis the separation of *ḥākimiyya* into a separate category of *tawḥīd* represented *bid'a*, a sinful and forbidden innovation. "There are [only] three types of *tawḥīd*," stated a fatwa from Permanent Committee for Scholarly Research and *Ifta'* [legal opinions]. "There is no fourth type…making *ḥākimiyya* a separate type of *tawḥīd* is an innovated act."[52] Instead they argue that *ḥākimiyya* forms a subordinate branch of *tawḥīd al-ulūhiyya* (the oneness of divinity) because implementing Allah's laws constitutes an act of worship and, as such, all acts of worship must fall under this classification. Abu Hamza was dismissive of such a view, concluding that the relationship between *ḥākimiyya* and *tawḥīd* is so close that it is impossible to call it an innovation. "Anything linked with *tawḥīd* could never be a *bid'a*," he wrote.[53]

Abu Basir al-Tartusi took a more lateral approach. He accepted that *ḥākimiyya* is a subordinate branch of *tawḥīd al-ulūhiyya* but argued that it should now be separated into its own distinct category—or just singled out for special attention—because its features, functions, and application have become so poorly understood among the modern Muslim masses. He explained:

> It was necessary to specify this important category of *tawḥīd* by mentioning it on its own to draw sight of the people towards its importance and that without it they have not [understood] *tawḥīd al-ulūhiyya* as it must be.[54]

This view was also shared by Abu Qatada al-Filastini who argued that ignorance about Islamic governance has become so widespread that *ḥākimiyya* must be separated into its own category. Both hoped this might lead to greater awareness of its importance.[55] Presenting the concept of *tawḥīd al-ḥākimiyya* in this way is very different to the quietist approach which absorbs it entirely within *tawḥīd al-ulūhiyya*.

This difference in approach accounts for the differing weight each of the two traditions attached to the idea. For Abu Hamza, Abu Basir and Abu Qatada, *ḥākimiyya* had become such a lost and poorly understood aspect of *tawḥīd* that it undermined the unity of God himself. Abu Hamza argued, for example, that those who reject a distinct category of *tawḥīd al-ḥākimiyya* are "very narrow minded," because all of these categorisations are ultimately invented by scholars anyway.[56] They are neither divinely mandated nor do they appear in the *Qur'an* or *sunna*, and are consequently open to scrutiny and debate. Some scholars have even changed the number of categories of *tawḥīd* over time. Figures from Islamic antiquity such as Ibn Qayyim al-Jawziyyah, the thirteenth-century expert on *ḥadīth* and jurisprudence, only classified *tawḥīd* in two ways: *tawḥīd al-'ilm wa-l-'atīqad* (the *tawḥīd* of knowledge and belief); and *tawḥīd al-qasd wa-l-irādah* (the *tawḥīd* of intention and purpose).[57] These distinctions were later expanded into the three categories expressed by 'Abd al-Wahhab, in order to better help Muslims understand the different obligations owed to God, through the commands of *tawḥīd*. "So how can someone claim that using a fourth or fifth classification of *tawḥīd* is an innovation?" asked Abu Huthayfah al-Kanadi.[58]

Abu Hamza took this argument forward. He noted that Islam stipulates 99 names for God, each of which refers to one of his attributes. Taken together, these names form the basis of *tawḥīd al-asmā' wa-l-ṣifāt*—something that Abu Hamza argued is a mirror image of *tawḥīd al-ulūhiyya*. "You must believe in the name," he said, "as well as its implications."[59] Thus, one of God's names is al-Hakam, which means "judge," giving rise to God's sovereignty over law and legislation.[60] Abu Hamza consequently argued that each of God's separate attributes can give rise to a different category of *tawḥīd*, if that helps "execute our duties towards this [particular] *tawḥīd*."[61] By contrast, if *tawḥīd al-ḥākimiyya* is to be rejected, then so too must *tawḥīd al-asmā' wa-l-ṣifāt*.

While *tawḥīd al-ḥākimiyya* is clearly a new distinction, disputes only exist over its necessity as a concept and its status as a *bid'a*. "There have been many terms introduced into the religion for the necessity to preserve it," Abu Hamza explained. "The scholars of Islam, however, are not as interested in the terms as they are in the implications of the term."[62]

The use of *tawḥīd al-ḥākimiyya* in this context is incredibly empowering. Abu Hamza explained that it could be used to measure the sincerity of a Muslim ruler by creating a standard by which they are judged. "The *īmān* of the rulers is based on action," he wrote.[63] As a result, he argued that *tawḥīd al-ḥākimiyya* is a more important concept than even the *'aqīda*, which is another invented term not found in the *Qur'an* or *sunna*. This is because the issues of doctrinal belief which relate to the *'aqīda* are all inner secrets of the heart. It allows the *murji'a* to postpone *takfīr* by claiming that what truly matters is what resides within an individual's heart. This makes it a passive and appeasing concept, whereas *tawḥīd al-ḥākimiyya* is empowering and aggressive. The argument surrounding *tawḥīd al-ḥākimiyya* is therefore deeply political and invested with ideological significance. Abu Hamza insisted that the real *bid'a*, therefore came not from introducing the concept into popular discussion but from abandoning the *shari'a* in favour of laws which negate the sovereignty of God. In response to state scholars who argued against this, Hamza scornfully asked, "how can they be trusted to protect *ḥākimiyya* when they have [already] sold it?"[64]

The relationship between shari'a, tawḥīd, *and the* shirk *of legislation*

The *shari'a* occupies a central place within the doctrine of *tawḥīd al-ḥākimiyya*, providing an umbilical cord between God and those in his servitude. "The association between [Allah] and the *shari'a* is the chain between creator and creation that *ḥākimiyya* represents," explained Abu Hamza.[65] Linking the *shari'a* to *tawḥīd* in this way carries a number of implications that have shaped Salafi-Jihadi responses to governments deemed to have fallen short of implementing divine law in its totality. The consequence of this belief was demonstrated in a letter written by Osama bin Laden to King Fahd in August 1995. With relations having already deteriorated significantly between Bin Laden and the House of al-Sa'ūd by this stage, the former issued a declaration of *takfir* against the Saudi government. "Whoever disobeys what God and His messenger have ordered and arbitrates between people by other than what God has revealed," Bin Laden explained, "he indeed has disbelieved and expelled himself from the folds of Islam."[66] His primary argument was that the House of al-Sa'ūd had negated *tawḥīd al-ḥākimiyya* by implementing laws that were not derived from the *shari'a*. This view is based on a very particular verse of the *Qur'an* which states:

> They (Jews and Christians) took their rabbis and their monks to be their lords besides Allah.[67]

Ḥadīths also report that when one of the Prophet's companions, Adi bin Hatim, first heard this verse he told the Prophet Muhammad that it was incorrect because Jews and Christians do not deify their clergy. The Prophet replied that they had become deities because they legislated to allow things God had forbidden and prohibited things he had allowed. This created two sins: the sin of those who legislated and the sin of those who acted in obedience to those laws.[68] This has profound implications for the manner in which Salafi-Jihadis understand the verse above, because it links legislation directly to *tawḥīd*. "The issue of legislative elections is an issue that is related to *tawḥīd* and it is not a jurisprudential subject," explained Abu Qatada.[69] This establishes a symbiotic relationship between God's unity and legislation, as Abu Hamza explained: "*tawḥīd* and the use of the *shari'a* are related."[70] Any abrogation of the *shari'a* risked undermining the unity and essence of

God, thereby propelling the offender into heresy. "The opposite of *tawḥīd* is *shirk*, thus to go against *tawḥīd* and violate it would cause the one that perpetrated the act to become a *mushrik*," he wrote.[71] Abu Qatada also argued that popular democratic models are unacceptable for Muslims because the ultimate authority to issue commands resides with Allah as part of his *al-ulūhiyya*, and cited the following verse of the *Qur'an* to establish this:

> Surely, His is the creation and the commandment.[72]

Abu Qatada deconstructed this verse into its constituent parts in order to explain its meaning. The first part of the verse which refers to Allah owning "the creation" is a reference to his *al-rubūbiyya*, while the second half, which refers to "the commandment" is a reference to his *al-ulūhiyya*.[73] The implications of this are emphatic. "It is proven that anyone who fails to rule by Allah's *shari'a* is *kafir*, not merely those who replace the *shari'a*," Abu Hamza wrote. "It is actually *kufr* just to fail to rule by it."[74] That view is in stark contrast to activist Salafis who believe that rulers must consciously abrogate the *shari'a* by thinking they know better, before *kufr* can be declared. The uncompromising nature of the Salafi-Jihadi view stems from their coupling of *shari'a* with *tawḥīd*, producing an absolutist and rigid doctrine. There is no room for even the limited or moderate accommodation suggested by the likes of Salman al-'Awda or Abu Basir—the latter of whom, despite being a Salafi-Jihadi, has adopted a more nuanced approach to this issue than his counterparts.

Almost all of the major theorists in the Salafi-Jihadi movement consequently reject democracy—however constructed. Democracy is not seen as a malleable administrative mechanism protecting individual rights, but is deemed to constitute its own distinct religion, according to Abu Muhammad al-Maqdisi.[75] "The new God in democracy is the desire of man," argues Sayyid Imam al-Sharif.[76] "This makes democracy a self-established religion in which the mastership is for the people." The sovereignty of man coupled with his right to legislate in the modern democratic system makes the entire concept a blasphemous anathema for Salafi-Jihadis. In his 1995 letter to King Fahd, Osama bin Laden had argued that "this issue constitutes the principal theme in the entire *Qur'an*."[77]

The sin of obedience

The sin of human legislation does not end with the legislator but also extends to those who recognise and obey it. Both Maqdisi and Abu Hamza cited verse 6:121 of the *Qur'an* to explain that it is *shirk* to obey a ruler who does not implement the *shari'a*, because it states: "And if you obey them, you will surely become an idolater."[78] Abu Hamza explained, "to obey and to serve is also a part of *tawḥīd*," with the natural result being that obedience to someone other than Allah results in *shirk*.[79] All of this reaches back to the ultimate aim of man himself, which is to serve God, prompting Maqdisi to conclude, "the followers of today's democracy are worse and more impure than such priests and monks [who legislated for themselves]."[80] This is because, although they changed some of God's laws, they did not codify those changes into a formal legal system or national constitution. Thus, in today's context, Madqisi argued:

> The legislators became gods to everyone who obeyed and followed them, or agreed with them in this disbelief and polytheism.[81]

This empowers the Salafi-Jihadi view of the need to confront existing Muslim regimes. Maqdisi told his readers to act in "avoidance of the deity," by making *barā'* from it and fighting against it. "The highest step of disbelief in this man made deity [democracy/human legislation] is the climax of Islam. By this I mean the jihad," he explained.[82] This is how Salafi-Jihadi movements have licensed their violence against Muslim states, all of whom they regard as errant and deficient in their application of Islam. All of them have failed to secure the *ḥākimiyya* of God and must therefore be fought—the ultimate manifestation of disavowal from a deity other than Allah.

Conclusion

This chapter reveals how Salafi-Jihadi theorists have developed the concept of *ḥākimiyya* as a separate branch of *tawḥīd*, elevating matters of governance to the level of doctrinal significance. Alternative political systems consequently promote *shirk* by giving prominence to the role of human legislators and individual sovereignty. Democracy is a religion, while secularism is a tool for undermining Islam with its promotion of *irjā'* and the separation of religion from public life. The Salafi-Jihadi understanding of this idea is particularly unique, even within the spectrum of Salafi debate.

Activist Salafis adopt a more liberal and tolerant view, which strives for reform (*iṣlāḥ*) over revolution. This is because they prioritise social order and view the relationship between sin and governance with greater nuance than their jihadi counterparts. Yes, rulers commit sin and have shortcomings—but these should be addressed through *naṣīḥa* unless there is evidence of indisputable *kufr*. In this context, the Salafi-Jihadi understanding of *ḥākimiyya* is particularly inflexible, uncompromising and confrontational. By linking it to *tawḥīd*, they have restricted their potential flexibility and are therefore forced to agitate for absolutist and revolutionary change. The alternative of this is the very antithesis of Islam itself: *shirk*.

CONCLUSION

Salafi-Jihadism is a broad and complex religious ideology. It draws from the religion as a whole—both conceptually and politically—combining a diverse set of ideas into a potent soteriological programme. This millenarian project believes in progress through regression, where the perfect life is realised by reviving the Islam of its first three generations. Taken as markers of both authenticity and purity, the legacy of these so-called "pious predecessors"—the *al-salaf al-ṣāliḥ*—provides the praxis for action in contemporary Salafism. Yet, Salafi belief is varied, with its most significant fault lines appearing over issues of power. Although Thomas Hegghammer correctly identifies Salafism as an essentially theological categorisation, its principal divergences almost always appear to be influenced by politics.[1] Movements within Salafism differ sharply over their views on the modern nation-state, its role and legitimacy. They consequently prescribe different methods (*manhaj*) for change, from inert quietism to revolutionary upheaval. It is this latter manifestation of Salafism that has been the subject of inquiry in this book.

Divergences of opinion within the Salafi-Jihadi tradition expose the bifurcation that occurs between the idealism of theory and reality of practice. This is where interpretative differences thrive, allowing different groups to arrange the contours of the ideology as they see fit. It explains why groups like Majlis Shura al-Mujahideen in Gaza, al-Shabaab in Somalia, al-Qaeda and Islamic State can all claim to be Salafi-Jihadi in orientation despite pronounced differences in their application of the same philosophical worldview. Ideologies are frequently pulled in new directions when transitioning from theory to practice, being shaped by context, time and setting. Salafism is an overarching and dense soteriology with differing opinions about how its aims are best actualised. The Harvard historian Peter Gordon notes that "when an idea gets taken up within the larger circuit of culture, it rarely manages to retain its original shape."[2]

Only by distilling the essence of Salafi-Jihadism can its ideological outlook be fully appreciated. This book has shown how five key features define this ideology more than anything else: jihad, *takfir, al-walā' wa-l-barā'*, *tawḥīd*, and *ḥākimiyya*. The development of each has been uneven and irregular, mutating at different times and in different ways. What can be seen, however, is that all the major periods of ideational shift have come in response to war. The Soviet invasion of Afghanistan birthed the foreign fighter movement, revived the spirit of jihad in the modern age, and renewed ideas about its primacy, importance and perceived virtuosity. The experience of war also shaped 'Abdallah 'Azzam's views about the necessity of jihad in order to satisfy the conditions of *tawḥīd al-ulūhiyya*. Only war could allow a true believer to fully establish their devotion to Allah by demonstrating their conviction in *al-qaḍā' wa-l-qadr, tawakkul*, and *khawf*. Concerns about the need for political reform and *ḥākimiyya* were later given renewed attention after Saddam Hussein invaded Kuwait. Even before this, the idea was borne from the colonial experience of Muslims in British India when theorists first began imagining how to secure God's rights within the political system. Social disorder can be said to have given birth not just to the concept of *ḥākimiyya* but also to the ideas of *takfir* and *al-walā' wa-l-barā'*.

What becomes clear is that war and its associated nomenclature have driven intellectual changes within Salafi-Jihadism. This is hardly surprising. Conflict is the wellspring of social change—whether political, cultural or intellectual. "The origins of Europe were hammered out on the anvil of war," noted Michael Howard in his celebrated work, *War in European History*.[3] Salafi-Jihadism is even more sensitive to this stimulus given that it is principally a militaristic ideology. For this reason, the greatest period of anti-Western intellectual development in Salafi-Jihadi thought took place in the years after the 9/11 terrorist attacks. Galvanised by the wars in Afghanistan and Iraq, a muscular and self-assured doctrine emerged that not only wanted to confront the West but which also sought to mobilise

Muslims in support of its cause. For the first time, too, it was non-state actors that were leading this campaign.

The Syrian war and ideological change

The ideology of militant Salafism is in a state of flux once again. Islamic State has emerged as perhaps the most powerful Salafi-Jihadi movement in history, acquiring control over large parts of Syria and Iraq. Yet it has many critics, including some of the most recognisable and well established Salafi theorists in the world such as Abu Muhammad al-Maqdisi, Abu Qatada al-Filastini, Ayman al-Zawahiri and 'Abdallah al-Mohaisany. Their criticisms of Islamic State will inevitably fuel the next stage in the ideological development of Salafi-Jihadism, just as the Algerian civil war spurred a series of changes two decades earlier. Abu Qatada has repeatedly dismissed the group as *khawārij* and claims they have not established a Caliphate but are instead a group of rogues and renegades. Part of the reason for this is because the group misunderstands, misapplies and abuses the concept of *takfir*. "We stand against ISIS [the acronym by which Islamic State was previously known] because they are targeting Muslims," Abu Qatada said. "They made *takfir* on [other Syrian jihadist groups], fought them, slaughtered them, enslaved their women and many other things."[4] Their application of *takfir* is held to be so deviant and promiscuous that Abu Qatada even considers them to have fallen outside the scope of *ahl al-sunna wa-l-jamā'a*. This necessarily invalidates their claims to the Caliphate.

The blasé attitude of Islamic State was on full display when they controversially burned to death the Jordanian pilot, Muath al-Kasasbeh. They knew this would be contentious within Islamic circles because the majority of mainstream scholarly opinions prohibit the use of fire in punishments, arguing that this is God's exclusive right over those condemned to hell. Islamic State responded by justifying their actions with reference to the principle of *mumathala*, which is a supplementary rule under the laws of *qiṣāṣ*.[5] *Mumathala* literally means "exact likeliness in retaliation" and stipulates that acts of reciprocity must be identical not just in their result, but also in method. Thus, while *qiṣāṣ* only stipulates the result—for example: X lost a limb, therefore Y must lose a limb too—it does not specify the method, although *mumathala* does. It states that the same method of harm inflicted by a perpetrator on their victim must be revisited upon them. "Some of the *ahl al-'ilm* [people of knowledge] have been of the opinion that burning with fire was prohibited originally, but [accept that] on retaliation it is permitted," stated an official document from Islamic State.[6] Although only a very small number of classical jurists have endorsed the idea of *mumathala*, its application by Islamic State already highlights one way in which the group is trying to bring more obscure and nihilistic theology into the foreground of Salafi thinking.

There is an important point to note about Islamic State in this respect. The statement regarding Kasasbeh was short and limited to one page. Other documents produced by Islamic State are similarly brief. It is almost as if they are content with the theoretical aspects of Salafi-Jihadism and assume that its tenets are understood. Al-Qaeda, by contrast, dedicated significant effort to producing lengthy books and treatises that explained the jurisprudence behind their actions. To that extent, al-Qaeda was keen to be seen as a religious movement and therefore spent time positioning itself within the Salafi-Jihadi tradition. This was important not just in order for them to retain their relevance, but also because they were the main operational group that could explain the disconnect between Salafi-Jihadi theory and the challenges it faced when moving from theory towards practical implementation. This explains why Abu Yahya al-Libi felt compelled to write a lengthy book on human shields (*tatarrus*) which did not challenge any of the classical opinions on the issue. Instead, Libi wanted to show why traditional thinking on the matter was out-dated and no longer relevant to the realities of modern warfare. When considering the output of Islamic State, the group is not known for written work but is instead famous for its production of filmic videos—many of them characterised by artistic sequences of extreme violence of the kind that might be expected from Stanley Kubrick or Quentin Tarantino. Its messaging is also simpler than that of al-Qaeda's, often presenting simple binary choices between two dichotomous and caricatured positions.

Although public and political attention is heavily focused on Islamic State because of the security challenges it presents, the main intellectual developments are still being undertaken by al-Qaeda's affiliates such as Jabhat al-Nusra in Syria. For example, Jabhat al-Nusra does not usually implement *ḥudūd* punishment in the areas it administers (although there have been cases of its fighters doing so in some limited instances), and has been compelled to explain its rationale for not doing so. "*Shari'a* is not just *ḥudūd*," said Abu Firas, a *shari'a* official with Jabhat al-Nusra. "It is a complete System. The *Qur'an* contains 6,200 verses, but only six are about *ḥudūd*. The *ḥadīth* are more than 10,000 but less than ten relate to the *ḥudūd*. The Prophet first taught the people, then he applied the *ḥudūd*."[7] Abu Firas explained that before the *ḥudūd* could be implemented, it was necessary to first educate people about the nature of the Islamic legal system. He also argued that *ḥudūd* can be suspended in times of war or calamity based on the example of Umar ibn al-Khattab who did just that during a famine in 640. One of *Ṣahāba*, Sa'd bin Abi Waqqas, also suspended the *ḥudūd* during the Battle of Qadisiyyah in 636 when Muslim armies launched their first missions into Persia. Given the dogmatic rigidity for which al-Qaeda was known in the years after 9/11, it is remarkable to find the group now adopting a more pragmatic and flexible approach to its own theology.

The Syrian civil war will continue to fuel further changes within the Salafi-Jihadi belief system over the coming years. It is too soon to fully understand precisely how these changes will take root and how the ideological contours of militant Salafism might be recast, but they are already being redefined in ways that did not seem possible just a few years ago. There are still large gaps in our understanding about how the Syrian conflict will incubate new phases in the development of Salafi-Jihadism. As more documents and theorists emerge, our understanding will grow, particularly as they relate to Islamic State.

What is clear, however, is that Salafi-Jihadism remains an extremely resilient soteriology. Despite domestic repression, civil war, and an international "War on Terror," it has endured and survived more than three decades of forceful repression. The collapse of civic society across parts of North Africa and the Levant has fuelled the rise of militant groups driven by this ideology. It seems as if wherever they emerge right now, they only grow stronger and more emboldened. This is remarkable considering the blood and treasure that has been expended in recent decades trying to contain the spread of militant Salafism, and makes the slogan of Islamic State particularly prescient. Whenever its name is called, supporters chant "*bāqiyya wa tatamaddad*"—remaining and expanding.

NOTES

1. INTRODUCTION

1. "*English subtitles of full sermon by ISIS's Abu Bakr al-Baghdadi, Caliph of the Islamic State*," YouTube. Accessed 20 Dec. 2014.
2. Abu Muhammad al-Adnani, "*This is the promise of Allah*," Al-Hayat Media, 29 June 2014.
3. Ibid.
4. Jalaluddin al-Suyuti, *History of the Caliphs* (Baptist Mission Press: Calcutta, 1881), 143.
5. Sermon by ISIS's Abu Bakr al-Baghdadi.
6. Ibid.
7. William McCants, *The ISIS Apocalypse: The History, Strategy, and Doomsday Vision of the Islamic State* (New York, NY: St Martin's Press, 2015).
8. Graeme Wood, "What ISIS Really Wants," *The Atlantic*, March 2015.
9. Rick Edmonds, "The best-read digital story of 2015? It's The Atlantic's "What ISIS Really Wants," *Poynter*, 31 Dec. 2015.
10. Wood, "What ISIS Really Wants."
11. Bernard Haykel, "On the nature of salafi thought and action," in Roel Meijer (ed.), *Global Salafism: Islam's New Religious Movement* (London: Hurst, 2009), 33.
12. Permanent Committee for Scholarly Research and Ifta', "What is "Al-Salafiyah?" What do you think of it?," *vol. 2: Al-'Aqidah* (2), Fatwa no. 1361.
13. Wasiullah ibn Muhammad Abbas, *Al-Ittiba: and the Principles of Fiqh of the Righteous Predecessors* (Brooklyn, NY: Dar ul Itibaa Publications, 2013), 111.
14. *Sahih Muslim*, Book 31, no. 6159.
15. The collected fatwas of Saudi Arabia's Permanent Committee for Scholarly Research and Fatwas arrange questions relating to *salafism* under the title of *ṭā'ifa al-manṣūra* (vol. 2).

16. Muhammad ibn Salih al-Uthaymin, *Explanation of a summary of al-'aqīda-tul-hamawiyyah of Ibn Taymiyyah* (np, nd), see chs 5 and 6.
17. Salih ibn Fawzan, al-Albani, and Taraheeb al-Dosri, "The difference between the Aqīda and the Manhaj," *Salaf-us-saalih*, http://salaf-us-saalih.com/2010/02/08/the-difference-between-the-aqeedah-and-the-manhaj/ accessed on 15 March 2013.
18. Ikram Chaghatai, *Shah Waliullah (1703–1762), His Religious and Political Thought* (Lahore: Sang-e-Meel Publications, 2005).
19. Natana DeLong-Bas, *Wahhabi Islam: From Revival and Reform to Global Jihad* (Oxford: Oxford University Press, 2008).
20. 'Abd al-'Aziz Bin Baz, "Speech during Sheikh Muhammad ibn 'Abd al-Wahhab week," *Fatwas of Bin Baz*, vol. 1:378.
21. Dore Gold, *Hatred's Kingdom: How Saudi Arabia Supports the New Global Terrorism* (Washington, D.C.: Regnery Publishing Inc., 2004). DeLong-Bas, *Wahhabi Islam*.
22. Madawi al-Rasheed, *Contesting the Saudi State: Islamic Voices from a New Generation* (Cambridge: Cambridge University Press, 2010).
23. Quintan Wiktorowicz, "Anatomy of the Salafi Movement," *Studies in Conflict & Terrorism*, 29 (2006), 207.
24. Ibid., 208.
25. Mohammed Hafez, *Suicide Bombers in Iraq: The Strategy and Ideology of Martyrdom* (Washington, D.C.: United States Institute of Peace, 2007), 65.
26. Jarret Brachman, *Global Jihadism*, 26. The various categories are as follows: establishment *salafis*, Madkhali *salafis*, Albani *salafis*, scientific *salafis*, *salafi* ikhwanis, Sururis, Qutbis, global *jihadists*.
27. Thomas Hegghammer, "Jihadi-Salafis or Revolutionaries? On Religion and Politics in the study of Militant Islamism," in Roel Meijer (ed.), *Global Salafism*, 246. Roel Meijer, "Introduction," in Roel Meijer (ed.), *Global Salafism*, 27.
28. Ibid.
29. Mordechai Abir, *Saudi Arabia: Society, Government and the Gulf Crisis* (Oxford: Routledge, 2006), 10.
30. Stéphane Lacroix, *Awakening Islam: The Politics of Religious Dissent in Contemporary Saudi Arabia*, trans. George Holoch (Cambridge, MA: Harvard University Press, 2011).
31. Abdelrezak Rejjam, "Communique no. 42, The Islamic Salvation Front National Provisional Executive Bureau," in John Calvert (ed.), *Islamism: A Documentary and Reference Guide* (Westport, CT: Greenwood Publishing Group, 2008), 160–161. Randall Law, *Terrorism: A History* (Cambridge: Polity Press, 2009), Kindle edn.

32. Aron Lund, "Syria's Salafi Insurgents: The Rise of the Syrian Islamic Front," *Swedish Institute of International Affairs*, no. 17, 2013.
33. John Esposito, *Islam and Politics* (Syracuse, NY: Syracuse University Press, 1998), 239.
34. Al-Qaeda, "Al-Qaeda's Path and Creed," in *Global Salafism*, trans. Bernard Haykel, ed. Roel Meijer, 53.
35. Frazer Egerton, *Jihad in the West: The Rise of Militant Salafism* (Cambridge: Cambridge University Press, 2011).
36. Meijer, "Introduction," 25.
37. Ibid. Also: Roel Meijer, "Yūsuf al-'Uyayrī and the making of a revolutionary salafi praxis," *Die Welt des Islams*, 47, 3–4 (2007), 422–459; Roel Meijer, "Yūsuf al-'Uyayrī and the transnationalisation of Saudi jihadism," in Madawi al-Rasheed (ed.), *Kingdom without Borders: Saudi Arabia's Political, Religious and Media Frontiers* (London: Hurst, 2008), 221–244.
38. Eli Alshech, "The doctrinal crisis within the salafi-jihadi ranks and the emergence of neo-takfirism: a historical and doctrinal analysis," *Islamic Law and Society*, 21 (2014), 431.
39. Hafez, *Suicide Bombers in Iraq*, 66–70.
40. Brachman, *Global Jihadism*, 41.
41. Abu Muhammad al-Maqdisi, *This is our Aqīda* (Al-Tibyān Publications, second edn, nd).
42. Ibid., 37.
43. Al-Qaeda, "Al-Qaeda's Path and Creed," 51–56.
44. Ibid., 55.
45. Raymond Ibrahim, *The al-Qaeda Reader: The Essential Texts of Osama Bin Laden's Terrorist Organization* (New York, NY: Broadway Books, 2007), 25.
46. Thomas Hegghammer, "Violent Islamism in Saudi Arabia 1979–2006, the Power and Perils of Pan-Islamic Nationalism" (PhD diss., Sciences Po, 2007), 61.
47. Ibid., 62.
48. Alison Pargeter, *The New Frontiers of Jihad: Radical Islam in Europe* (London: I.B. Tauris, 2008), 119.
49. Ibid.
50. Gilles Kepel, *Jihad: The Trail of Political Islam* (London: I.B. Tauris, 2006); Olivier Roy, *The Failure of Political Islam* (London, I.B. Tauris, 2007); Jan-Erik Lane and Hamadi Redissi, *Religion and Politics: Islam and Muslim Civilization* (Farnham: Ashgate Publishing, 2009), 158.
51. Quintan Wiktorowicz, "The new global threat: transnational salafis and jihad," *Middle East Policy*, vol. VIII, no. 4, Dec. 2001.
52. Pargeter, *The New Frontiers of Jihad*, 119.
53. Abu Musab al-Zarqawi, "Our Creed and Methodology," 24 March 2005.

54. Ibid.
55. The only exception to this is Abu Basir al-Tartusi, who has periodically participated in the Syrian jihad by fighting alongside opposition forces since 2012.
56. Josef Van Ess, "Political ideas in early Islamic religious thought," *British Journal of Middle Eastern Studies* (hereafter *BJMES*), vol. 28, no. 2 (Nov., 2001), 151–164.
57. Roel Meijer, "Yūsuf al-'Uyayrī and the making of a revolutionary salafi praxis," *Die Welt des Islams*, vol. 47, 3–4 (2007), 422.
58. Although this interview was conducted with al-Qimmah it was reproduced on the Ansar al-Mujahideen internet forum a week later. Accessed at: http://ansar1.info/showthread.php?t=8500. For confirmation of Yazid's role as an al-Qaeda financer see: National Commission on Terrorist Attacks, *The 9/11 Commission Report: Final Report of the National Commission on Terrorist Attacks Upon the United States* (Washington, D.C.: Claitor's Law Books and Publishing, 2004). Note that Yazid appears in the report under the name Saeed al-Masri.
59. "Biography of Abu Musab Al-Zarqawi," Ansar al-Mujahideen Forum. Accessed 29 Dec. 2011. http://ansar1.info/showthread.php?t=9579
60. Shiraz Maher and Amany Soliman, "Al-Qaeda confirms death of Bin Laden," ICSR Insight, 6 May 2011. Accessed May 2011 at: http://icsr.info/2011/05/icsr-insight-al-qaeda-confirms-death-of-bin-laden/
61. "The blood of the martyr is light and fire; a statement about the martyrdom of shaykh Anwar al-Awlaqi and his comrades," *Ansar al-Mujahideen Forum*, accessed on 3 April 2012 at: http://ansar1.info/showthread.php?t=36355
62. John Berger, *Jihad Joe: Americans Who Go to War in the Name of Islam* (Washington, D.C.: Potomac Books, 2011); Brynjar Lia, *Architect of Global Jihad: The Life of al-Qaeda Strategist Abu Mus'ab Al-Suri* (London: Hurst, 2009).
63. Jarret M. Brachman and Alix N. Levine, "You too can be Awlaki!," *The Fletcher Forum of World Affairs*, vol. 35, 1, Winter 2011.
64. Dominick LaCapra, *Rethinking Intellectual History: Texts, Contexts, Language* (Ithaca, NY: Cornell University Press, 1983); The History of Ideas Club, *Studies in Intellectual History* (Baltimore, MD: The Johns Hopkins Press, 1953); Donald Kelley, *The Descent of Ideas: the History of Intellectual History* (Aldershot: Ashgate, 2002); Joseph Levine, "Intellectual History as History," *Journal of the History of Ideas*, vol. 66, no. 2 (April, 2005), 189–200; Franklin Baumer, "Intellectual history and its problems," *The Journal of Modern History*, vol. 21, no. 3 (Sept., 1949), 191–203; John Higham, "Intellectual history and its neighbours," *Journal of the History of Ideas*, vol. 15, no. 3 (June, 1954), 339–347; Felix Gilbert, "Intellectual history:

its aims and methods," *Daedalus*, vol. 100, no. 1, Historical Studies Today (Winter, 1971), 80–97.

65. Peter E. Gordon, "What is Intellectual History? A frankly partisan introduction to a frequently misunderstood field," Harvard History Department website. http://history.fas.harvard.edu/people/faculty/documents/pgordon-whatisintellhist.pdf
66. Arthur Lovejoy, *The Great Chain of Being: A Study of the History of an Idea* (Harvard, MA: Harvard University Press, 2001).
67. Lovejoy, *The Great Chain of Being*, 4–5.
68. Gordon, "What is Intellectual History?."
69. Stefan Collini, "What is intellectual history," *History Today*, vol. 35, 10, Oct. 1985.
70. LaCapra, *Rethinking Intellectual History*, 23–71; John Dunn, *The History of Political Theory and Other Essays* (Cambridge: Cambridge University Press, 1996); John Dunn, "The identity of the history of ideas," *Philosophy*, 43 (April 1968), 85–104.
71. Abdul Wahid, "Hizb ut Tahrir's distinction," OpenDemocracy (14 Aug. 2005), accessed on 7 Dec. 2011 at: http://www.opendemocracy.net/conflict-terrorism/criticism_2755.jsp
72. John Austin, *How to do Things with Words* (Oxford: Oxford University Press, 1976).
73. Ibid. See lecture nine in particular, 109–120.
74. Palonen, *Quentin Skinner*, 56–60.
75. Hannah Arendt, *The Origins of Totalitarianism* (Geo Allen & Unwin, 1967) 468.
76. Ian Adams, *Political Ideas Today* (Manchester: Manchester University Press, 2001), 1.
77. Ibid., 2.
78. Karl Mannheim, *From Karl Mannheim with an Introduction by Volker Meja and David Kettler* (New Jersey: Transaction Publishers, 1993), 52.
79. Steven B. Smith, *The Cambridge Companion to Leo Strauss* (Cambridge: Cambridge University Press, 2009).
80. Kenneth Deutsch, "Leo Strauss's friendly criticism of American liberal democracy: neoconservative or aristocratic liberalism?" in Kenneth Deutsch and Ethan Fishman (eds.), *The Dilemmas of American Conservatism* (Kentucky: University Press of Kentucky, 2010).
81. Kenneth Deutsch and Walter Nicgorski, "Introduction," in Kenneth Deutsch and Walter Nicgorski (eds.), *Leo Strauss: Political Philosopher and Jewish Thinker* (Lanham, MD: Rowman & Littlefield Publishers, 1984), 19.
82. Thierry Gontier, "From 'political theology' to 'political religion': Eric Voegelin and Carl Schmitt,' *Review of Politics*, 75, 2013, 25–43; Eric

Voegelin, *The New Science of Politics: An Introduction* (Chicago, IL: University of Chicago Press, 1987).

83. Anthony James Gregor, *Totalitarianism and Political Religion: An Intellectual History* (Stanford, CA: Stanford University Press, 2012); Barry Cooper, *New Political Religions, or an Analysis of Modern Terrorism* (Missouri: University of Missouri Press, 2005).
84. David Martin Jones and M.L.R. Smith, *Sacred Violence: Political Religion in a Secular Age* (London: Palgrave Macmillan, 2014), 2.

2. THE OBLIGATION OF FIGHTING

1. Ibn Kathir, *The Battles of the Prophet*, trans. Wa'il Abdul Mut'aal Shihab (Cairo: Dar al-Manarah, 2001).
2. 'Abdallah 'Azzam, *al-Jihad: Linguistically and Legally* (unpubl, nd).
3. Ibid.
4. Ibid.
5. The idea of a jihad against oneself constituting "the greater jihad" is disputed among scholars because it is based on a *ḥadīth* which some do not regard as *ṣaḥiḥ*, meaning genuine or authentic.
6. Ibn Nuhaas, *The Book of Jihad*, trans. Noor Yamani (np, nd).
7. Anwar al-Awlaki, *The Book of Jihad by ibn Nuhaas—Commentary by al-Awlaki* (np, nd).
8. Ibn Nuhaas, *The book of Jihad*.
9. *Qur'an* 2:251.
10. 'Abdallah 'Azzam, *The Defence of the Muslim Lands: the First Obligation After Īmān* (unpubl, 1984).
11. 'Azzam, *Defence of the Muslim Lands*.
12. Abu Musab al-Zarqawi, "Our Creed and Methodology," Ansar al-Mujahideen forum, 24 March 2005. Accessed 30 April 2014 at: http://thesis.haverford.edu/dspace/bitstream/handle/10066/5026/AQI20050321.pdf
13. Zawahiri, *The Exoneration*.
14. Abu Qatada, *Characteristics of the Victorious Party in the Foundation of the State of the Believers, the Land of ash-Sham* (Al-Tibyān publications, nd), 46.
15. 'Azzam, *Defence of the Muslim Lands*.
16. 'Abdallah 'Azzam, *Join the Caravan* (np, 1987).
17. Ibid.
18. Sayyid Qutb, *In the Shade of the Qur'an*, vol. 2, quoted in 'Azzam, *Join the Caravan* (unpubl, 1987).
19. Ibn Nuhaas, *The Book of Jihad*.
20. *Qur'an* 9:19. The incident is narrated in Ibn Nuhaas, *The Book of Jihad*.
21. Ibn Nuhaas, *The Book of Jihad*.

22. For more on Yusuf al-'Uyayri see: Meijer, "Yūsuf al-'Uyayrī and the making of a revolutionary salafi praxis"; see also: Anwar al-Awlaki, "*Thawābit 'ala darb al-Jihad, Constants on the Path of Jihad by Yūsuf al-'Uyayrī, lecture series delivered by Anwar al-Awlaki*" (Np, nd); Yusuf al-'Uyayri, '*Haqīqat al-Harb al-Salībiyyah al-Jadīdah,*' [The Truth of the New Crusader War] translated version in *The Clarification Regarding Intentionally Targeting Women and Children* (Al-Tibyān Publications, nd).
23. Zarqawi, "Our Creed and Methodology."
24. Qatada, *Characteristics of the Victorious Party*, 46.
25. Akbar Shah Najibabadi, *The History of Islam*, vol. 3 (London: Darussalam Publications, 2001), 311–313; Percy Sykes, *A History Of Persia*, vol. 2 (Oxford: Routledge, 2006), 86–99.
26. David Ayalon, "Studies on the Transfer of The ʿAbbāsid Caliphate from Baġdād to Cairo," *Arabica*, T. 7, Fasc. 1 (Jan., 1960), 41–59.
27. Muhammad Nasir al-Din al-Albani, *"Debate with a Jihadi," Jihad in the Qur'an and Sunnah* (Salafi Publications, nd).
28. Ibid.
29. Ibid.
30. Meijer, "Introduction," 18.
31. 'Azzam, *Defence of the Muslim Lands*.
32. Ibid.
33. 'Abdallah al-Ghunayman, "Question #11275: Is it a condition of jihad that there be a leader?" (www.islam-qa.com), accessed on 4 Oct. 2013 at: https://muwahhidmedia.wordpress.com/2013/07/24/is-having-a-ruler-a-condition-for-the-defensive-and-offensive-jihad/
34. 'Azzam, *Defence of the Muslim Lands*.
35. Ibid.
36. Ibid.
37. Awlaki, "Constants on the Path of Jihad."
38. Paul Middleton, *Martyrdom: A Guide for the Perplexed* (London: T&T Clark, 2011).
39. David Cook, *Martyrdom in Islam* (Cambridge: Cambridge University Press, 2007), 14.
40. *Qur'an* 22:39. It is important to note that the *Qur'an* uses the term *qitāl* here (which means "fighting"), rather than jihad. The first specific use of jihad as a term comes in verse 25:52.
41. Clinton Bennett, *Interpreting the Qur'an: A Guide for the Uninitiated* (London: Continuum International Publishing Group, 2010), 130.
42. Barnaby Rogerson, *The Prophet Muhammad: A Biography* (London: Hachette Digital, 2003), Kindle edn.

3. APPLYING JIHAD IN SALAFI THOUGHT

1. 'Abdallah 'Azzam, *The Lofty Mountain* ('Azzam publications, nd), Part I; "Interview with shaykh Tameem al Adnani," Iraq war collection, accessed on 11 May 2015 at: https://archive.org/details/interview-sheikh-tameem-adnani
2. National Commission on Terrorist Attacks, *The 9/11 Commission Report*, section 2.4.
3. The term "far enemy" has become widespread since 9/11. See: Fawaz Gerges, *The Far Enemy: Why Jihad Went Global* (Cambridge: Cambridge University Press, 2005).
4. "Bin Laden Interviewed on Jihad Against US," by Abdel Bari Atwan, Al-Quds al-Arabi (27 Nov. 1996, London, in *Compilation of Osama Bin Laden Statements 1994—Jan. 2004* by Foreign Broadcast Information Service (FBIS) (Jan. 2004), 5.
5. Osama bin Laden, *Letter to Bin Baz Regarding the Invalidity of his Fatwa About Peace Treaties with the Jews*, 27 Dec. 1994.
6. Mahan Abedin, "A Saudi oppositionist's view: an interview with Dr Muhammad al-Massari," *Terrorism Monitor*, vol. 1, Issue: 7, The Jamestown Foundation (Dec., 2003).
7. Osama bin Laden, *"Osama bin Laden, statement no. 3, 7 June 1994,"* Counter-Terrorism Centre, Westpoint, Harmony Index (AFPG-2002–003345).
8. Osama bin Laden, *"Osama bin Laden, statement no. 18, 11 Aug. 1995,"* Counter-Terrorism Centre, Westpoint, Harmony Index (AFPG-2002-003345).
9. John Miller, "A conversation with the most dangerous man in the world," *Esquire Magazine*, Feb. 1999, in *Compilation of Osama Bin Laden Statements 1994—Jan. 2004* by Foreign Broadcast Information Service (FBIS), 96.
10. Magnus Ranstorp, "Interpreting the broader context and meaning of Bin Laden's Fatwa," *Studies in Conflict & Terrorism*, 21, vol. 4 (1998), 324.
11. Osama bin Laden, *Declaration of War against the Americans Occupying the Land of the Two Holy Places*, 1996.
12. Miller, "The most dangerous man in the world," 99.
13. Ibid.
14. Osama bin Laden, "Letter to the American people," Nov. 2002.
15. Ibid.
16. Ibid.
17. John Kelsay, *Islam and War: A Study in Comparative Ethics, The Gulf War and Beyond* (Louisville, KY: John Knox Press, 1993); Niaz Shah, *Islamic Law and the Law of Armed Conflict: The Conflict in Pakistan* (New York, NY: Routledge, 2011), 29–90; James Turner Johnson, *The Holy War Idea in Western and Islamic Traditions* (University Park, PA: Pennsylvania State University Press, 1997).

18. Mohammed Abu-Nimer, "Framework for nonviolence and peace building," in Abdul Aziz Said, Mohammed Abu-Nimer, Meena Sharify-Funk (eds.) *Contemporary Islam: Dynamic, Not Static* (New York, NY: Routledge, 2006), 149.
19. Shah, *Islamic Law*.
20. *Qur'an* 2:190.
21. *Essay Regarding the Basic Rule of the Blood, Wealth, and Honour of the Disbelievers* (Al-Tibyān Publications, 2004); *The Clarification Regarding Intentionally Targeting Women and Children* (Al-Tibyān Publications, 2004).
22. Mohammad Hashim Kamali, *Principles of Islamic Jurisprudence* (Cambridge: Islamic Texts Society, 1991), 130–137.
23. Narrated by Muslim, *The book of Faith*, Chapter 8, no. 124.
24. *Essay Regarding the Basic Rule of the Blood, Wealth, and Honour of the Disbelievers*, 10.
25. Ibid.
26. Imran Ahsan Khan Nyazee, *Islamic Jurisprudence: Usūl Al-Fiqh* (London: International Institute of Islamic Thought, 2000), 282–290; Muhammad M. Yunis Ali, *Medieval Islamic Pragmatics: Sunni Legal Theorists' Models of Textual Communication* (Oxford: Routledge, 2009), 14.
27. Kamali, *Principles of Islamic Jurisprudence*, 133–4.
28. *Clarification Regarding Intentionally Targeting Women and Children*, 9.
29. Although he now claims to have renounced the movement, he was still considered a member in 2004 when this book was written.
30. *Essay Regarding the Basic Rule of the Blood, Wealth, and Honour of the Disbelievers*.
31. *The Clarification Regarding Intentionally Targeting Women and Children*, 18.
32. Quintan Wiktorowicz and John Kaltner, "Killing in the name of Islam: al-Qaeda's justification for Sept. 11," *Middle East Policy Council*, vol. X, Summer 2003, no. 2.
33. Al-Qaeda, 'A statement from al-Qaeda al-jihad regarding the mandates of the heroes and the legality of the operations in New York and Washington," 24 April 2004.
34. Ibid.
35. M. Cherif Bassiouni, *The Shari'a and Islamic Criminal Justice in Time of War and Peace* (Cambridge: Cambridge University Press, 2014), 139–141.
36. Morris J. Fish, "An eye for an eye: proportionality as a moral principle of punishment," *Oxford Journal of Legal Studies*, vol. 28, no. 1 (Spring, 2008), 57–71.
37. Gamil Muhammed Hussein, "Basic guarantees in the Islamic criminal justice system," in Muhammad Abdel Haleem, Adel Omar Sharif, and Kate Daniels (eds.), *Criminal Justice in Islam: Judicial Procedure in the Shari'ah*, (London: I.B. Tauris, 2003), 35–56; Mahfodz Mohamed, "The concept

of Qisās in Islamic law," *Islamic Studies*, vol. 21, no. 2 (Summer 1982), 77–88.

38. Susan C. Hascall, "Restorative justice in Islam: should qisas be considered a form of restorative Justice?," *Berkeley Journal of Middle Eastern & Islamic Law* (2012).
39. *Qur'an* 2:178.
40. *Qur'an* 5:45.
41. Kamali, *Principles of Islamic Jurisprudence*, 132.
42. 'Uyayri, '*Haqīqat al-Harb,*' 63.
43. Bin Laden, "Letter to America," Nov. 2002.
44. 'Uyayri, '*Haqīqat al-Harb,*' 63.
45. All of their fatwas are contained in *The Clarification Regarding Intentionally Targeting Women and Children*, 48–96.
46. Muhammad ibn al-Uthaymin, "The verdict of shaykh Muhammad ibn Salih al-Uthaymeen," in *The Clarification Regarding Intentionally Targeting Women and Children*, 73.
47. *The Clarification Regarding Intentionally Targeting Women and Children*, 46.
48. Nasir ibn Hamad al-Fahd, *A Treatise on the Legal Status of Using Weapons of Mass Destruction Against Infidels* (np, 2003), 11–12.
49. Ayman al-Zawahiri, *The Treatise Exonerating the Nation of the Pen and the Sword from the Blemish of Weakness and Fatigue* (np, 2008); Rolf Mowatt-Larssen, *Islam and the Bomb: Religious Justification For and Against Nuclear Bombs* (Massachusetts: Belfer Center for Science and International Affairs, 2011), 34.
50. *Qur'an* 2:194.
51. Miller, "The most dangerous man in the world," 96.
52. Mohammed M. Hafez, "From marginalization to massacres: a political process explanation of GIA violence in Algeria," in Quintan Wiktorowicz (ed.), *Islamic Activism: A Social Movement Theory Approach* (Bloomington, IN: Indiana University Press, 2004), 37–60.
53. Martha Crenshaw, "Crisis in Algeria," in Richard Gillespie (ed.), *Mediterranean Politics*, vol. 1 (London: Pinter Publishers, 1994), 191–211.
54. Adam Robinson, *Bin Laden: Behind the Mask of the Terrorist* (Edinburgh: Mainstream Publishing Company, 2001), 115; Mohammed M. Hafez, *Why Muslims Rebel: Repression and Resistance in the Islamic World* (London: Lynne Rienner Publishers Inc, 2003), 41.
55. Wiktorowicz, "A Genealogy of Radical Islam," 87.
56. Lia, *Architect of Global Jihad*, 156.
57. Montasser al-Zayat, *The Road to al-Qaeda: The Story of Bin Laden's Right-Hand Man*, trans. Ahmed Fikry (London: Pluto, 2004).
58. Reuven Paz, "Islamic legitimacy for the London bombings," *Global Research*

in *International Affairs* (GLORIA), The Project For The Research Of Islamist Movements (PRISM), Occasional Papers, vol. 3, no. 4 (2005).

59. Abu Basir al-Tartusi, *Refutation Regarding the Targeting of Women and Children* (np, 24 July 2005).
60. Ibid.
61. *Qur'an* 2:194.
62. Paul Kamolnick, "al-Qaeda's sharia crisis: Sayyid Imam and the jurisprudence of lawful military jihad," *Studies in Conflict & Terrorism*, 36 (2013), 399.
63. *Qur'an* 6:16.
64. Sayyid Imam al-Sharif, *Doctrine for Rationalising Jihad in Egypt and the World* (2006), part 6.
65. Tartusi, *Refutation*.
66. Ibid.
67. Paz, "Islamic Legitimacy for the London Bombings."
68. Osama bin Laden, "Why we are fighting you," in Raymond Ibrahim (ed.), *The al-Qaeda Reader* (New York, NY: Broadway Books, 2007), 197–200.
69. Ibid., 200.
70. Ibid.
71. "Interview with shaykh Ayman al-Zawahiri, part 3," *Al-Sahab Media*, April 2007.
72. "Transcript of CBS Morning Show," in *Compilation of Osama Bin Laden Statements 1994—Jan. 2004* by Foreign Broadcast Information Service (FBIS), 102.
73. "Fatwa on Recent Events by shaykh Humud al-Uqla."
74. There are two books covering this in the English language. Ibn Taymiyya, *The Political Shariyah on Reforming the Ruler and the Ruled* (UK: Dar ul Fiqh, 2006); Ibn Taymiyya, *The Religious and Moral Doctrine of Jihad* (Birmingham: Maktabah al Ansar Publications, 2001).
75. Ibn Taymiyya, *The Religious and Moral Doctrine of Jihad*, 28.
76. Al-Qaeda, *"A statement from al-Qaeda al-jihad regarding the mandates of the heroes and the legality of the operations in New York and Washington,"* 24 April 2004.
77. Ibid.
78. Safi-ur-Rahman al-Mubarkpuri, *Ar-Raheeq Al-Makhtum (The Sealed Nectar), Biography of the Prophet* (Riyadh: Dar–us-Salam Publications, 1996), 262.
79. Benjamin Buchholz, "The human shield in Islamic jurisprudence," *Military Review* (May–June 2013), 49.
80. Sahih Muslim, Book 19, no. 4321.
81. Ibid.
82. Ibn Hajar al-Asqalani, *Selections from the Fath al-Bārī*, trans. Abdul Hakim Murad (Cambridge: Muslim Academic Trust, 2000).

83. Joseph Edmund Lowry, *Early Islamic Legal Theory: The Risāla of Muhammad Ibn Idrīs Al-Shāfiʿī* (Leiden: Brill, 2007), 131; Muhammad ibn Idris al-Shafi'I, *Al-Shafi'I's Risala: Treatise on the Foundations of Islamic Jurisprudence* (Cambridge: Islamic Texts Society, 2008), 220; For more on abrogation see: John Burton, "The exegesis of Q. 2: 106 and the Islamic theories of naskh: mā nansakh min āya aw nansahā na'ti bi khairin minhā aw mithlihā," *BSOAS*, University of London, vol. 48, no. 3 (1985), 452–469.
84. Abu Yahya al-Libi, *Human Shields in Modern Jihad* (np), 6 Jan. 2006.
85. Ibid.
86. Ibid.
87. Jasser Auda, *Maqasid Al-Shariah as Philosophy of Islamic Law: A Systems Approach* (London: International Institute of Islamic Political Thought, 2008); Imam Nawawi, *Al-Maqasid: Nawawi's Manual of Islam*, trans. Nuh Ha Min Keller (Beltsville, MD: Amana Publications, 2002).
88. Mohammad Hashim Kamali, "Maqāsid al-Sharʿiah: The objectives of Islamic law," *Islamic Studies*, vol. 38, no. 2 (Summer 1999), 193–208; Mohammad Hashim Kamali, "Istiḥsān and the renewal of Islamic law," *Islamic Studies*, vol. 43, no. 4 (Winter 2004), 561–581; Mohammad Hashim Kamali, "Qawa'id al-Fiqh: The legal maxims of Islamic law," *The Association of Muslim Lawyers*.
89. Libi, *Human Shields in Modern Jihad*.
90. "Periodical Review: Fatwas—Feb. 2011," *ICT's Jihadi Websites Monitoring Group*, ICT, April 2011.
91. Ayman al-Zawahiri, "Jihad, martyrdom, and the killing of innocents," in Raymond Ibrahim (ed.), *The Al-Qaeda Reader* (New York, NY: Broadway Books, 2007), 137–171.
92. Ibid., 162.
93. Ibid., 168.
94. Ibid., 169.
95. Ibid.
96. Ibid.
97. Ibid.; also see: Andrew F. March, "Anwar al-Awlaqi against Islamic tradition," in Asma Afsaruddin (ed.) *Islam, the State, and Political Authority: Medieval Issues and Modern Concerns* (New York, NY: Palgrave Macmillan, 2011), 231.
98. Nibras Kazimi, "A virulent ideology in mutation: Zarqawi upstages Maqdisi," *Current Trends*, Hudson Institute (12 Sept. 2005), 67.
99. Ibid.
100. Libi, *Human Shields*.
101. Zawahiri, *The Exoneration*.
102. Libi, *Human Shields*.
103. Ibid.

104. Zawahiri, *The Exoneration*.
105. James D. Le Sueur, *Uncivil War: Intellectuals and Identity Politics During the Decolonization of Algeria* (London: University of Nebraska Press 2005), 311.
106. John C. Hawley, "Jihad as a rite of passage: Tahar Djaout's *The Last Summer of Reason* and Slimane Benaïssa's *The Last Night of a Damned Soul*," in Fiona Tolan, Stephen Morton, Anastasia Valassopoulos, Robert Spencer (eds.), *Literature, Migration and the 'War on Terror'* (Oxford: Routledge, 2012), 141.
107. "Interview shaykh Tameem al Adnani," Iraq War Archive, archive.org, accessed on 5 May 2016, available at: https://archive.org/details/interview-sheikh-tameem-adnani
108. March, "Awlaqi Against Islamic Tradition," 231.
109. Sayyid Imam al-Sharif, *Doctrine for Rationalising Jihad in Egypt and the World* (np, 2007). This was a series of letters sent by Sayyid Imam to the *Asharq al-Awsat* newspaper in London from his prison cell in Egypt.
110. Paul Kamolnick, "Al-Qaeda's Sharia crisis," 395.
111. Ibid.
112. Abu Basir al-Tartusi, *The Dangers of Martyrdom or Suicide Bombings* (np, 2005).

4. ESTABLISHING DISBELIEF

1. Safar al-Hawali, "Ẓahiratu al-Irjā' fi al-Fikr al-Islami," quoted in Mansoor Jassem Alshamsi, *Islam and Political Reform in Saudi Arabia: The Quest for Political Change and Reform* (Oxford: Routledge, 2011), 70.
2. *Qur'an* 57:20.
3. Abu Hamza al-Masri, *Be Aware of Takfir* (np, nd).
4. Muhammad ibn 'Abd al-Wahhab, *Kitāb al-Tawḥīd*, ch 2. Also see: Muhammad ibn 'Abd al-Wahhab, Risālah Aslu Dīn al-Islām wa Qā'idatuhu.
5. Masri, *Be Aware of Takfir*; Daurius Figueira, *Salafi Jihadi Discourse of Sunni Islam in the 21st Century: The Discourse of Abu Muhammed al Maqdisi and Anwar al Awlaki* (Bloomington, IN: iUniverse books, 2011), 129–30; Daniel Lav, *Radical Islam and the Revival of Medieval Theology* (Cambridge: Cambridge University Press, 2012), 69.
6. According to Abu Hamza these include: *Juhūd*—denying key tenets of Islam; *Takdhib*—denying the promise of Allah; *Istakbār*—denying aspects of faith through pride or arrogance; *Istihazā*—mocking the faith; *I'rād*—avoiding the truth or commandments of Allah; *Istibdāl*—replacing Allah's laws with something else.
7. Imam Nawawi, *Riyad-Us-Saliheen: The Paradise of the Pious* (Leicester: Dar-us-Salam Publications, 1999) ch 49.

8. The Battle of Badr holds particular significance in Islam because it was the first battle waged by the Prophet Muhammad. A number of contemporary militant movements explicitly reference the number of muslims who participated in it (which was 313). For example, there is the "313 Brigade" led by Ilyas Kashmiri in Pakistan.
9. Anwar al-Awlaki, "Tawfique Chowdhury's alliance with the West," *Anwar al-Awlaki blog*, Feb. 12, 2009.
10. Ibid.
11. Sahih Bukhari, vol. 8, Book 73, no. 125.
12. Masri, *Be Aware of Takfir*; Abu Muhammad al-Maqdisi, *Ar-Risālah Ath-Thalathīniyah Fit-Tahdhīr min al-Ghūluw Fit-Takfir* (np, 1998/9); Omar 'Abd al-Rahman, *The present rulers, are they Muslim or not?* (np, nd); Abu Basir al-Tartusi, *Principles of Takfir* (np, 1994).
13. Abu Muhammad al-Maqdisi, *This is our Aqīda* (Al-Tibyān Publications, nd), 56.
14. Ibid., 58.
15. Khaled Abou El Fadl, *Rebellion and Violence in Islamic Law* (Cambridge: Cambridge University Press, 2001), particularly chs 1 and 2.
16. A useful consolidation of various opinions from across the centuries of quietist salafi opinion on this matter is contained in: *"Fatawa from the imams of salafiyyah concerning rallies and demonstrations, and additional guidelines concerning revolt and takfeer in light of the Algerian affair,"* TROID publications.
17. El Fadl, *Rebellion and violence*, 32.
18. David Nicolle, *The Great Islamic Conquests AD 632–750* (Oxford: Osprey Publishing, 2009), 23–25.
19. Nabia Abbott, *Aisha, the Beloved of Mohammed* (Chicago: Chicago University Press, 1942), 158.
20. Tayeb El-Hibri, *Parable and Politics in Early Islamic History: The Rashidun Caliphs* (New York, NY: Columbia University Press, 2010), ch 5. Ira M. Lapidus, *A History of Islamic Societies* (Cambridge: Cambridge University Press, 2010), 46–51; Martin Hinds, "The murder of the Caliph Uthman," *International Journal of Middle East Studies*, vol. 3, no. 4 (Oct., 1972), 450–469.
21. El Fadl, *Rebellion and violence*, 34.
22. For an excellent discussion of the idioms, language, and conceptualisation of these ideas among the various factions see: G. R. Hawting, "The significance of the slogan "lā hukma illā lillāh" and the references to the "hudūd" in the traditions about the fitna and the murder of Uthman," *BSOAS*, University of London, vol. 41, no. 3 (1978), 453–463; Josef Van Ess, "Political ideas in early Islamic religious thought," *BJMES*, vol. 28, no. 2 (Nov., 2001), 151–164.

23. Khaled Keshk, "When did Mu'āwiya become Caliph?," *Journal of Near Eastern Studies*, vol. 69, no. 1 (April 2010), 31–42. This article provides an unusually sympathetic view of Muawiyah.
24. Thomas Hodgkin, "The revolutionary tradition in Islam," *History Workshop*, no. 10 (Autumn, 1980), 138–150.
25. Thomas Sizgorich, *Violence and Belief in Late Antiquity: Militant Devotion in Christianity and Islam* (Philadelphia, PA: University of Pennsylvania Press, 2009), 196–230; Hussam S. Timani, *Modern Intellectual Readings of the Kharijites* (New York, NY: Peter Lang, 2008).
26. Muhammad Nasir al-Din al-Albani, *Descriptions of the Khawārij*, accessed on 17 Oct. 2014 at: http://www.authentic-translations.com/trans-pub/ae_mnaa_2.pdf
27. Abul A'la Maududi, *Khilafat-o-Malookeyat* [The Caliphate and kingship] (Lahore: Urdu Bazar, nd).
28. Abu 'Abd al-Rahman Aadil bin Ali Al-Furaydaan, *The Characteristics of the Extremist Khawarij* (USA: Al-Ibaanah Publishing, 2005); Ibrahim al-Ruhayli, *A Concise Introduction to the Khawārij* (np, nd).
29. Ali was not, of course, the Prophet Muhammad's nephew but was instead his significantly younger cousin and, later, his son-in-law through marriage to Fatima.
30. Tom Holland, *In the Shadow of the Sword, The Battle for Global Empire and the End of the Ancient World* (London: Little Brown, 2012), 363.
31. Daniel Lav, *Radical Islam*, 15; Michael Cook, *Early Muslim Dogma: A Source-Critical Study* (Cambridge: Cambridge University Press, 1981), 22–50; 68–88.
32. Lav, *Radical Islam*, 16; Cook, *Early Muslim Dogma*, 27.
33. Cook, *Early Muslim Dogma*, 27.
34. Lav, *Radical Islam*, 18–22.
35. Ibid., 30.
36. This need not just relate to ritual acts such as the failure to observe prayer. Jurists who oppose Abu Hanifa's view also hold that acts of personal morality can lead to kufr, such as engaging in heterosexual anal sex. For a normative *salafi* view on this see: Ibn al-Qayyim, "Madarij us-Salikin," trans. Salafi Publications, *'Ibn al-Qayyim on the Types of Kufr and Ruling by Other than What Allah has Revealed,'* Salafi Publications, nd.
37. Many of Abu Hanifa's students later added caveats to this view, arguing that there were some acts that are inextricably intertwined with faith, such as prayer, and that these constitute stipulated acts of faith, *shara'i al-īmān*. See: A. Kevin Reinhart, "Like the difference between night and day: Hanafi and Shāfi discussions on Wājib and Fard," in Bernard G. Weiss (ed.), *Studies in Islamic Legal Theory* (Leiden: Brill, 2002), 222–3.
38. Toshihiko Izutsu, *The Concept of Belief in Islamic Theology, a Semantic Analysis of Imān and Islam* (Kuala Lumpur: Islamic Book Trust, 2006).

39. Kamali, *Principles of Islamic jurisprudence*. Gibril Fouad Haddad, *The Four Imāms and Their Schools: Abū Hanīfa, Mālik, Al-Shāfi'ī, Ahmad* (London: Muslim Academic Trust 2007).
40. Lacroix, *Awakening Islam*, 212.
41. Taqi ad-din Ahmad ibn Taymiyya, *Kitāb al-Īmān: Book of Faith* (Indiana: Īmān Publishing House, 2009), 18–47.
42. Ibid., 171.
43. Imam Bukhari, *Sahih al-Bukhari: The Early Years of Islam*, trans. Muhammad Asad (Kuala Lumpur: Islamic Book Trust, 2013), 360.

5. PRAXIS IN ACTION

1. Al-Qaeda, *Our Creed and Methodology* (March, 2005).
2. Reuven Amitai, "The Mongol occupation of Damascus in 1300: a study of Mamluk loyalties," in Michael Winter and Amalia Levanoni (eds.), *The Mamluks in Egyptian and Syrian Politics and Society* (Leiden: Brill, 2004), 29; Ahmad ibn 'Abd al-Halim Ibn Taymiyya, *Sharh al-Aqīda al-Wasatiyyah: Fundamental beliefs of Islam and rejection of false concepts* (Riyadh: Dar-us-Salam Publications, 1996), 12.
3. Yahya Michot, "Ibn Taymiyya's "New Mardin Fatwa." Is genetically modified Islam (GMI) carcinogenic?" *The Muslim World*, vol. 101 (April 2011), 131.
4. Yahya Michot, *Muslims under Non-Muslim Rule. Ibn Taymiyya on fleeing from sin, kinds of emigration, the status of Mardin (domain of peace/war, domain composite), the conditions for challenging power; Texts translated, annotated and presented in relation to six modern readings of the Mardin fatwa* (Oxford: Interface Publications, 2006), 26.
5. Majmu al-Fatawa, publisher Daru-l-Wafa, 3rd edn, 2005, vol. 28, 240, reproduced in "Fatwa of shaykh al-Islam Ibn Taymiyya about the country in which Muslims live and which are ruled by infidels," KavKaz Center, accessed on 4 April 2012 at: http://www.kavkazcenter.com/eng/content/2011/03/01/17640_print.html
6. Baber Johansen, "A perfect law in an imperfect society: Ibn Taymiyya's concept of "governance in the name of the sacred law,"' in P. Bearman, W. Heinrichs, and B. G. Weiss (eds.), *The Law Applied: Contextualizing the Islamic Shari'a* (London: I.B. Tauris, 2008), 276.
7. Hamza Yusuf, 'The Mardin fatwa and al-Qaeda,' *Rethinking Islamic Reform Conference*, Oxford University Islamic Society, University of Oxford, 2010.
8. Anwar al-Awlaki, 'The new Mardin declaration: an attempt at justifying the new world order,' *Inspire*, 2, Fall 2010, 34.
9. Lorenzo Vidino, *The New Muslim Brotherhood in the West* (New York, NY: Columbia University Press, 2010).

10. Bassam Tibi, *Islam's Predicament with Modernity: Religious Reform and Cultural Change* (Oxford: Routledge, 2009), 278.
11. Sayyid Qutb, *Milestones Along the Way* (Birmingham: Maktabah al-Ansar, 1996).
12. Sayed Khatab, *The Political Thought of Sayyid Qutb: The Theory of Jahiliyyah* (London: Routledge, 2006), 10.
13. A case could be made that Ibn Taymiyya indirectly influenced Qutb because of his influence on Maududi who, in turn, had influenced Qutb. Yet, given the centrality of Ibn Taymiyya in radical literature and thought, if he had been deemed important to Qutb then it is likely he would have been referenced directly.
14. Falah 'Abdallah al-Mdaires, *Islamic Extremism in Kuwait: From the Muslim Brotherhood to Al-Qaeda and Other Islamist Political Groups* (London: Routledge, 2010), 162.
15. Emmanuel Sivan, *Radical Islam: Medieval Theology and Modern Politics* (New Haven, CT: Yale University Press, 1990).
16. Michael Youssef, *Revolt Against Modernity: Muslim Zealots and the West* (Leiden: Brill, 1985), 78–80.
17. Nadine Gurr and Benjamin Cole, *New Face of Terrorism: Threats from Weapons of Mass Destruction* (London: I.B. Tauris, 2005), 133.
18. Daniel Byman, *The Five Front War: The Better Way to Fight Global Jihad* (Hoboken, NJ: John Wiley & Sons), 24.
19. Wiktorowicz, "A Genealogy of Radical Islam," 88.
20. Ibid.
21. Assaf Moghadam, *The Globalization of Martyrdom: al-Qaeda, Salafi Jihad, and the Diffusion of Suicide Attacks* (Baltimore, MD: Johns Hopkins University Press, 2008), 161.
22. Gabriel G. Tabarani, *Jihad's New Heartlands: Why The West Has Failed to Contain Islamic Fundamentalism* (Milton Keynes: Author House, 2011), 290.
23. Christopher Anzalone, "Revisiting Shaykh Atiyyatullah's work on takfir and mass violence," *CTC Sentinel*, April 2012.
24. Mohammed Hafez gives similar categorisations, although I differ slightly with his exact criteria. Mine are given above, but are adapted from his work. Mohammed M. Hafez, "Tactics, takfir, and anti-Muslim violence," in Assaf Moghadam and Brian Fishman (eds.), *Fault Lines in Global Jihad: Organizational, Strategic, and Ideological Fissures* (London: Routledge, 2011), 27.
25. Bruce Riedel, *The Search for al-Qaeda: Its Leadership, Ideology, and Future* (Washington, D.C.: The Brookings Institution, 2010), 15.
26. Ibn Kathir, *Stories of the Prophets* (Riyadh: Maktaba Dar-ur-Salam), 344.
27. Muhammad 'Abd al-Salam Faraj, *Jihad: The Absent Obligation* (Birmingham: Maktabah al-Ansar, 2000), 20.

28. Ibid.
29. Ibid., 21.
30. *Qur'an* 5:44.
31. Abu Hamza al-Masri, *Ruling by Man Made Law, is it Major or Minor Kufr? Explaining the Words of ibn Abbas* (Supporters of Shariah, 1996).
32. Wagemakers, *A Quietist Jihadi*, 65.
33. Ibid. Abu Hamza explains the same concept in *Be aware of Takfir*, although not as succinctly.
34. Ali ibn Khudair al-Khudair, Ma Ḥukm al-hakim bi-ghayri ma anzala Allah? Wa ma al-wajib tajahahu? [What is the ruling on the one who rules by other than what God has sent down? And what must one do to him?], *Minbar al-tawḥīd wa-l-jihad*, accessed on 17 Nov. 2014 at: http://www.tawhed.ws/pr?i=6441
35. Omar 'Abd al-Rahman, "The Present Rulers, are they Muslims or not?" trans from Al-Mawa'ithat ul-Hasana (np, nd).
36. Ibid.
37. Ibid.
38. Faraj, *Jihad: The Absent Obligation*, 24.
39. Patrick Gaffney, *The Prophet's Pulpit: Islamic Preaching in Contemporary Egypt* (Berkeley, CA: University of California Press, 1994), 252.
40. Sayyid Imam al-Sharif, "The stating of the ijmā' on the kufr of the rulers who rule by what Allah has not revealed," taken from *Al-Jamit Fi Talab el-Ilm al-Sharif*, vol. 2 (np, 1995), 880–882, reproduced on Salafi Media UK, accessed on 12 Nov. 2014 at: http://salafimediauk.com/2014/03/13/the-ijma-on-the-kuffr-of-the-rulers-who-rule-by-other-then-what-allah-swt-has-revealed/
41. Faraj, *Jihad: the absent obligation*, 27.
42. Laura Mansfield, *His Own Words: Translation and Analysis of the Writings of Dr. Ayman al-Zawahiri* (United States: TLG Publications, 2006), 95.
43. Masri, *Be Aware of Takfir*.
44. Abu Basir al-Tartusi, *Fatwa Regarding the Saudi Regime* (np, nd).
45. Omar 'Abd Al-Rahman, *The Present Rulers, are they Muslim or not?*; Masri, *Be Aware of Takfir*; Wagemakers, *A Quietist Jihadi*, 92.
46. *Badr ar-Riyadh*, al-Sahab Media, 2004.
47. *The Open Meeting with Shaykh Ayman al-Zawahiri: Part One*, Al-Sahab Media, 2009.
48. Wagemakers, *A Quietist Jihadi*, 89.
49. Tartusi, *Fatwa Regarding the Saudi Regime*.
50. Abu Basir al-Tartusi, *Ruling Regarding Signing up for the Armies of the Kuffār*.
51. Ibid.
52. Abu Basir al-Tartusi, *Principles of Takfir*; Masri, *Be Aware of Takfir*.
53. Ibid.

54. Jamal bin Farihan al-Harithi, *The Khawarij Perform Takfir on Account of Major Sins (*Salafi Publications, nd).
55. Ibid.
56. Ibid.
57. Salih al-Fawzan, *Are the Terrorists of Today the Khawārij?* (np, nd).
58. 'Abd al-Muhsin al-'Ubaykan, *The Khawarij and their Renewed Ideology* (Sunnah Publishing, nd); Muhammad Nasir al-Din al-Albani, *Descriptions of the Khawarij*.
59. 'Abd al-Muhsin al-'Ubaykan, "Fear Allah and do not Sympathize with al-Zarqawi and the Takfiri Agenda," *Ash-Sharq al-Awsat*; see also: 'Abd al-Muhsin al-Ubaykan, *The Khawarij and their Renewed Ideology* (sunnahpublishing.net, nd).
60. Hegghammer, *Jihad in Saudi Arabia*, 211.
61. I visited the second site on assignment for the BBC in 2008.
62. Al-Qaeda, "Our Creed and Methodology," (March, 2005).
63. Ibid.
64. *The Open Meeting with Shaykh Ayman al-Zawahiri*.
65. Ibid.
66. Abu Hamza al-Baghdadi, "Stop them, do not kill them," *Al-Fajr Media Center*, March 23, 2010.
67. Abu Hamza al-Baghdadi's full name is: Hamid Dawud Mohamed Khalil al Zawi. He is also sometimes referred to as Abu Omar al-Qurashi al-Baghdadi.
68. Baghdadi, "Stop them, do not kill them."
69. *Qur'an* 49:12.
70. Abu Yahya al-Libi, *Guidance on the Ruling of the Muslim Spy* (Al-Fajr Media Center, 2008), Open Source Center: Jihadist Website Posts Al-Libi's "Guidance on the Ruling of the Muslim Spy," (GMP20090708342001).
71. Ibid.
72. Ibid. A point must be made on spies here. Whereas some jihadis pronounce *takfir* on these groups in general, when it comes to spies there are a number of further caveats and considerations needed before *takfir* is pronounced. This comes from an incident during the Prophet Muhammad's life when one of the companions, Hatib ibn Abi Baltah, effectively spied on the *Sahāba* for the Quraysh. The Prophet forgave him and did not declare him an apostate. The exact details of the exemptions and caveats are not relevant here—but it is important to demonstrate an awareness of this. The caveats in this regard are even acknowledged by al-Qaeda theorists. Al-Libi, for example, discusses the case of Hatib extensively in his tract on spies and argues: "It is not necessary that spying, in all its forms, is infidelity, and here come the conflicts among the scholars concerning the Muslim spy."

73. *Fatwas of Bin Baz*, "Clarification on the Shi'a sects," vol. 4: 439.
74. *Fatwas of Bin Baz*, "Ruling on a Ma'dhun forbidding a Shi'a girl from concluding marriage," vol. 4: 437.
75. Nibras Kazimi, "Zarqawi's anti-Shi'a legacy: original or borrowed?," *Current Trends in Islamist Ideology*, Nov. 1st, 2006.
76. Ibid.
77. For more analysis of the book, see: Frederic M. Wehrey et al., *Saudi-Iranian Relations Since the Fall of Saddam: Rivalry, Cooperation, and Implications for U.S. Foreign Policy* (Arlington, VA: Rand Corporation, 2009), 15; Jerrold D. Green, Frederic M. Wehrey, Charles Wolf, *Understanding Iran* (Arlington, VA: Rand Corporation, 2009), 121; Frederic M. Wehrey, *Sectarian Politics in the Gulf: From the Iraq War to the Arab Uprisings* (New York, NY: Columbia University Press, 2014), 122–136.
78. Alshamsi, *Islam and Political Reform in Saudi Arabia*, 74.
79. Ibid.
80. Fatwas of Bin Baz, "Clarification on the Shi'a sects," vol. 4: 439.
81. *Dialogue with shaykh Abu Musab Al-Zarqawi, Part One*, al-Furqan Media (2005).
82. Ibid.
83. "A new audio message from commander Abu-Musab al-Zarqawi to the nation of Islam," *Text of Al-Zarqawi Message Threatening More Attacks*, Federation of American Scientists, accessed on April 2014 at: https://www.fas.org/irp/world/para/zarqawi040604.html
84. Ibid.
85. Kazimi, "Zarqawi's anti-Shi'a legacy."
86. Michael Schwartz, *War Without End: The Iraq War in Context* (Chicago, IL: Haymarket Books, 2008), 110.
87. Ibid.
88. *Dialogue With Shaykh Abu Musab Al-Zarqawi, Part One*.
89. Ibid.
90. "Letter from Zawahiri to Zarqawi," *CTC Harmony Index Documents*, 9 July 2005.
91. Masri, *Be Aware of Takfir*.

6. THE MAKING OF LOVE AND HATE

1. For generalised texts see: Basheer M. Nafi, "Fatwa and war: on the allegiance of the American Muslim soldiers in the Aftermath of Sept. 11," *Islamic Law and Society*, vol. 11, no. 1 (2004), 78–116; Uriya Shavit, "The Wasati and Salafi approaches to the religious law of Muslim minorities," *Islamic Law and Society*, vol. 19, no. 4 (2012), 416–457; Meir Hatina, "Redeeming Sunni Islam: Al-Qaida's polemic against the Muslim Brethren,"

BJMES, vol. 39, no. 1 (April, 2012), 101–113. For Wagemakers works see: Joas Wagemakers, "The enduring legacy of the second Saudi state: quietist and radical Wahhabi contestations of al-walā' wa-l-barā," *International Journal of Middle East Studies*, 44, 2012, 93–110; Joas Wagemakers, "Framing 'the threat to Islam': al-walā' wa-l-barā' in Salafi discourse," *Arab Studies Quarterly*, vol. 30, no. 4 (Fall 2008), 1–22; Joas Wagemakers, "A purist jihadi-salafi: the ideology of Abu Muhammad al-Maqdisi," *BJMES*, vol. 36, no. 2 (Aug. 2009), 281–297; Joas Wagemakers, "The transformation of a radical concept: al-walā' wa-l-barā' in the ideology of Abu Muhammad al-Maqdisi," in Meijer (ed.), *Global Salafism*, 81–106; Wagemakers, *A Quietist Jihadi*, 147–190.

2. It is worth stating upfront that the relatively recent politicisation of *al-walā' wa-l-barā'* as a concept means that much of the primary source material presented in this chapter is the same as that used by Wagemakers. This inevitably creates some areas of analytical overlap, although the focus and scope of this chapter frames the discussion of *al-walā' wa-l-barā'* with reference to the salafi-jihadi movement as a whole.
3. 'Abd al-Malik Mujahid, *Affection and Aversion (al-walā' and al-barā')* (Riyadh: Dar-us-Salam, 2002), 8. Also see: Saleh bin 'Abd al-'Aziz Al ash-Sheikh, "Shariah principles for the position of a Muslim in times of tribulation," Oct. 1990, transcribed by Salafi Publications under the title: *"Concerning Tawallī and Muwālāt"* (Salafi Publications, nd); Muhammad Saeed al-Qahtani, *Al-Walā' wa-l-Barā' According to the 'Aqīda of the Salaf, part 2* (np, 1984), 8.
4. Mujahid, *Affection and Aversion*, 8. Also see Wagemakers, *A Quietist Jihadi*, 148.
5. Al-Qahtani, *al-walā' wa-l-barā', part 2*, 10.
6. Muhammad Saeed al-Qahtani, *Al-Walā' wa-l-Barā': According to the Aqīda of the Salaf* (np, 1984), vols 1–3.
7. Qahtani, *Al-Walā' wa-l-Barā', part 2*, 11.
8. Ibid.
9. Wagemakers, *A Quietist Jihadi*, 149.
10. Bernard Lewis, "Islamic Revolution," *The New York Review of Books*, Jan. 21, 1988.
11. Joas Wagemakers, "The enduring legacy of the second Saudi state: quietist and radical Wahhabi contestations of al-walā' wa-l-barā', *International Journal of Middle East Studies*, 44 (2012), 93–110.
12. Wagemakers, "The enduring legacy of the second Saudi state," 96; James Wynbrandt, *A Brief History of Saudi Arabia* (New York, NY: Checkmark Books, 2010), ch 6: 117–142.
13. David Commins, *The Wahhabi Mission and Saudi Arabia* (London: I.B. Tauris, 2006), 77.

14. Khaled Fahmy, *All The Pasha's Men: Mehmed Ali, His army and the Making of Modern Egypt* (Cairo: American University in Cairo Press, 2002), 48; Donald Quataert, *The Ottoman Empire, 1700–1922* (Cambridge: Cambridge University Press, 2005), 61.
15. Sulayman ibn Muhammad ibn 'Abd al-Wahhab, *The Evidences for the Ruling Regarding Alliances with the In fidels: Ad-Dalā'il fī Ḥukm Muwālāt ahl al-Ishrāk* (Al-Tibyān Publications, 2004).
16. Ibid., 78.
17. Ibid., 80. In this context, the reference to *qibāb* is presumably a derogatory reference to Sufi practices which involve visiting the graves of notable saints, holy men, and scholars.
18. Ibid., 76.
19. Tim Niblock, *Saudi Arabia: Power, Legitimacy and Survival* (Oxford: Routledge, 2006), 23.
20. Pascal Ménoret, *The Saudi Enigma: A History* (London: Zed Books Ltd, 2005), 77.
21. James Wynbrandt, *A Brief History of Saudi Arabia* (York, PA: Maple Vail Publishing, 2010), 162.
22. Ibid.
23. Hamad ibn 'Atiq, *The way of Cutting Relations off From the Polytheist and Apostate: Sabil an-Najāt wa-l-Fikāk min Muwalat al-Murtadin wa ahl al-Ishrāk* (Mustaqeem Publications, nd).
24. Wagemakers, "The enduring legacy of the second Saudi state," 96.
25. Wynbrandt, *A Brief History of Saudi Arabia*, 161–2.
26. 'Atiq, *The way of Cutting Relations off From the Polytheist and Apostate.*
27. Sulayman ibn 'Abd al-Wahhab, *Ruling Regarding Alliances with the Infidels*, 77.
28. 'Abd al-'Aziz bin 'Abdallah Bin Baz, *The undeniably known duties about the relations between the ruler and the ruled* (np, nd) 22–23.
29. Meijer, "Introduction," *Global Salafism*, 18.
30. Abu Muhammad al-Maqdisi, *Millat Ibrahim and the Calling of the Prophets and Messengers and the Methods of the Transgressing Rulers in Dissolving it and Turning the Callers Away From it* (Al-Tibyān Publications, 1984).
31. Maqdisi, *Millat Ibrahim*, 10–11.
32. "Major Police Raids: Salafist Organization Banned in Germany," *Der Spiegel*, June 14, 2012.
33. Maqdisi, *Millat Ibrahim*, 19.
34. Ibn Kathir, *Stories of the Prophets* (Jeddah, Dar us-Salam: 2003), 130–195.
35. *Qur'an* 21:59–67.
36. Maqdisi, *Millat Ibrahim*, 21.

37. Ibid., 42.
38. 'Abd al-Qadir ibn 'Abd al-'Aziz, *Fundamental Concepts Regarding Al-Jihad* (Al-Tibyān Publications, nd).
39. Ibid., 23.
40. Ibid., 35.
41. Ibid.
42. Ibid., 35–45.

7. *AL-WALĀ'WA-L-BARĀ'* AS SOCIAL EMPOWERMENT

1. 'Azzam, *Defence of Muslim Lands*.
2. Ibid.
3. Ibid.
4. "Sheikh 'Abd al-'Aziz bin Baz: his childhood and youth," *Fatwas of Bin Baz, vol. 1* (np, nd), 9. The website is no longer functional but can be accessed through the internet archive on: http://web.archive.org/web/20080320110244/http://www.bin-baz.org.sa/aboutbinbaz2.asp.
5. "Complaints by Arab fanatics against King ibn Sa'ūd," despatch of U.S. Minister, Jedda, 4 Dec. 1944, in Ibrahim Rashid (ed.), *Saudi Arabia enters the modern world: secret U.S. documents on the emergence of the Kingdom of Saudi Arabia as a world power, 1936–1949*, vol. 1 (Salisbury, N.C.: Documentary Publications, 1980).
6. Now Saudi Aramco.
7. Guido Steinberg, "The Wahhabi ulama and the Saudi State: 1745 to the present" in Paul Aarts and Gerd Nonneman (eds.), *Saudi Arabia in the Balance: Political Economy, Society, Foreign Affairs* (London: Hurst, 2005), 25.
8. Ibid.
9. Niblock, *Saudi Arabia*, 23.
10. "Complaints by Arab fanatics against King ibn Sa'ūd."
11. "Employing non-Muslim servants," *Fatwas of Bin Baz*, Question 8 (np, nd). Available online at: http://www.alifta.net/
12. Madawi al-Rasheed, "Saudi religious transnationalism in London" in Madawi al-Rasheed (ed.), *Transnational Connections and the Arab Gulf* (New York, NY: Routledge, 2005), 154.
13. Steinberg, "The Wahhabi ulama and the Saudi State: 1745 to the Present," 29.
14. *Fatwas of Bin Baz*, vol. 6 (nd, np), 75.
15. Ibid.
16. Ibid., 76.
17. Ibid., 79.
18. Felicitas Opwis, *Maslaha and the Purpose of the Law: Islamic Discourse on Legal Change from the 4th/10th to 8th/14th Century* (Leiden: Brill, 2010), section

1 of chapter 1 is particularly useful: 9–13; as is ch 3: 133–174; Felicitas Opwis, "Islamic law and legal change: the concept of maslaha in classical and contemporary Islamic legal theory," in Abbas Amanat and Frank Griffel (eds.), *Sharia: Islamic Law in the Contemporary Context* (Stanford, CA: Stanford University Press, 2007), 62–82; John Esposito, *What Everyone Needs to Know About Islam: Answers to Frequently Asked Questions from one of America's Leading Experts* (Oxford: Oxford University Press, 2011), 140–141.

19. For more on this see: Nuh Amin Keller, *Al-Maqasid: Nawawi's Manual of Islam* (Beltsville, MD: Amana Publications, 2002); Jasser Auda, *Maqasid al-Shariah as Philosophy of Islamic Law: A Systems Approach* (London: International Institute of Islamic Thought, 2008); Mohammed Umer Chapra, *The Islamic Vision of Development in the Light of Maqasid Al-Shariah* (London: International Institute of Islamic Political Thought, 2008).
20. *Fatwas of Bin Baz, vol. 6* (np, nd), 79.
21. Ibn Taymiyya, *Enjoining Right and Forbidding Wrong*, trans. Salim 'Abdallah ibn Morgan (unpubl, nd).
22. Michael Cook, *Commanding Right and Forbidding Wrong in Islamic Thought* (Cambridge: Cambridge University Press, 2002), 154.
23. Ibn Taymiyya, *Enjoining Right and Forbidding Wrong*.
24. Lacroix, *Awakening Islam*.
25. Safar al-Hawali, *Al-Masrah al-Islamiyya wa-l-hayat fi wa athar hawathorah anashatha al-amaniyat* [Secular origins, evolution, and its impact on contemporary Islamic life]. Accessed 27 Nov. 2014 at: http://www.alhawali.com/index.cfm?method=home.showcontent&contentID=1. Safar al-Hawali, *Muqadama fi tdhowar al-fikr al-arabiwa al-khadatha* [Introduction to the evolution of Western thought and modernity]. Accessed 27 Nov. 2014 at: http://www.alhawali.com/index.cfm?method=home.show content&contentID=2
26. Safar al-Hawali, *Wa'd Kissinger: al-Ahdaf al-Amrikiyya fil Khalij* [*Kissinger's Promise: American goals in the Gulf*], 158, quoted in Sonia Alianak, *Middle Eastern Leaders and Islam: A Precarious Equilibrium* (New York, NY: Peter Lang, 2007), 69.
27. Ibid.
28. *Fatwas of Bin Baz*, vol. 18, 216.
29. Ibid., 218–9.
30. Ibid., 225.
31. Ibid.
32. Ibid., 240.
33. Ibid.
34. *Fatwas of Bin Baz*, vol. 6, 183.
35. Ibid., 187.

36. Ibid., 188. The issue kept Bin Baz exceptionally busy. To get an idea of just how much output he was dedicating to this subject consider the number of edicts collected in his volumes of fatwas: *Fatwas of Bin Baz*, vol. 18, 167–284; and *Fatwas of Bin Baz*, vol. 6, 75–188.
37. National Commission on Terrorist Attacks, *The 9/11 Commission Report*.
38. *"Dadullah and Yazid on ties between al-Qaeda and the Taliban,"* al-Sahab media (Nov., 2009). Transcript provided at: Bill Roggio, "Dadullah and Yazid on ties between al Qaeda and the Taliban," *Long War Journal*, Nov. 19, 2009.
39. Abu Zubair Adel bin 'Abdallah al-Abab, "Loyalty to the believers," *Al-Malahim Publications and the Global Islamic Media Front*, June 22, 2010.
40. Some of the most important texts in this regard include: Muhammad ibn Idrees al-Shafi'i, *Al-Risala fi Usūl al-Fiqh, Treaties on the Foundations of Islamic Jurisprudence*, trans. Majid Khadduri (Cambridge: The Islamic Texts Society, 1961), ch 15, 333–352. A good source of secondary literature includes: Brannon M. Wheeler, *Applying the Canon in Islam: The Authorization and Maintenance of Interpretive Reasoning in Hanafi scholarship* (Albany, NY: State University of New York Press, 1996), Franz Rosenthal, *The History of al-Tabari vol. 1: General Introduction and From the Creation to the Flood* (Albany, NY: State University of New York Press, 1989); Mohammad Hashim Kamali, *Shari'ah Law: An Introduction* (Oxford: Oneworld Publications, 2010), ch 5, 99–122.
41. Abu Zubair Adel bin 'Abdallah al-Abab, "Loyalty to the believers."
42. *Ijtihād* is a theological term meaning "independent reasoning" and applies to issues on which *ikhtilāf* can be made.
43. Abu Zubair Adel bin 'Abdallah al-Abab, "Loyalty to the believers."
44. Nasir bin Hamad al-Fahd, *The Exposition Regarding the Disbelief of the One that Assists the Americans* (Al-Tibyān, 2003), 168–169.
45. Hegghammer, *Jihad in Saudi Arabia*, 83–98; Hegghammer, *Violent Islamism in Saudi Arabia*, 314–332.
46. Hegghammer, *Violent Islamism in Saudi Arabia*, 316.
47. Hegghammer, *Jihad in Saudi Arabia*, 83.
48. All these men continue to pose a challenge to the Saudi state. They are all incarcerated at the time of writing.
49. Hamud al-Uqla al-Shu'aybi, *"Fatwa on the Shariah Implementation of the Taliban Government in Afghanistan,"* (np, 29 Nov. 2000).
50. Fahd, *The Exposition Regarding the Disbelief of the One that Assists the Americans*.
51. Ibid., 47.
52. Ibid., 32, 65, 78, 84. Also Ali ibn Khudair al-Khudair, *The Dividing Boundary Between Muwālāt and Tawallī Towards the Kuffār [al-Hadd al-Fāsil Bayn Muwalat wa Tawalli Kuffār]* (np, nd).
53. Khudair, *The Dividing Boundary*. Ali al-Khudair classified four ways in which a person could perform *tawallī*. These include: having love (*maḥabba*) for

non-Muslims; offering them aid (*nusra*) or assistance (*I'anah*); through alliance (*Tahaluf*); or agreement (*Muwafaqa*).

54. Khudair, *The Dividing Boundary*.
55. Mohammad Ali Amir-Moezzi, *The Spirituality of Shi'i Islam: Belief and Practices* (London: I.B. Tauris, 2011), 262.
56. Ayman al-Zawahiri, "Loyalty and Enmity: an inherited doctrine and a lost reality," in Raymond Ibrahim (ed.), *The al-Qaeda Reader* (New York, NY: Broadway Books, 2007), 63–115.
57. Ibid., 94.
58. Ibid., 93.
59. Ibid., 104.
60. *"Bin Laden Contests Legality of Saudi Rulers, Praises Attack on US Consulate,"* Open Source Centre, Report: GMP20041216000222 (Dec. 16, 2004).
61. Ibid.
62. *"What We're Fighting for: A Letter From America,"* Institute for American Values, Feb. 2002.
63. *"How We Can Coexist,"* Islam Today, May 2002.
64. Osama bin Laden, "Moderate Islam is a prostration to the West," in Raymond Ibrahim (ed.), *The al-Qaeda Reader*, 17–62.
65. Ibid., 30.
66. Khaled Abou El Fadl, *Rebellion and Violence in Islamic Law* (Cambridge: Cambridge University Press, 2001).
67. Abu Zubair Adel bin 'Abdallah al-Abab, *"Loyalty to the Believers,"* Al-Malahim Publications and the Global Islamic Media Front, June 22, 2010.

8. REALISING MONOTHEISM

1. Sayyid Abul Ala Maududi, *Towards Understanding Islam* (Leicester: The Islamic Foundation, 2013), 58.
2. 'Abd al-'Aziz bin 'Abdallah bin Baz, *Explanation of important lessons for every Muslim* (Riyadh: Dar-us-salam Publications, 2002), 157–160. Also see "Lesson Four," 207–231.
3. Maududi, *Towards Understanding Islam*, 58.
4. Muhammad bin 'Abd al-Wahhab, *Kashf ash-Shubuhat: The Removal of Doubts* (np, nd).
5. Abu Muhammad al-Maqdisi, *This is our Aqīda* (Al-Tibyān Publications, 2nd edn), 23–29.
6. Badmas Lanre Yusuf, *Sayyid Qutb: A Study of His Tafsir* (Selangor: Islamic Book Trust, 2009), 254.
7. 'Abdallah 'Azzam, *The Tawḥīd of Action* (Tibyān publications, nd).
8. Ibid.
9. Maududi, *Towards Understanding Islam*, 58.

10. 'Azzam, *The Tawḥīd of Action.*
11. Ibid.
12. Ibid.
13. Maududi, *Towards Understanding Islam*, 59.
14. Wahhab, *Kashf al-Shubuhat.*
15. Muhammad bin 'Abd al-Wahhab, *Kitāb al-Tawḥīd* (unpubl, nd). See chapter 2, 'Definition of Tawḥīd and 'Ibāda.'
16. *Fatwas of Bin Baz*, vol. 8, 15. Available at: http://www.alifta.net/
17. *Fatwas of Bin Baz*, vol. 1, 131.
18. *Fatwas of Bin Baz*, vol. 28, 209–210.
19. Ibn Taymiyya, *al-Aqidah al-Wasitiyyah: The Principles of Islamic Faith* (unpubl, nd).
20. *Fatwas of Bin Baz*, vol. 6, 295.
21. *Qur'an* 20:82.
22. Osama bin Laden, *An Open Letter to King Fahd on the Occasion of the Recent Cabinet Reshuffle* (np, 1995).
23. Ibid.
24. Osama bin Laden, *"Osama bin Laden, statement no. 3, 7 June 1994,"* Counter-Terrorism Centre, Westpoint, Harmony Index (AFPG-2002–003345). Also see, Osama bin Laden, *"Osama bin Laden, statement no. 4, 11 July 1994,"* Counter-Terrorism Centre, Westpoint, Harmony Index (AFPG-2002-003345).
25. Osama bin Laden, *Letter to Bin Baz regarding the invalidity of his fatwa about peace treaties with the Jews* (np, nd).
26. Osama Bin Laden, *"Exposing the New Crusader War—Osama Bin Laden,"* Al-Sahab Media (Feb. 14, 2003).
27. Osama Bin Laden, *"The Wills of the Heroes of the Raids on New York and Washington,"* Al-Sahab Media (Sept. 2007).
28. Ayman al-Zawahiri, *"Realities of the Conflict Between Islam and Unbelief,"* Al-Sahab Media (Dec. 2006).
29. Ibid.
30. *Qur'an* 3:103.
31. *"Interview with shaykh Ayman al-Zawahiri,"* Al-Sahab Media (April/May 2007).
32. *"Al-Zawahiri: Six Years Since the Invasion of Iraq,"* Al-Sahab Media (April 2009).
33. *"The Open Meeting with Sheikh Ayman al-Zawahiri: Part One,"* Al-Sahab Media (2008).
34. Ayman al-Zawahiri, *A Victorious Ummah, a Broken Crusade: Nine Years After the Start of the Crusader Campaign*, Al-Sahab Media (Aug. 2010).

9. HOLY WAR AND THE ESSENCE OF MONOTHEISM

1. 'Abd al-Qadir ibn 'Abd al-'Aziz, *Fundamental Concepts Regarding al-Jihad* (np, 2004).
2. Abu Muhammad al-Maqdisi, *Monotheism and Jihad—The Distinguished Title, Minbar al-Tawḥīd wa-l-Jihad* (24 July 2009).
3. 'Azzam, *The Defence of the Muslim Lands.*
4. Ibid.
5. 'Azzam, *The Tawḥīd of Action.*
6. 'Abdallah 'Azzam, *The Signs of Ar-Rahman (Allah the most merciful) in the Jihad of Afghanistan* (Birmingham: Maktabah Booksellers, nd).
7. 'Abdallah 'Azzam, *The Lofty Mountain* (London: 'Azzam publications, nd); see also: Wright, *The Looming Tower.*
8. 'Azzam, *The Lofty Mountain*
9. William Maley, *The Afghanistan Wars* (Basingstoke: Palgrave Macmillan, 2002), 49.
10. 'Azzam, *The Tawḥīd of Action*
11. Peter Bergen, *The Osama Bin Laden I Know: An Oral History of al-Qaeda's Leader* (New York, NY: Simon & Schuster, 2006). A number of accounts of the battle can be found on 51–58. Also see Peter Bergen, *The Longest War: the Enduring Conflict Between America and al-Qaeda* (New York, NY: Simon & Schuster, 2011), 16.
12. 'Azzam, *The Lofty Mountain.*
13. Ibid.
14. 'Azzam, *The Tawḥīd of Action.*
15. 'Azzam, *The Lofty Mountain.*
16. Ibid.
17. 'Azzam, *The Tawḥīd of Action*; 'Azzam, *The Lofty Mountain.*
18. 'Azzam, *The Tawḥīd of Action.*
19. Saleh Al-Saleh, *The Salaf's Understanding of Al-Qadaa' wa-l-Qadar* (2006) Accessed 11 Nov. 2011 at: http://understand-islam.net/site/index.php?option=com_wrapper&view=wrapper&Itemid=42
20. Sahih Muslim, The Book of Faith (*Kitāb al-Īmān*), book 1, no. 1.
21. Muhammad 'Abd al-Wahhab, *Kitāb al-Tawḥīd* (Riyadh, 1998), 312.
22. Ibid., 314; also see: 'Abd al-'Aziz bin Baz, *A lecture in Aqīda: Al-Qadā wa-l-Qadr*, trans. Abu Sulayman Muhammad ibn Baker (unpubl, nd). A particularly good discussion of *al-Qadā wa-l-Qadr* also takes place in: Taqiuddin an-Nabahani, *The System of Islam: Nidham ul Islam* (London: Khilafah Publications, 2002), 21–32.
23. *Qur'an* 3:145.
24. *Qur'an* 7:34.
25. *Ḥadīth* reported on the authority of Ubadah ibn al-Samit and recorded

in Tirmidhi. It is also cited and discussed in Wahhab, *Kitāb al-Tawḥīd*, 314. Also see: Salih Al-Fawzan, *Concise Commentary on the Book of Tawḥīd* (Riyadh: Al-Maiman Publishing House, 2005), 418.

26. Meir Hatina, *Martyrdom in Modern Islam: Piety, Power, and Politics* (Cambridge: Cambridge University Press, 2014), 48. Rebecca Molloy, "Deconstructing Ibn Taymiyya's views on suicidal missions," *CTC Sentinel*, vol. 2, 3, March 2009.
27. 'Azzam, *The Tawḥīd of Action*.
28. Salih bin Fawzan al-Fawzan, *Haqīqat-ut-Tawakkul 'ala Allah: The meaning of reliance on Allah* (np, nd), 7.
29. *Qur'an* 5:23.
30. Al-Fawzan, *The Meaning of Reliance*, 7.
31. Wahhab, *Kitāb al-Tawḥīd*, 206.
32. Oliver Leaman, *The Qur'an: an Encyclopedia* (Oxford: Taylor & Francis, 2006), 650.
33. Ibid.
34. Al-Fawzan, *The Meaning of Reliance*, 7–16.
35. 'Azzam, *The Tawḥīd of Action*.
36. Wahhab, *Kitāb ut-Tawḥīd*, 197. Also see: Imam al-Nawawi, *Riyadh al-Saliheen* [Gardens of the Righteous], trans. Muhammad Amin and Abu Usamah Al-Arabi bin Razduq (Riyadh: Dar-us-salam Publications, 1995), chs 50–53.
37. *Qur'an* 3:175.
38. Wahhab, *Kitāb al-Tawḥīd*, 197.
39. Ibid.
40. 'Azzam, *The Tawḥīd of Action*.
41. Musnad Ahmad 1145.
42. 'Azzam, *The Tawḥīd of Action*.
43. Ibid.
44. Ibid.
45. Sura al-Tawba is also sometimes—but uncommonly—also called sura al-Bara'ā (the dispensation). For more on the background to this verse see: Ibn Kathir, *Tafsir Ibn Kathir Juz' 10 (Part 10), Al-Anfal 41 To At-Tauba 92* (London: MSA Publication, 2009), 85–96.
46. 'Azzam, *The Tawḥīd of Action*.
47. Ibid.

10. THE DAWN OF MODERN POLITICAL ISLAM

1. Reza Pankhurst, *The Inevitable Caliphate? A History of the Struggle for Global Islamic Union, 1924 to the Present* (London: Hurst, 2013), 131–160.
2. Abu al-Hasan al-Mawardi, *al-Aḥkām al-Sulṭāniyya, the Ordinances of Government* (London: Ta-Ha Publishers, 1998), 270.

3. Daniel Lerner, *The Passing of Traditional Society: Modernizing the Middle East* (London: Collier-Macmillan, 1964).
4. Ibid., 405.
5. Roy, *Globalised Islam*; Kepel, *Jihad: The Trail of Political Islam*.
6. Robert Pape, *Dying to Win: The Strategic Logic of Suicide Terrorism* (New York, NY: Random House, 2005).
7. For an authoritative survey of conflicting views see: Bassam Tibi, *The Challenge of Fundamentalism: Political Islam and the New World Disorder* (Berkeley, CA: University of California Press, 2002), 159–164.
8. Interestingly, some contemporary scholars such as Gamal al-Banna (brother of Hasan al-Banna) argue that '*dīn wa dawla*,' represents an unattainable golden age of the rightly guided Caliphs—the *rāshidūn* period. A more appropriate alternative they advocate for modern times is 'dīn wa ummah,' religion and community. For more on this, see: Augustus Richard Norton, "Thwarted Politics: The Case of Egypt's Hizb al-Wasat," in Robert Hefner (ed.), *Remaking Muslim Politics: Pluralism, Contestation, Democratization* (Princeton, NJ: Princeton University Press, 2005), 133–160.
9. Elie Kedourie, *Afghani and 'Abduh: An Essay on Religious Unbelief and Political Activism in Modern Islam* (London: Frank Cass, 1997). Kosugi Yasushi, "Al-Manār revisited: the "lighthouse" of the Islamic revival," in Stéphane A. Dudoignon, Komatsu Hisao, Kosugi Yasushi (eds.), *Intellectuals in the Modern Islamic World: Transmission, Transformation and Communication* (New York, NY: Routledge, 2006), 3–39; John L. Esposito, *Islam and Politics* (New York, NY: Syracuse University Press, 1998), 62–78.
10. Hamid Enayat, *Modern Islamic Political Thought* (London: I.B. Tauris, 2005), 8. Mohammed Abed al-Jabri, *Formation of Arab Reason: Text, Tradition and the Construction of Modernity in the Arab World* (London: I.B. Tauris, 2005), 134–145.
11. Samira Haj, "Reordering Islamic Orthodoxy: Muhammad ibn 'Abdul Wahhab," *The Muslim World*, vol. 92, Nos. 3&4 (Fall 2002), 333–370.
12. Muhammad 'Abduh, "Laws should change in accordance with the conditions of nations," in Charles Kurzman (ed.), *Modernist Islam, 1840–1940: A Sourcebook* (Oxford: Oxford University Press, 2002), 50–54.
13. Rashid Rida, "Renewal, renewing, and renewers," in Charles Kurzman (ed.), *Modernist Islam, 1840–1940: A Sourcebook* (Oxford: Oxford University Press, 2002), 77–85.
14. Ibid., 78.
15. Ibid.
16. Souad Ali, *A Religion, not a State: Ali 'Abd al-Raziq's Islamic Justification of Political Secularism* (Salt Lake City: University of Utah Press, 2009).
17. Gudrun Krämer, "Islamist notions of democracy," in Joel Beinin and Joe

Stork (eds.), *Political Islam: Essays from Middle East Report* (Berkeley, CA: University of California Press, 1997), 73; Sulaiman al-Farsi, *Democracy and Youth in the Middle East: Islam, Tribalism and the Rentier State in Oman* (London: I.B. Tauris, 2013), 38.

18. Jan-Peter Hartung, *A System of Life: Mawdudi and the Ideologisation of Islam* (London: Hurst, 2013).
19. Abul A'la Maududi, *The Islamic Law and Constitution*, trans. Khurshid Ahmad (Lahore: Islamic Publications, nd), vi.
20. For a thorough biographical assessment see: Hartung, *A System of Life*.
21. Maududi, *The Islamic Law and Constitution*, 133–4.
22. Ibid., 1.
23. Ibid., 138.
24. Iqbal Singh Sevea, *The Political Philosophy of Mohammed Iqbal: Islam and Nationalism in Late Colonial India* (Cambridge: Cambridge University Press, 2012), 83.
25. Mohammed Iqbal, *The Reconstruction of Religious Thought in Islam* (London: Oxford University Press, 1930).
26. Mohammed Iqbal, *Poems from Iqbal: Renderings in English Verse with Comparative Urdu text*, trans. Victor G. Kiernan (Oxford: Oxford University Press, 1955), 93.
27. Maududi, *The Islamic Law and Constitution*, 141.
28. Ibid., 140.
29. Ibid., 7.
30. Ayesha Jalal, *Self and Sovereignty: Individual and Community in South Asian Islam Since 1850* (Oxford: Oxford University Press, 2001).
31. Asyraf A.B. Rahman and Nooraihan Ali, "The influence of al-Mawdudi and the Jama'at al Islami Movement on Sayyid Qutb's Writings," *World Journal of Islamic History and Civilisation*, vol. 2, no. 4 (2012), 232–236.
32. John Calvert, *Sayyid Qutb and the Origins of Radical Islamism* (London: Hurst, 2010).
33. For a comprehensive discussion of how Maududi's views were appropriated by Qutb—and many others besides—see: Jan-Peter Hartung, *A System of Life*, 193–254.
34. Adnan Musallam, *From Secularism to Jihad: Sayyid Qutb and the Foundations of Radical Islamism* (Westport, CT: Greenwood Publishing, 2005), 151.
35. For more on Nadwi see: Yoginder Sikand, "Sayyed Abul Hasan 'Ali Nadwi," in Ibrahim Abu-Rabi (ed.), *The Blackwell Companion to Contemporary Islamic Thought* (Oxford: Blackwell Publishing, 2006), 88–104; Yoginder Sikand, *Muslims in India Since 1947: Islamic Perspectives on Inter-Faith Relations* (London: Routledge Curzon, 2004), 31–48.
36. Roxanne L. Euben and Mohammed Qasim Zaman, "Sayyid Abu'l-Hasan 'Ali Nadwi," in Roxanne L. Euben and Mohammed Qasim Zaman (eds.),

Princeton Readings in Islamist Thought, Texts and Contexts from al-Banna to Bin Laden (Princeton, NJ: Princeton University Press, 2009), 107.

37. Sayyid Abul Hasan Nadwi, *Islam and the World: The Rise and Decline of the Muslims and its Effect on Mankind* (Leicester: UK Islamic Academy, 2003).
38. For a good discussion of Qutb prior to his activist phase see Ibrahim M. Abu-Rabi, *Intellectual Origins of Islamic Resurgence in the Modern Arab World* (New York, NY: State University of New York, 1996), ch 4: 92–137, and ch 5: 138–165.
39. That said, Qutb did publish *al-Taswir al-Fanni fi'l-Qu'ran* [Artistic Imagery in the *Qur'an*] in 1945, although its focus was neither political nor social.
40. Sayyid Abul-Hasan 'Ali Nadwi, "Muslim decadence and revival," in Roxanne L. Euben and Mohammed Qasim Zaman (eds.), *Princeton Readings in Islamist Thought, Texts and Contexts from al-Banna to Bin Laden* (Princeton, NJ: Princeton University Press, 2009), 125–126.
41. Ibid., 128.
42. Ibid., 108.
43. Nadwi, *Islam and the World: The Rise and Decline of the Muslims and its Effect on Mankind* (Leicester: UK Islamic Academy, 2003), vi.
44. Ibid.
45. Sayyid Abul A'la Maududi, *Tanqihaz* [Inquiries] (Lahore, 1989).
46. Qutb, *Milestones*.
47. Sayyid Qutb, *The America I have seen* (np, 1951).
48. Ibid.
49. *Tawḥīd* appears five times in the text, while *shirk* appears six times. By contrast, *jāhil* or *jāhiliyya* appears on 114 occasions.
50. Sayed Khatab, *The Political Thought of Sayyid Qutb: The Theory of Jahiliyyah* (London; Routledge: 2006), 10; Karen Armstrong, *Muhammad: A Prophet for Our Time* (New York, NY: Harper Perennial, 2007). See chapter 2 for a particularly useful discussion of *jāhiliyya*: 41–76.
51. An excellent overview of this period is found in: Kepel, *Muslim Extremism in Egypt*, 26–35. (The first three chapters are also relevant to understanding the evolution of Islamist thought in the Egyptian context, 26–102).
52. Ibid., 70.
53. Carrie Rosefsky Wickham, *The Muslim Brotherhood: Evolution of an Islamist Movement* (Princeton, NJ: Princeton University Press, 2013), 20–45; Alison Pargeter, *The Muslim Brotherhood: The Burden of Tradition* (London: Saqi Books, 2010); Barry Rubin, *The Muslim Brotherhood: The Organization and Policies of a Global Islamist Movement* (London: Palgrave Macmillan, 2010); Brynjar Lia, *The Society of the Muslim Brothers in Egypt: The Rise of an Islamic Mass Movement, 1928–1942* (Reading: Ithaca Press, 2006).
54. The exact month is unknown due to his use of Islamic calendar which simply states that it was written in Rajab 1366.

55. Hasan al-Banna, "Toward the Light," in Roxanne L. Euben and Mohammed Qasim Zaman (eds.), *Princeton Readings in Islamist Thought, Texts and Contexts from al-Banna to Bin Laden* (Princeton, NJ: Princeton University Press, 2009), 57.
56. Ibid., 58.
57. Ibid.
58. Ibid., 74–78.
59. See, for example, Abu Jihad ash-Shami, *A Strategic Study of the Prophetic Sirah* (nd, np).
60. Abul A'la Maududi, *Islam: An Historical Perspective* (Leicester: Islamic Foundation, 1980).
61. Safi ur Rahman Al Mubarakpuri, *When The Moon Split: A Biography of Prophet Muhammad* (Riyadh: Dar-us-salam, 2002), 65.
62. Mohammed Mohar Ali, *Sīrat al-Nabī and the Orientalists: with Special Reference to the Writings of William Muir, D.S. Margoliouth and W. Montgomery Watt, vol. 1B from the Early Phase of the Prophet's Mission to his Migration to Madinah* (Medina: King Fahd Complex, 1997), 656.
63. Sayyid Qutb, *In the Shade of the Qur'an* (np, 1951).
64. Anwar al-Awlaki, "The rule on dispossessing the disbelievers' wealth in Dar al-Harb," *Inspire magazine* (Winter, 2010), 60.
65. 'Azzam, *Defence of the Muslim Lands.*

11. SECURING GOD'S RIGHTS

1. Lacroix, *Awakening Islam.*
2. Safar al-Hawali, *Secularism: Its Emergence, Development and Influence on Islamic Life* (np, nd).
3. See Safar al-Hawali's website: www.alhawali.com for a list of his books, articles and lectures.
4. Safar al-Hawali, *al-masrah al-Islamiyya wa-l-hayat fi wa athar hawathorah anashatha al-amaniyat* [Secular origins, evolution, and its impact on contemporary Islamic life] (np, nd); Safar al-Hawali, *muqadama fi tdhowar al-fikr al-arabiwa al-khadatha* [Introduction to the evolution of Western thought and modernity] (np, nd).
5. Safar al-Hawali, *Al-masrah al-Islamiyya wa-l-hayat fi wa athar hawathorah anashatha al-amaniyat*, quoted in Mansoor Jassem Alshamsi, *Islam and Political Reform in Saudi Arabia: The Quest for Political Change and Reform* (Oxford: Routledge, 2011), 67.
6. Safar al-Hawali, *Ẓahiratu al-irjā'fi al-fikr al-Islami*, quoted in Alshamsi, *Islam and Political Reform*, 70.
7. Alshamsi, *Islam and Political Reform*, 15.
8. Ibid.

9. Lacroix, *Awakening Islam*, 143.
10. Alshamsi, *Islam and Political Reform*, 112.
11. Steinberg, "The Wahhabi ulama and the Saudi State," 31.
12. Osama bin Laden, *Letter to Bin Baz Regarding the Invalidity of his Fatwa about Peace Treaties with the Jews* (27 Dec. 1994).
13. Alshamsi, *Islam and Political Reform*, 100.
14. Ibid., 100–101.
15. Ibid.
16. Tim Niblock, *Saudi Arabia: Power, Legitimacy and Survival* (New York, NY: Routledge, 2006), 96.
17. Ibid.
18. Alshamsi, *Islam and Political Reform*, 107.
19. Madawi al-Rasheed, *A History of Saudi Arabia* (Cambridge: Cambridge University Press, 2002), 171.
20. Ibid.
21. 'Abdallah 'Azzam, "Lessons and insights for jihad in modern times," quoted in Ayman al-Zawahiri, *Knights Under the Banner of the Prophet* (al-Sahab Media, 2010), 84.
22. Rashid Khalidi, *Palestinian Identity* (New York, NY: Columbia University Press, 1997); Baruch Kimmerling and Joel Migdal, *The Palestinian People: A History* (Cambridge, MA: Harvard University Press, 2003); Mohammed Muslih, *The Origins of Palestinian Nationalism* (New York, NY: Columbia University Press, 1988).
23. 'Azzam, *Join the Caravan*.
24. 'Azzam, *Defence of the Muslim Lands*.
25. 'Asharq Al-Awsat interviews Umm Muhammad: The Wife of Bin laden's Spiritual Mentor,' *Asharq Al-Awsat* (April, 2006).
26. 'Azzam, *Join the Caravan*.
27. John L. Esposito (ed.), *The Oxford Dictionary of Islam* (Oxford: Oxford University Press, 2003), 335.
28. Syed Saleem Shahzad, "Al-Qaida: the unwanted guests," *Le Monde Diplomatique* (July, 2007).
29. Talal Asad, *Genealogies of Religion: Discipline and Reasons of Power in Christianity and Islam* (Baltimore, MD: Johns Hopkins University Press, 1993), 214.
30. Peter Mandaville, *Global Political Islam* (Oxford: Routledge, 2007), 163.
31. Salman al-'Awda, "Religion is Sincerity," *IslamToday.net* (nd; accessed in July 2014).
32. Salman al-'Awda, "How we can Forbid Wrongdoing," *IslamToday.net* (nd; accessed in July 2014).
33. Ibid.
34. 'Awda, "Religion is sincerity."
35. Salman al-'Awda, "Reform is the Best Option," *IslamToday.net* (Jan. 2012; accessed in July 2014).

36. Ibid.
37. Salman al-'Awda, "Criticism Requires Self-Control," *IslamToday.net* (Jan. 2012; accessed in July 2014).
38. Ibid.
39. Salman al-'Awda, *As'ilat al-Thawra [Questions of Revolution]*
40. Salman al-'Awda, "An Open Letter to the Saudi People," *IslamToday.net* (nd; accessed in July 2014); Salman al-'Awda, "History Need Not Repeat Itself," *IslamToday.net* (May 2012; accessed in July 2014); Salman al-'Awda, "Reform is the Best Option," *IslamToday.net* (Jan. 2012; accessed in July 2014); Salman al-'Awda, "Criticism Requires Self-Control," *IslamToday.net* (Jan. 2012; accessed in July 2014); Salman al-'Awda, *As'ilat al-Thawra [Questions of Revolution]*.
41. Salman al-'Awda, "Democracy as a System of Government," *IslamToday.net* (undated; accessed in Sept. 2014).
42. Ibid.
43. 'Abdallah Nasir al-Subayh, 'Towards an Islamic Concept of Democracy,' *IslamToday.net* (Feb., 2005; accessed Sept. 2014).
44. Ibid.
45. Ibid.
46. D. Hazan, "Salafi-Jihadi Cleric Abu Basir Al-Tartusi Presents His Position on Democracy: The Principle of the Rule of the People is Heresy—But Some Mechanisms of Democracy can be Adopted," *MEMRI Inquiry & Analysis Series Report no. 786* (Jan. 19, 2012).
47. William McCants, "The Lesser of Two Evils: The Salafi Turn to Party Politics in Egypt," *Brookings Middle East Memo no. 23*, May 2012; William McCants, "The Sources of Salafi Conduct," *Foreign Affairs*, Snapshot (Sept. 19, 2012).
48. Ibid.
49. Ibid.
50. Abu Hamza al-Masri, *Allah's Governance on Earth* (np, 1999).
51. Ibid., 268.
52. *Fatwas of the Permanent Committee*, Group 2, vol. 1, Aqidah; Taghuts and ruling by other than Allah's Law: *"Adding Tawḥīd al-Ḥākimiyya to types of Tawḥīd,"* Part no. 1; Page no. 376 [Part 5 of fatwa no. 18870]; *Fatwas of Bin Baz*, vol. 30, Miscellaneous issues, "Observing Taqwa and Adhering to Allah's Religion."
53. Masri, *Allah's Governance on Earth*, 270.
54. Abu Basir al-Tartusi, "What is Tawḥīd al-Ḥākimiyya?" (np, nd). Accessed in May 2014.
55. Abu Qatada al-Filastini, "Divisions ofTawḥīd," (ClearGuidance.com, nd), accessed in May 2014.
56. Masri, *Allah's Governance on Earth*, 270.

57. Abu Huthayfah Yusuf al-Kanadi, "Is Tawḥīd al-Ḥākimiyya a bid'a?" (ClearGuidance.com, nd) accessed in May 2014.
58. Ibid.
59. Masri, *Allah's Governance on Earth*, 268.
60. Talib Samat, *The 99 Most Eminent Names of Allah* (Kuala Lampur: Utusan Publications, 2001), 104–107; 169–172.
61. Masri, *Allah's Governance on Earth*, 272.
62. Ibid., 273.
63. Ibid., 274.
64. Ibid., 278.
65. Ibid., 271.
66. "*An Open Letter to King Fahd On the Occasion of the Recent Cabinet Reshuffle, Osama bin Muhammad bin Laden*," CTC Westpoint Harmony Documents (AFGP-2002–000103-HT-NVTC), 3 Aug. 1995. For a better translation of the document see: Brad Berner, *Jihad: Bin Laden in His Own Words: Declarations, Interviews, and Speeches* (New Delhi: Atlantic Books, 2007), 1–29.
67. *Qur'an* 9:31.
68. Muhammad Saed Abdul-Rahman, *Tafsir Ibn Kathir Juz' 10 (Part 10), Al-Anfal 41 to At-Tauba 92* (London: MSA Publication, 2009), 137–139.
69. Abu Qatada, *Condemnation of the Democratic Process, Voting and the Islamic Stances on these Issues* (Al-Tibyān Publications, nd), 19.
70. Masri, *Allah's Governance on Earth*, 98.
71. Ibid.
72. *Qur'an* 7:54.
73. Abu Qatada, *Condemnation of the Democratic Process*, 12.
74. Abu Hamza al-Masri, *Ruling by Man Made Law, is it Minor or Major Kufr? Explaining the words of Ibn Abbas* (Supporters of Shariah Publications, 1996).
75. Abu Muhammad al-Maqdisi, *Democracy: A Religion!* (np, nd).
76. 'Abd al-Qadir bin 'Abd al-'Aziz, *The Criticism of Democracy and the Illustration of its Reality*, taken from *al-Jame'a fi talab el-ilm esh-sharif, vol. 1* (np, nd), 146–155.
77. Bin Laden, "*An Open Letter to King Fahd On the Occasion of the Recent Cabinet Reshuffle.*"
78. *Qur'an* 6:121.
79. Masri, *Allah's Governance on Earth*, 98.
80. Maqdisi, *Democracy: A Religion!*
81. Ibid.
82. Ibid.

CONCLUSION

1. Hegghammer, "Jihadi-Salafis or Revolutionaries?," 246. Meijer, "Introduction," *Global Salafism*, 27.
2. Peter E. Gordon, "What is Intellectual History? A frankly partisan introduction to a frequently misunderstood field," Harvard History Department website. http://history.fas.harvard.edu/people/faculty/documents/pgordon-whatisintellhist.pdf
3. Michael Howard, *War in European History* (Oxford: Oxford University Press, 2009), 1.
4. "Abu Qatada Interview Part 2 of 3," YouTube. Accessed March 9, 2015.
5. "Islamic State Justification for Burning Alive the Jordanian Pilot: Translation and Analysis," *Islamic State Document Archive*, housed on website of Aymenn Jawad Ali al-Tamimi, accessed on 6 May 2016. Availabe here: http://www.aymennjawad.org/2015/02/islamic-state-justification-for-burning-alive
6. Ibid.
7. "1 of 3 Bilal Abdul Kareem Interviews Jabha Nusra Shura Member Abu Firas,"YouTube, accessed on 4 Oct. 2015. Available at: https://www.youtube.com/watch?v=0RIsR9LXiWU

BIBLIOGRAPHY

Primary Sources

"*Abu Qatada Interview Part 2 of 3*," YouTube. Accessed on 9 March 2015.

"*An interview with the shaheed Abu Dujanah al-Khorasani, hero of the raid of the shaheed amir Baytullah Mehsud*," Ansar al-Mujahideen Forum.

Badr ar-Riyadh, al-Sahab Media, 2004.

"*Bin Laden Contests Legality of Saudi Rulers, Praises Attack on US Consulate*," Combatting Terrorism Center, Open Source Centre (GMP20041216000222). December 16, 2004.

"*Bin Laden Interviewed on Jihad Against US*," Al-Quds al-Arabi, 27 November 1996, in "Compilation of Osama Bin Laden Statements 1994—January 2004" by Foreign Broadcast Information Service (FBIS).

"*Biography of Abu Musab Al-Zarqawi*." Ansar al-Mujahideen Forum.

"Complaints by Arab fanatics against King ibn Saud," despatch of US Minister, Jedda, 4 December 1944, in Ibrahim Rashid (ed.), *Saudi Arabia enters the modern world: secret U.S. documents on the emergence of the Kingdom of Saudi Arabia as a world power, 1936–1949*, Volume 1. Salisbury, N.C.: Documentary Publications, 1980.

"*Dadullah and Yazid on ties between al-Qaeda and the Taliban*." Al-Sahab media, November, 2009.

"*Dialogue with Shaykh Abu Musab Al-Zarqawi, Part One*," al-Furqan Media. 2005.

"*English subtitles of full sermon by ISIS's Abu Bakr al-Baghdadi, Caliph of the Islamic State*," YouTube.

Essay Regarding the Basic Rule of the Blood, Wealth, and Honour of the Disbelievers. Al-Tibyān Publications, 2004.

"*Fatawa from the Imams of Salafiyyah Concerning Rallies and Demonstrations, and Additional Guidelines Concerning Revolt and Takfir in Light of the Algerian Affair*," TROID publications.

"*Fatwa on Recent Events by Shaykh Humud al-Uqla*."

"Glad tidings for the Islamic Ummah—2 brothers from Ansar Al-Mujahideen Arabic (Saleel Al-Soyoof and Qahar El-Saleeb) reported shaheed inshallah," Ansar al-Mujahideen Forum.

"How we can coexist," Islam Today, May 2002.

"Interview with Shaykh Ayman al-Zawahiri, Part 3," Al-Sahab Media, April 2007.

"Interview with Shaykh Tameem al Adnani," Iraq war collection, accessed on 11 May 2015. https://archive.org/details/interview-sheikh-tameem-adnani

Majmu al-Fatawa, Daru-l-Wafa, 3rd edition, 2005, vol. 28, 240, reproduced in *'Fatwa of Shaykh al-Islam Ibn Taymiyyah about country in which Muslims live and which ruled by infidels,'* KavKaz Center.

"Periodical Review: Fatwas—Jan. 2011," ICT's Jihadi Websites Monitoring Group, ICT, April 2011.

"Salafi-Jihadi Cleric Abu Basir Al-Tartusi Presents His Position on Democracy: The Principle of the Rule of the People Is Heresy—But Some Mechanisms of Democracy Can Be Adopted." MEMRI Inquiry & Analysis Series Report no. 786, Jan. 19, 2012.

"The Blood of the Martyr is Light and Fire; A Statement about the Martyrdom of Shaykh Anwar Al-Awlaqi and His Comrades," Ansar al-Mujahideen Forum.

The Clarification Regarding Intentionally Targeting Women and Children. Al-Tibyān Publications, 2004.

"The Open Meeting with Shaykh Ayman al-Zawahiri." Al-Sahab Media, 2008.

"Transcript of CBS Morning Show," in "Compilation of Osama bin Laden Statements 1994—Jan. 2004" by Foreign Broadcast Information Service (FBIS).

"*What We're Fighting for: A Letter from America,*" Institute for American Values, Jan. 2002.

Abab, Abu Zubair Adel bin 'Abdallah al-. *Loyalty to the Believers*. Al-Malahim Publications and the Global Islamic Media Front, June 22, 2010.

'Abduh, Muhammad. 'Laws should change in accordance with the conditions of nations,' in Charles Kurzman (ed.), *Modernist Islam, 1840–1940: A Sourcebook*. Oxford: Oxford University Press, 2002.

Abedin, Mahan. 'A Saudi Oppositionist's View: An Interview with Dr. Muhammad Al-Massari,' *Terrorism Monitor*, vol. 1, Issue: 7, The Jamestown Foundation. December, 2003.

Adnani, Abu Muhammad al-. '*This is the promise of Allah*,' Al-Hayat Media, 29 June 2014.

Al-Qaeda. "Al-Qaeda's Path and Creed," in Roel Meijer (ed.), *Global Salafism: Islam's New Religious Movement*, trans. Bernard Haykel. London: Hurst, 2009.

Al-Qaeda. *'A Statement from al-Qaeda al-Jihad Regarding the Mandates of the Heroes and the Legality of the Operations in New York and Washington,'* 24 April 2004.

BIBLIOGRAPHY

Albani, Muhammad Nasir al-Din al-. *'Debate with a Jihadi,' Jihad in the Qur'an and Sunnah*. Salafi Publications, nd.

———. *Descriptions of the Khawārij*. Np, nd., accessed on 5 May 2016. http://www.authentic-translations.com/trans-pub/ae_mnaa_2.pdf

———. Salih ibn Fawzan and Taraheeb ad-Dosri, *'The difference between the aqīda and the Manhaj,'* Salaf-us-salih. Accessed on 15 March 2013. http://salaf-us-saalih.com/2010/02/08/the-difference-between-the-aqeedah-and-the-manhaj/

Asqalani, Ibn Hajar al-. *Selections from the Fath al-Bārī*, trans. Abdul Hakim Murad. Cambridge: Muslim Academic Trust, 2000.

'Atiq, Hamad ibn. *The Way of Cutting Relations off from the Polytheist and Apostate: Sabil an-Najāt wa-l-Fikāk min Muwalat al-Murtadin wa ahl al-Ishrāk*. Mustaqeem Publications, nd.

'Awda, Salman al-. 'An Open Letter to the Saudi People.' IslamToday.net, nd.

———. *As'ilat al-Thawra* [Questions of Revolution].

———. 'Criticism Requires Self-Control.' IslamToday.net, Jan. 2012.

———. 'Democracy as a System of Government,' IslamToday.net, nd.

———. 'History Need Not Repeat Itself.' IslamToday.net, May 2012.

———. 'How We Can Forbid Wrongdoing.' IslamToday.net, nd.

———. 'Reform is the Best Option.' IslamToday.net, Jan. 2012.

———. 'Religion is Sincerity.' IslamToday.net, nd.

Awlaki, Anwar al-. 'Tawfique Chowdhury's Alliance with the West,' *Anwar al-Awlaki blog*, Jan. 12, 2009.

———. *Thawābit 'ala darb al-Jihad, Constants on the Path of Jihad by Yusuf al-'Uyayri, lecture series delivered by Anwar al-Awlaki*. Np, nd.

———. *The Book of Jihad by ibn Nuhaas—Commentary by al-Awlaki*. Np, nd.

———. 'The New Mardin Declaration: An Attempt at Justifying the New World Order,' *Inspire*, 2, Fall 2010, 34.

———. 'The Rule on Dispossessing the Disbelievers Wealth in Dar al-Harb,' *Inspire*, Winter, 2010.

Aziz, 'Abd al-Qadir ibn 'Abd al-'. *Fundamental Concepts Regarding Al-Jihad*. Al-Tibyan Publications, 2004.

———. *The Criticism of Democracy and the Illustration of its Reality*. Np, nd.

'Azzam, 'Abdallah. *Join the Caravan*. Np, 1987.

———. *The Defence of the Muslim Lands: the First Obligation after Iman*. Np, 1984.

———. *The Lofty Mountain*. London: 'Azzam publications, nd.

———. *The Signs of Ar-Rahman (Allah the most merciful) in the Jihad of Afghanistan*. Birmingham: Maktabah Booksellers, nd.

———. *The Tawḥīd of Action*. Tibyan publications, nd.

Baghdadi, Abu Hamza al-. *'Stop Them, Do Not Kill Them,'* Al-Fajr Media Center, March 23, 2010.

Banna, Hasan al-. 'Toward the Light,' in Roxanne L. Euben and Muhammad Qasim Zaman (eds.), *Princeton Readings in Islamist Thought, Texts and Contexts from al-Banna to Bin Laden*. Princeton: Princeton University Press, 2009.

Baz, 'Abd al-'Aziz bin. *A lecture in Aqīda: Al-Qadaa wa-l-Qadr*, trans. Abu Sulayman Muhammad Ibn Baker. Np, nd.

———. *Explanation of important lessons for every Muslim*. Riyadh: Dar-us-salam Publications, 2002.

———. *The undeniably known duties about the relations between the ruler and the ruled*. Np, nd.

———. *Fatwas of Ibn Baz, vol. 1–30*, General Presidency of Scholarly Research and Ifta, Kingdom of Saudi Arabia.

———. "Speech during Shaykh Muhammad ibn 'Abdul-Wahhab week," *Fatwas of Ibn Baz*, vol. 1: 378.

Berner, Brad. *Jihad: Bin Laden in His Own Words: Declarations, Interviews, and Speeches*. New Delhi: Atlantic Books, 2007.

Bukhari, Imam. *Sahih al-Bukhari: The Early Years of Islam*, trans. Muhammad Asad. Kuala Lumpur: Islamic Book Trust, 2013.

Cook, Michael. *Early Muslim Dogma: A Source-Critical Study*. Cambridge: Cambridge University Press, 1981.

Fahd, Nasir ibn Hamad al-. *A Treatise on the Legal Status of Using Weapons of Mass Destruction Against Infidels*. Np, 2003.

———. *The Exposition Regarding the Disbelief of the One That Assists the Americans*. Al-Tibyan, 2003.

Faraj, Muhammad 'Abd al-Salam. *Jihad: The Absent Obligation*. Birmingham: Maktabah al-Ansar, 2000.

Fawzan, Salih al-. *Are the Terrorists of Today the Khawārij?* Np, nd.

———. *Concise Commentary on the Book of Tawḥīd*. Riyadh: Al-Maiman Publishing House, 2005.

———. *Haqīqat-al-Tawakkul 'ala Allah: The Meaning of Reliance on Allah*. Np, nd.

Filastini, Abu Qatada al-. *Characteristics of the Victorious Party in the Foundation of the State of the Believers, the Land of ash-Sham*. Al-Tibyan publications, nd.

———. *Condemnation of the Democratic Process, Voting and the Islamic Stances on these Issues*. Al-Tibyan Publications, nd.

———. 'Divisions of Tawheed,' ClearGuidance.com, nd.

Furaydan, Abu 'Abd al-Rahman Aadil bin 'Ali Al-. *The Characteristics of the Extremist Khawarij*. USA: Al-Ibaanah Publishing, 2005.

Ghunayman, 'Abdallah al-. 'Question #11275: Is it a Condition of Jihad That There be a Leader?' (www.islam-qa.com).

Harithi, Jamal bin Farihan al-. *The Khawarij Perform Takfir on Account of Major Sins*. Salafi Publications, nd.

Hawali, Safar al-. *Al-masrah al-Islamiyya wa-l-hayat fi wa athar hawathorah anashatha al-amaniyat* [Secular origins, evolution, and its impact on contemporary Islamic life].

———. *Muqadama fi tdhowar al-fikr al-arabiwa al-khadatha* [Introduction to the evolution of Western thought and modernity].

———. *Wa'd Kissinger: al-Ahdaf al-Amrikiyya fil Khalij* [*Kissinger's Promise: American goals in the Gulf*] quoted in Sonia Alianak, *Middle Eastern leaders and Islam: a precarious equilibrium*. New York, NY: Peter Lang Publishing, 2007.

———. '*Ẓahiratu* al-Irjā' fi al-Fikr al-Islami,' quoted in Mansoor Jassem Alshamsi, *Islam and Political Reform in Saudi Arabia: The Quest for Political Change and Reform*. Oxford: Routledge, 2011.

Iqbal, Mohammed. *Poems from Iqbal: Renderings in English Verse with Comparative Urdu text*, trans. Victor Keirnan. Oxford: Oxford University Press, 1955.

———. *The Reconstruction of Religious Thought in Islam*. London: Oxford University Press, 1930.

Kanadi, Abu Huthayfah Yusuf al-. 'Is Tawḥīd al-Ḥākimiyya a bid'a?' ClearGuidance.com, nd.

Kathir, Ismail ibn. *Stories of the Prophets*. Riyadh: Maktaba Dar-ur-Salam, 2003.

———. *Tafsir Ibn Kathir Juz' 10 (Part 10): Al-Anfal 41 To At-Tauba 92*. London: MSA Publication, 2009.

———. *The Battles of the Prophet*, trans. Wa'il Abdul Mut'al Shihab (Cairo: Dar al-Manarah, 2001)

Keller, Nuh Amin. *Al-Maqasid: Nawawi's Manual of Islam*. Beltsville, MD: Amana Publications, 2002.

Khudair, 'Ali ibn Khudair al-. *Ma ḥukm al-hakim bi-ghayri ma anzala Allah? wa ma al-wajib tajahahu?* [What is the ruling on the one who rules by not what God has sent down? And what must one do to him?], Minbar al-tawḥīd wa-l-jihad.

———. *The Dividing Boundary between Muwālāt and Tawallī Towards the Kuffār* [al-Hadd al-Fāsil Bayn Muwalat wa Tawallī Kuffār]. Np, nd.

Laden, Osama bin. '*An Open Letter to King Fahd On the Occasion of the Recent Cabinet Reshuffle, 3 Aug. 1995*.' Counter-Terrorism Centre, Westpoint, Harmony Index. AFGP-2002–000103-HT-NVTC.

———. *Declaration of War against the Americans Occupying the Land of the Two Holy Places*, 1996.

———. *Exposing the New Crusader War*. Al-Sahab Media, Jan. 2003.

———. *Letter to Ibn Baz Regarding the Invalidity of his Fatwa About Peace Treaties with the Jews*, 27 December 1994.

———. '*Letter to the American people*.' November 2002.

———. "Moderate Islam is a Prostration to the West," in Raymond Ibrahim (ed.), *The al-Qaeda Reader*. New York, NY: Broadway Books, 2007.

———. '*Osama bin Laden, statement no. 3, 7 June 1994*,' Counter-Terrorism Centre, Westpoint, Harmony Index. AFPG-2002–003345.

———. '*Osama bin Laden, statement no. 4, 11 July 1994*,' Counter-Terrorism Centre, Westpoint, Harmony Index. AFPG-2002–003345.

———. '*Osama bin Laden, statement no. 18, 11 Aug. 1995*,' Counter-Terrorism Centre, Westpoint, Harmony Index. AFPG-2002–003345.

———. *The Wills of the Heroes of the Raids on New York and Washington*. Al-Sahab Media, Sept. 2007.

———. 'Why We Are Fighting You,' in Raymond Ibrahim (ed.), *The al-Qaeda Reader*. New York, NY: Broadway Books, 2007.

Libi, Abu Yahya al-. *Guidance on the Ruling of the Muslim Spy* (Al-Fajr Media Center, 2008), Open Source Center: Jihadist Website Posts Al-Libi's 'Guidance on the Ruling of the Muslim Spy,' (GMP20090708342001).

———. *Human Shields in Modern Jihad*. Np, Jan. 2006.

Mansfield, Laura. *His Own Words: Translation and Analysis of the Writings of Dr. Ayman al-Zawahiri*. United States: TLG Publications, 2006.

Maqdisi, Abu Muhammad al-. *Democracy: A Religion!* Np, nd.

———. *Millat Ibrahim and the Calling of the Prophets and Messengers and the methods of the Transgressing Rulers in Dissolving it and Turning the Callers Away from it*. Al-Tibyan Publications, 1984.

———. *Monotheism and Jihad—The Distinguished Title, Minbar al-tawḥīd wa-l-jihad*. 24 July 2009.

———. *Takfir Based Upon the Rule "the Principle Ruling Over the People is Kufr" because the Dār is Dār Kufr*. Np, 1998/9.

———. *This is our Aqīda*. Al-Tibyan Publications, second edition, nd.

Masri, Abu Hamza al-. *Allah's Governance on Earth*. Np, 1999.

———. *Be Aware of Takfir*. Np, nd.

———. *Ruling by Man Made Law, is it Major or Minor Kufr? Explaining the words of Ibn Abbas*. Supporters of Shariah, 1996.

Maududi, Sayyid Abul A'la. *Islam: An Historical Perspective*. Leicester: Islamic Foundation, 1980.

———. *Khilafat-o-Malookeyat* [The Caliphate and kingship]. Lahore: Urdu Bazar, nd.

———. *Tanqihaz* [Inquiries]. Lahore, 1989.

———. *Towards Understanding Islam*. Leicester: The Islamic Foundation, 2013.

———. *The Islamic law and constitution* trans. Khurshid Ahmad. Lahore: Islamic Publications, nd.

Mawardi, Abu al-Hasan al-. *al-Aḥkām al-Sulṭāniyya, the Ordinances of Government*. London: Ta-Ha Publishers, 1998.

Miller, John. 'A conversation with the most dangerous man in the world,' *Esquire Magazine*, Jan. 1999, in "Compilation of Osama Bin Laden Statements 1994—Jan. 2004" by Foreign Broadcast Information Service (FBIS).

Mubarkpuri, Safi-ur-Rahman al-. *Ar-Raheeq Al-Makhtum (The Sealed Nectar): Biography of the Prophet*. Riyadh: Dar-us-Salam Publications, 1996.

Mujahid, 'Abd al-Malik. *Affection and Aversion (Al-Walā' and Al-Barā')*. Riyadh: Dar-us-Salam, 2002.

Nabahani, Taqiuddin an-. *The System of Islam: Nidham ul Islam*. London: Khilafah Publications, 2002.

Nadwi, Sayyid Abul Hasan. *Islam and the World: The Rise and Decline of the Muslims and Its Effect on Mankind*. Leicester: UK Islamic Academy, 2003.

———. 'Muslim decadence and revival,' in Roxanne L. Euben and Muhammad Qasim Zaman (eds.), *Princeton Readings in Islamist Thought, Texts and Contexts from al-Banna to Bin Laden*. Princeton: Princeton University Press, 2009.

National Commission on Terrorist Attacks, *The 9/11 Commission Report: Final Report of the National Commission on Terrorist Attacks Upon the United States*. Washington, D.C.: Claitor's Law Books and Publishing, 2004.

Nawawi, Imam Abu Zakaria Muhiy ad-Din al-. *Al-Maqasid: Nawawi's Manual of Islam*, trans. Nuh Ha Min Keller. Beltsville, MD: Amana Publications, 2002.

———. *Riyad-Us-Saliheen: The Paradise of the Pious*. Leicester: Dar-us-Salam Publications, 1999.

Nuhaas, Ahmad Ibrahim Muhammad al Dimashqi ibn. *The book of Jihad*, trans. Noor Yamani. Np, nd.

Permanent Committee for Scholarly Research and Ifta', "What is "Al-Salafiyah?" "What do you think of it?," *Volume 2: Al-'Aqidah*, (2), Fatwa no. 1361.

Qahtani, Muhammad Saeed al-. *Al-Walā' wa-l-Barā' According to the 'Aqīda of the Salaf*, Vol 1–3. Np, 1984.

Qayyim, Ibn al-. 'Madarij us-Salikin,' trans. Salafi Publications, *'Ibn al-Qayyim on the Types of Kufr and Ruling by Other than What Allah has Revealed,'* Salafi Publications, nd.

Qutb, Sayyid. *In the Shade of the Qur'an*, vol. 1–14. Leicester: Islamic Foundation, 2001.

———. *Milestones Along the Way*. Birmingham: Maktabah al-Ansar, 1996.

———. *The America I have seen*. Np, 1951.

Rahman, Omar 'Abd Al-. *The Present Rulers, Are They Muslim or Not?* Np, nd.

Rejjam, Abdelrezak. "Communique no. 42, The Islamic Salvation Front National Provisional Executive Bureau," in John Calvert (ed.), *Islamism: A Documentary and Reference Guide*. Westport, CT: Greenwood Publishing Group, 2008.

Rida, Rashid. 'Renewal, renewing, and renewers,' in Charles Kurzman (ed.), *Modernist Islam, 1840–1940: A Sourcebook*. Oxford: Oxford University Press, 2002.

Rosenthal, Franz. *The History of al-Tabari vol. 1: General Introduction and From the Creation to the Flood*. Albany, NY: State University of New York, 1989.

Ruhayli, Ibrahim al-. *A Concise Introduction to the Khawārij*. Np, nd.

Saleh, Saleh Al-. *The Salaf's Understanding of Al-Qadaa' wa-l-Qadar*. Np. 2006.
Shafi'i, Muhammad ibn Idris Al-. *Al-Shafi'i's Risala: Treatise on the Foundations of Islamic Jurisprudence*. Cambridge: Islamic Texts Society, 2008.
Shami, Abu Jihad ash-. *A Strategic Study of the Prophetic Sirah*. Np, nd.
Sharif. Sayyid Imam al-. 'Doctrine for rationalising Jihad in Egypt and the World,' parts 1–7, (unpublished, 2007).
———. 'The Stating of the Ijmā' on the Kufr of the Rulers Who Rule by what Allah has Not Revealed,' taken from *Al-Jamit Fi Talab el-Ilm al-Sharif*, vol. 2 (np, 1995), 880–882, reproduced on Salafi Media UK.
Sheikh, Saleh bin 'Abd al-'Aziz Al ash-. *"Concerning Tawallī and Muwālāt."* Salafi Publications, nd.
Shu'aybi, Hamud al-Uqla al-. *Fatwa on the Shariah Implementation of the Taliban Government in Afghanistan*. Np, 29 November 2000.
Subayh, 'Abdallah Nasir al-. 'Towards an Islamic Concept of Democracy.' IslamToday.net, Jan., 2005.
Tabari, Muhammad ibn Jarir al-. *The History of al-Tabari vol. 9: The Last Years of the Prophet*, trans. Ismail K. Poonawala. Albany, New York: State University of New York, 1990.
Tartusi, Abu Basir al-. *Fatwa Regarding the Saudi Regime*. Np, nd.
———. *Principles of Takfir*. Np, 1994.
———. *Refutation Regarding the Targeting of Women and Children*. Np, July 2005.
———. *Ruling regarding signing up for the Armies of the Kuffār*. Np, nd.
———. *The Dangers of Martyrdom or Suicide Bombings*. Np, 2005.
———. *'What is Tawḥīd al-Ḥākimiyya?'* Np, nd.
Taymiyya, Taqi ad-Din Ahmad ibn. *Al-Aqidah al-Wasitiyyah: The Principles of Islamic Faith*. Np, nd.
———. *Enjoining Right and Forbidding Wrong*, trans. Salim 'Abdallah ibn Morgan. Np, nd.
———. *Kitāb Al-Īmān: Book of Faith*. Indiana: Iman Publishing House, 2009.
———. *Sharh al-Aqīda al-Wasatiyyah: Fundamental Beliefs of Islam and Rejection of False Concepts*. Riyadh: Dar-us-Salam Publications, 1996.
———. *The Political Shariyah on Reforming the Ruler and the Ruled*. UK: Dar ul Fiqh, 2006.
———. *The Religious and Moral Doctrine of Jihad*. Birmingham: Maktabah al Ansar Publications, 2001.
'Ubaykan, 'Abd al-Muhsin al-. 'Fear Allah and do not Sympathize with al-Zarqawi and the Takfiri Agenda,' *Ash-Sharq al-Awsat*.
———. *The Khawarij and their Renewed Ideology*. Sunnah Publishing, nd.
'Uthaymin, Muhammad ibn Salih al-. *Explanation of a Summary of al-'Aqīdatul-Hamawiyyah of Ibn Taymiyyah*. Np, nd.
———. 'The verdict of Shaykh Muhammad ibn Salih al-Uthaymeen,' in *The Clarification Regarding Intentionally Targeting Women and Children*. Np, nd.

'Uyayri, Yusuf al-. Ḥaqīqat al-ḥarb al-Ṣalībiyyah al-Jadīda, [The Truth of the New Crusader War], translated version in *The Clarification Regarding Intentionally Targeting Women and Children*. Al-Tibyan Publications, nd.

Wahhab, Muhammad bin 'Abd al-. *Kashf ash-Shubuhat: The Removal of Doubts*. Np, nd.

———. *Kitāb al-Tawḥīd*. Riyadh, 1998.

Wahhab, Sulayman ibn Muhammad ibn 'Abd al-. *The Evidences for the Ruling Regarding Alliances with the Infidels: Ad-Dalā'il fī Ḥukm Muwālāt ahl al-Ishrāk*. Al-Tibyān Publications, 2004.

Wahid, Abdul. 'Hizb ut Tahrir's distinction,' *OpenDemocracy*, 14 Aug. 2005.

Yusuf, Hamza. 'The Mardin Fatwa and al-Qaeda,' *Rethinking Islamic Reform Conference*, Oxford University Islamic Society, University of Oxford, 2010.

Zarqawi, Abu Musab al-. *'A new audio message from commander Abu-Musab al-Zarqawi to the nation of Islam,' Text of al-Zarqawi Message Threatening More Attacks*, Federation of American Scientists.

———. *'Our Creed and Methodology.'* 24 March 2005.

Zawahiri, Ayman al-. *A Victorious Ummah, a Broken Crusade: Nine Years After the Start of the Crusader Campaign*. Al-Sahab Media, Aug. 2010.

———. *"Al-Zawahiri: "Six Years Since the Invasion of Iraq."* Al-Sahab Media, April 2009.

———. 'Jihad, Martyrdom, and the Killing of Innocents,' in Raymond Ibrahim (ed.), *The Al-Qaeda Reader*. New York, NY: Broadway Books, 2007.

———. *Knights Under the Banner of the Prophet*. Al-Sahab Media, 2010.

———. 'Loyalty and enmity: an inherited doctrine and a lost reality,' in Raymond Ibrahim (ed.), *The Al-Qaeda Reader*. New York, NY: Broadway Books, 2007.

———. *Realities of the Conflict Between Islam and Unbelief*. Al-Sahab Media, December 2006.

———. *The Exoneration: A Treatise on the Exoneration of the Nation of the Pen and Sword of the Denigrating Charge of Being Irresolute and Weak* (np, 2008).

———. *Zawahiri's Letter to Zarqawi*, Combating Terrorism Center, Harmony Index.

Secondary Sources

Aarts, Paul, and Gerd Nonneman (eds.), *Saudi Arabia in the Balance: Political Economy, Society, Foreign Affairs*. London: Hurst, 2005.

Abbas, Wasiullah ibn Muhammad. *Al-Ittiba: and the Principles of Fiqh of the Righteous Predecessors*. Brooklyn, NY: Dar ul Itibaa Publications, 2013.

Abbott, Nabia. *Aisha, the beloved of Mohammed*. Chicago, IL: University of Chicago Press, 1942.

Abir, Mordechai. *Saudi Arabia: Society, Government and the Gulf Crisis*. Abingdon: Routledge, 2006.

BIBLIOGRAPHY

Abu-Nimer, Mohammed. "Framework for nonviolence and peace building," in Abdul Aziz Said, Mohammed Abu-Nimer, Meena Sharify-Funk (eds.), *Contemporary Islam: Dynamic, Not Static*. New York, NY: Routledge, 2006.

Adams, Ian, *Political Ideas Today* (Manchester: Manchester University Press, 2001).

Ali, Muhammad M. Yunis. *Medieval Islamic Pragmatics: Sunni Legal Theorists' Models of Textual Communication*. Oxford: Routledge, 2009.

Ali, Muhammad Mohar. *Sīrat al-Nabī and the Orientalists: with Special Reference to the Writings of William Muir, D.S. Margoliouth and W. Montgomery Watt, vol. 1B from the Early Phase of the Prophet's Mission to his Migration to Madinah*. Medina: King Fahd Complex, 1997.

Ali, Souad. *A Religion, not a State: Ali 'Abd al-Raziq's Islamic Justification of Political Secularism*. Salt Lake City: University of Utah Press, 2009.

Alshamsi, Mansoor Jassem. *Islam and Political Reform in Saudi Arabia: The Quest for Political Change and Reform*. Abingdon: Routledge, 2011.

Alshech, Eli. "The Doctrinal Crisis within the Salafi-Jihadi Ranks and the Emergence of Neo-Takfirism: a Historical and Doctrinal Analysis," *Islamic Law and Society*, 21 (2014): 419–452

Amir-Moezzi, Mohammad Ali. *The Spirituality of Shi'i Islam: Belief and Practices*. London: I.B. Tauris, 2011.

Amitai, Reuven. "The Mongol Occupation of Damascus in 1300: A Study of Mamluk Loyalties," in Michael Winter and Amalia Levanoni (eds.), *The Mamluks in Egyptian and Syrian Politics and Society*. Leiden: Brill, 2004.

Anzalone, Christopher. "Revisiting Shaykh Atiyyatullah's Work on Takfir and Mass Violence," *CTC Sentinel*, April 2012.

Asad, Talal. *Genealogies of Religion: Discipline and Reasons of Power in Christianity and Islam*. Baltimore, MD: Johns Hopkins University Press, 1993.

Auda, Jasser. *Maqasid Al-Shariah as Philosophy of Islamic Law: A Systems Approach*. London: International Institute of Islamic Political Thought, 2008.

Austin, John. *How to do Things with Words*. Oxford: Oxford University Press, 1976.

Awan, Akil N. "Jihadi ideology in the new-media environment," in Jeevan Deol and Zaheer Kazmi (eds.), *Contextualising Jihadi Thought*. London: Hurst, 2012.

Ayalon, David. "Studies on the Transfer of The 'Abbāsid Caliphate from Baġdād to Cairo," *Arabica*, T. 7, Fasc. 1 (Jan., 1960): 41–59.

Ayoob, Mohammed, and Hasan Kosebalaban (eds.), *Religion and Politics in Saudi Arabia: Wahhabism and the State*. Boulder, CO: Lynne Rienner Publishers, 2009.

Bakker, Edwin. "Jihadi terrorists in Europe and global salafi jihadis," in Rik Coolsaet (ed.), *Jihadi Terrorism and the Radicalisation Challenge in Europe*. Aldershot: Ashgate, 2008.

Bassiouni, M. Cherif. *The Shari'a and Islamic Criminal Justice in Time of War and Peace*. Cambridge: Cambridge University Press, 2014.

Baumer, Franklin. "Intellectual History and Its Problems," *The Journal of Modern History*, vol. 21, no. 3 (Sept., 1949): 191–203.

Bennett, Clinton. *Interpreting the Qur'an: A Guide for the Uninitiated* (London: Continuum International Publishing Group, 2010), 130.

Bergen, Peter. *Holy war, Inc: Inside the Secret World of Osama Bin Laden*. New York, NY: Touchstone, 2002.

———. *The Osama Bin Laden I Know: An Oral History of Al Qaeda's Leader*. New York, NY: Simon & Schuster, 2006.

———. *The longest war: the enduring conflict between America and al-Qaeda*. New York, NY: Simon & Schuster, 2011.

Berger, John. *Jihad Joe: Americans who go to war in the name of Islam*. Washington, DC: Potomac Books, 2011.

Bergesen, Albert J. *The Sayyid Qutb Reader: Selected Writings on Politics, Religion, and Society: Selected Writings on Politics, Peligion, and Society*. New York, NY: Routledge, 2008.

Black, Antony. *The History of Islamic Political Thought from the Prophet to the Present*. New York, NY: Routledge, 2001.

———. *The West and Islam: Religion and Political Thought in World History*. Oxford: Oxford University Press, 2008.

Brachman, Jarret. *Global Jihadism: Theory and Practice*. Abingdon: Routledge, 2009.

Buchholz, Benjamin. "The Human Shield in Islamic Jurisprudence," *Military Review* (May–June 2013): 48–52

Burgat, François. *Face to Face with Political Islam*. London: I.B. Tauris and Co, 2005.

———. *Islamism in the Shadow of al-Qaeda*. Austin, TX: University of Texas Press, 2008.

Burke, Jason. *Al-Qaeda: the True Story of Radical Islam*. London: Penguin Books, 2003.

Burkhardt, Jacob. *The Civilisation of the Renaissance in Italy*. Mineola, NY: Dover Publications Inc., 2010,

Burleigh, Michael. *Sacred Causes: The Clash of Religion and Politics, from the Great War to the War on Terror*. London: HarperCollins, 2006.

———. *Blood and Rage: a Cultural History of Terrorism*. London: Harper Perennial, 2008.

Burton, John. "The Exegesis of Q. 2: 106 and the Islamic Theories of naskh: mā nansakh min āya aw nansahā na'ti bi khairin minhā aw mithlihā," *Bulletin of the School of Oriental and African Studies*, University of London, vol. 48, no. 3 (1985): 452–469.

Butterworth, Charles. "Political Islam: The Origins," *Annals of the American*

Academy of Political and Social Science, vol. 524, Political Islam (Nov., 1992): 26–37.

———. *Political Aspects of Islamic Philosophy: Essays in Honor of Muhsin S. Mahdi*. Cambridge, MA: Harvard University Press, 1992.

Byman, Daniel. *The Five Front War: The Better Way to Fight Global Jihad*. Hoboken, NJ: John Wiley & Sons.

Calvert, John. *Sayyid Qutb and the Origins of Radical Islamism*. London: Hurst, 2010.

Chapra, Muhammad Umer. *The Islamic Vision of Development in the Light of Maqasid Al-Shariah*. London: International Institute of Islamic Political Thought, 2008.

Chaghatai, Ikram. *Shah Waliullah (1703–1762): His Religious and Political Thought*. Lahore: Sang-e-Meel Publications, 2005.

Collini, Stefan. "What is Intellectual History," *History Today*, vol. 35, 10 Oct. 1985.

Commins, David Dean. *The Wahhabi Mission and Saudi Arabia*. New York, NY: I.B. Tauris, 2006.

Cook, David. *Martyrdom in Islam* (Cambridge: Cambridge University Press, 2007), 14.

Cook, Michael. *Commanding Right and Forbidding Wrong in Islamic Thought*. Cambridge: Cambridge University Press, 2002.

Cooper, Barry, *New Political Religions, or an Analysis of Modern Terrorism* (Missouri: University of Missouri Press, 2005).

Crawford, Michael. *Ibn 'Abd al-Wahhab: Makers of the Muslim World*. London: Oneworld Publications, 2014.

Crenshaw, Martha. "Crisis in Algeria," in Richard Gillespie (ed.), *Mediterranean Politics*, vol. 1. London: Pinter Publishers, 1994.

DeLong-Bas, Natana. *Wahhabi Islam: From Revival and Reform to Global Jihad*. Oxford: Oxford University Press, 2008.

Deutsch, Kenneth, "Leo Strauss's friendly criticism of American liberal democracy: neoconservative or aristocratic liberalism?" in Kenneth Deutsch and Ethan Fishman (eds.), *The Dilemmas of American Conservatism* (Kentucky: University Press of Kentucky, 2010).

Deutsch, Kenneth, and Walter Nicgorski, "Introduction," in Kenneth Deutsch and Walter Nicgorski (eds.), *Leo Strauss: Political Philosopher and Jewish Thinker.* Lanham, MD: Rowman & Littlefield Publishers, 1984.

Dumbe, Yunus. "The Salafi Praxis of Constructing Religious Identity in Africa: A Comparative Perspective of the Growth of the Movements in Accra and Cape Town," *Islamic Africa*, vol. 2, no. 2 (Winter 2011): 87–116.

Dunn, John. *The History of Political Theory and Other Essays*. Cambridge: Cambridge University Press, 1996.

———. "The Identity of the History of Ideas," *Philosophy*, 43 (April 1968): 85–104.

Edmonds, Rick. "The best-read digital story of 2015? It's The Atlantic's 'What ISIS Really Wants'," *Poynter*, December 31, 2015.

Egerton, Frazer. *Jihad in the West: The Rise of Militant Salafism*. Cambridge: Cambridge University Press, 2011.

Enayat, Hamid. *Modern Islamic Political Thought*. London: I.B. Tauris, 2005.

Esposito, John. *Islam and Politics*. Syracuse, NY: Syracuse University Press, 1998.

———. *What Everyone Needs to Know About Islam: Answers to Frequently Asked Questions from one of America's Leading Experts*. Oxford: Oxford University Press, 2011.

Esposito John L. *The Oxford Dictionary of Islam*. Oxford: Oxford University Press, 2003.

Esposito, John, and François Burgat (eds.), *Modernizing Islam: Religion in the Public Sphere in Europe and the Middle East*. London: Hurst, 2003.

Ess, Josef Van. "Political ideas in early Islamic religious thought," *British Journal of Middle Eastern Studies*, vol. 28, no. 2 (Nov., 2001): 151–164.

Euben, Roxanne L., and Muhammad Qasim Zaman, "Sayyid Abu'l-Hasan 'Ali Nadwi," in Roxanne L. Euben and Muhammad Qasim Zaman (eds.), *Princeton Readings in Islamist Thought, Texts and Contexts from al-Banna to Bin Laden*. Princeton, NJ: Princeton University Press, 2009.

Fadl, Khaled Abou El. *Rebellion and Violence in Islamic Law*. Cambridge: Cambridge University Press, 2001.

Fahmy, Khaled. *All the Pasha's Men: Mehmed Ali, His Army and the Making of Modern Egypt*. Cairo: American University in Cairo Press, 2002.

Fakhry, Majid. *A Short Introduction to Islamic Philosophy, Theology and Mysticism*. Oxford: Oneworld Publications, 1997.

Farsi, Sulaiman al-. *Democracy and Youth in the Middle East: Islam, Tribalism and the Rentier State in Oman*. London: I.B. Tauris, 2013.

Figueira, Daurius. *Salafi Jihadi Discourse of Sunni Islam in the 21st Century: The Discourse of Abu Muhammed al Maqdisi and Anwar al Awlaki*. Bloomington, IN: iUniverse books, 2011.

Fish, Morris J. "An Eye for an Eye: Proportionality as a Moral Principle of Punishment," *Oxford Journal of Legal Studies*, vol. 28, no. 1 (Spring, 2008): 57–71

Fukuyama, Francis. *The End of History and the Last Man*. London: Penguin Books, 2012.

Gaffney, Patrick. *The Prophet's Pulpit: Islamic Preaching in Contemporary Egypt*. Berkeley, CA: University of California Press, 1994.

Gallagher, John, and Ronald Robinson. "The Imperialism of Free Trade," *Economic History Review, New Series*, vol. 6, no. 1 (1953): 1–15.

Gerges, Fawaz. *The Far Enemy: Why Jihad Went Global*. Cambridge: Cambridge University Press, 2005.

Gilbert, Felix. "Intellectual History: Its Aims and Methods" *Daedalus*, vol. 100, no. 1, Historical Studies Today (Winter, 1971): 80–97

Gold, Dore. *Hatred's Kingdom: How Saudi Arabia Supports the New Global Terrorism*. Washington, D.C.: Regnery Publishing Inc., 2004.

Gontier, Thierry, "From 'Political Theology' to 'Political Religion': Eric Voegelin and Carl Schmitt," *Review of Politics*, 75, 2013, 25–43;

Goodwin, Barbara, *Using Political Ideas*. Chichester: John Wiley & Sons Ltd, 1998.

Gordon, Peter E., "What is Intellectual History? A frankly partisan introduction to a frequently misunderstood field," Harvard History Department website.

Green, Jerrold D., Frederic M. Wehrey, Charles Wolf, *Understanding Iran*. Arlington, VA: Rand Corporation, 2009.

Gregor, Anthony James, *Totalitarianism and Political Religion: An Intellectual History*. Stanford, CA: Stanford University Press, 2012.

Gurr, Nadine, and Benjamin Cole, *New Face of Terrorism: Threats from Weapons of Mass Destruction*. London: I.B. Tauris, 2005.

Haddad, Gibril Fouad. *The four Imāms and their schools: Abū Hanīfa, Mālik, Al-Shāfi'ī, Ahmad*. London: Muslim Academic Trust 2007.

Hafez, Mohammed. *Suicide Bombers in Iraq: The Strategy and Ideology of Martyrdom*. Washington, D.C.: United States Institute of Peace, 2007.

———. "From Marginalization to Massacres: A Political Process Explanation of GIA Violence in Algeria," in Quintan Wiktorowicz (ed.), *Islamic Activism: A Social Movement Theory Approach*. Bloomington, IN: Indiana University Press, 2004.

———. "Tactics, Takfir, and anti-Muslim Violence," in Assaf Moghadam and Brian Fishman (eds.), *Fault Lines in Global Jihad: Organizational, Strategic, and Ideological Fissures*. London: Routledge, 2011.

———. *Why Muslims Rebel: Repression and Resistance in the Islamic World*. London: Lynne Rienner Publishers Inc, 2003.

———. "From Marginalization to Massacres: A Political Process Explanation of GIA Violence in Algeria," in Quintan Wiktorowickz (ed.), *Islamic Activism: A Social Movement Theory Approach*. Indiana University Press: Indiana, 2004.

———. "Tactics, Takfir, and anti-Muslim Violence," in Assaf Moghadam and Brian Fishman (eds.), *Fault Lines in Global Jihad: Organizational, Strategic, and Ideological Fissures*. London: Routledge, 2011.

———. *Why Muslims Rebel: Repression and Resistance in the Islamic World*. London: Lynne Rienner Publishers Inc, 2003.

Haj, Samira. *Reconfiguring Islamic Tradition: Reform, Rationality, and Modernity*. Stanford, CA: Stanford University Press, 2009.

———. "Reordering Islamic orthodoxy: Muhammad ibn 'Abdul Wahhab," *The Muslim World*, vol. 92, Nos. 3&4 (Fall 2002): 333–370.

Hascall, Susan C. "Restorative Justice in Islam: Should Qisas be Considered a Form of Restorative Justice?" *Berkeley Journal of Middle Eastern & Islamic Law* (2012): 35–78.

Hartung, Jan-Peter. *A System of Life: Mawdudi and the Ideologisation of Islam*. London: Hurst, 2013.

Hatina, Meir. *Martyrdom in Modern Islam: Piety, Power, and Politics*. Cambridge: Cambridge University Press, 2014.

Hawley, John C., "Jihad as a rite of passage: Tahar Djaout's *The Last Summer of Reason* and Slimane Benaïssa's *The Last Night of a Damned Soul*," in Fiona Tolan, Stephen Morton, Anastasia Valassopoulos, Robert Spencer (eds.), *Literature, Migration and the "War on Terror."* Oxford: Routledge, 2012.

Hawting, G. R. "The Significance of the Slogan "lā hukma illā lillāh" and the References to the "Hudūd" in the Traditions about the Fitna and the Murder of 'Uthmān," *BSOAS*, University of London, vol. 41, no. 3 (1978): 453–463.

Haykel, Bernard. "On the nature of salafi thought and action,' in Roel Meijer (ed.), *Global Salafism: Islam's New Religious Movement*. London: Hurst, 2009.

Hegghammer, Thomas. "Jihadi-Salafis or Revolutionaries? On Religion and Politics in the study of Militant Islamism," in Roel Meijer (ed.), *Global Salafism: Islam's New Religious Movement*. London: Hurst, 2009.

———. "Violent Islamism in Saudi Arabia 1979–2006, the Power and Perils of Pan-Islamic Nationalism." PhD diss., Sciences Po, 2007.

———. "Islamist Violence and Regime Stability in Saudi Arabia," *International Affairs* (Royal Institute of International Affairs 1944–) vol. 84, no. 4 (Jul., 2008): 701–715.

———. *Jihad in Saudi Arabia: Violence and Pan-Islamism since 1979*. Cambridge: Cambridge University Press, 2010.

———. "Abdallah 'Azzam and Palestine," *Die Welt des Islams*, 53, (2013): 353–387.

Hegghammer, Thomas, & Joas Wagemakers, "The Palestine Effect: The Role of Palestinians in the Transnational Jihad Movement," *Die Welt des Islams*, 53, (2013): 281–314.

Hegghammer, Thomas, and Stéphane Lacroix, *The Meccan Rebellion: The Story of Juhayman Al-Utaybi Revisited*. London: Amal Press, 2011.

———, "Rejectionist Islamism in Saudi Arabia: The Story of Juhayman Al-Utaybi Revisited," *International Journal of Middle East Studies*, vol. 39, no. 1 (Feb., 2007): 103–122.

Hibri, Tayeb El-. *Parable and Politics in Early Islamic History: The Rashidun Caliphs*. New York, NY: Columbia University Press, 2010.

Higham, John. "Intellectual History and its Neighbours," *Journal of the History of Ideas*, vol. 15, no. 3 (June, 1954): 339–347.

Hinds, Martin. "The Murder of the Caliph Uthman," *International Journal of Middle East Studies*, vol. 3, no. 4 (Oct., 1972): 450–469.

Hodgkin, Thomas. "The Revolutionary Tradition in Islam," *History Workshop*, no. 10 (Autumn, 1980): 138–150.

Holland, Tom. *In the Shadow of the Sword, The Battle for Global Empire and the End of the Ancient World*. London: Little Brown, 2012.

Hourani, Albert. *A History of the Arab Peoples*. New York, NY: Warner Books, 1991.

———. *Arabic Thought in the Liberal Age, 1798–1939*. Cambridge: Cambridge University Press, 1962.

Howard, Michael. *War in European History*. Oxford: Oxford University Press, 2009.

Hughes, Henry Stuart. *Consciousness and Society: the Reorientation of European Social Thought 1890–1930*. Frogmore: Granada Publishing Limited, 1974.

Huntington, Samuel. *The Clash of Civilisations and the Remaking of the World Order*. New York, NY: Simon and Schuster, 2011.

Hussein, Gamil Muhammed. "Basic guarantees in the Islamic Criminal Justice System," in Muhammad Abdel Haleem, Adel Omar Sharif, and Kate Daniels (eds.), *Criminal Justice in Islam: Judicial Procedure in the Shari'ah*. London: I.B. Tauris, 2003.

Ibrahim, Raymond. *The Al Qaeda Reader: The Essential Texts of Osama Bin Laden's Terrorist Organization*. New York, NY: Broadway Books, 2007.

Izutsu, Toshihiko. *The Concept of Belief in Islamic Theology, a Semantic Analysis of Īmān and Islam*. Kuala Lumpur: Islamic Book Trust, 2006.

Jabri, Mohammed Abed al-. *Formation of Arab Reason: Text, Tradition and the Construction of Modernity in the Arab World*. London: I.B. Tauris, 2005.

Jalal, Ayesha. *Partisans of Allah: Jihad in South Asia*. Harvard: Harvard University Press, 2008.

Jalal, Ayesha. *Self and Sovereignty: Individual and Community in South Asian Islam Since 1850*. Oxford: Oxford University Press 2001.

Johansen, Baber. "A Perfect law in an imperfect society: Ibn Taymiyyah's concept of 'Governance in the name of the Sacred Law'," in P. Bearman, W. Heinrichs, and B. G. Weiss (eds.), *The Law Applied: Contextualizing the Islamic Shari'a*. London: I.B. Tauris, 2008.

Johnson, James Turner. *The Holy War Idea in Western and Islamic Traditions*. University Park, PA: Pennsylvania State University Press, 1997.

Jones, David Martin, and M.L.R. Smith, *Sacred Violence: Political Religion in a Secular Age*. London: Palgrave Macmillan, 2014.

Kamali, Mohammed Hashim. *Principles of Islamic Jurisprudence*. Cambridge: Islamic Texts Society, 1991.

———. *Shari'ah Law: An Introduction*. Oxford: Oneworld Publications, 2010.

———. "Maqāsid al-Shar'iah: The Objectives of Islamic Law," *Islamic Studies*, vol. 38, no. 2 (Summer 1999): 193–208.

———. "Istiḥsān and the Renewal of Islamic Law," *Islamic Studies*, vol. 43, no. 4 (Winter 2004), 561–581.

———. "Qawa'id al-Fiqh: The Legal Maxims of Islamic Law," *The Association of Muslim Lawyers*.

Kamolnick, Paul. "Al-Qaeda's Sharia Crisis: Sayyid Imam and the Jurisprudence of Lawful Military Jihad," *Studies in Conflict & Terrorism*, 36 (2013): 394–418.

Kazimi, Nibras. "A Virulent Ideology in Mutation: Zarqawi Upstages Maqdisi," *Current Trends, Hudson Institute*. 12 Sept. 2005.

———. "Zarqawi's Anti-Shi'a Legacy: Original or Borrowed?," *Current Trends in Islamist Ideology*, November 1, 2006.

Kedourie, Elie. *Afghani and 'Abduh: An Essay on Religious Unbelief and Political Activism in Modern Islam*. London: Frank Cass & Co, 1997.

Kelley, Donald. *The Descent of Ideas: the History of Intellectual History*. Aldershot: Ashgate, 2002.

Kenney, Jeffrey T., *Muslim Rebels: Kharijites and the Politics of Extremism in Egypt*. Oxford: Oxford University Press, 2006.

Kepel, Gilles. *Jihad: The Trail of Political Islam*. London: I.B. Tauris, 2006.

———. *The Roots of Radical Islam*. London: Saqi Books, 2005.

———. *Bad Moon Rising: a chronicle of the Middle East today*. London: Saqi Books, 2003.

———. *Beyond Terror and Martyrdom: the Future of the Middle East*. Harvard: Belknap Press, 2008.

Keshk, Khaled. "When Did Muʿāwiya Become Caliph?," *Journal of Near Eastern Studies*, vol. 69, no. 1 (April 2010): 31–42.

Khalidi, Rashid. *Palestinian Identity*. New York, NY: Columbia University Press, 1997.

Khatab, Sayed. *The Power of Sovereignty: The Political and Ideological Philosophy of Sayyid Qutb*. Abingdon: Routledge, 2006.

———. *The Political Thought of Sayyid Qutb: The Theory of Jahiliyyah*. Abingdon: Routledge, 2006.

Kimmerling, Baruch and Joel Migdal, *The Palestinian People: A History*. Cambridge, MA: Harvard University Press, 2003.

Kohlmann, Evan. "A Beacon for Extremists: The Ansar al-Mujahideen Web Forum" *CTC Sentinel*, vol. 3, no. 2. Jan. 2010.

Krämer, Gudrun. "Islamist notions of democracy," in Joel Beinin and Joe Stork (eds.), *Political Islam: Essays from Middle East Report*. Berkeley, CA: University of California Press, 1997.

LaCapra, Dominick. *Rethinking intellectual history: texts, contexts, language*. Ithaca, NY: Cornell University Press, 1983.

Lacroix, Stéphane. *Awakening Islam: The Politics of Religious Dissent in Contemporary Saudi Arabia*, trans. George Holoch. Cambridge, MA: Harvard University Press, 2011.

Lane, Jan-Erik, and Hamadi Redissi, *Religion and Politics: Islam and Muslim Civilization*. Farnham: Ashgate Publishing, 2009.

Lapidus, Ira M. *A History of Islamic Societies*. Cambridge: Cambridge University Press, 2010.

Lav, Daniel. *Radical Islam and the Revival of Medieval Theology*. Cambridge: Cambridge University Press, 2012.

Law, Randall. *Terrorism: A History*. Cambridge: Polity Press, 2009. Kindle edition.

Leaman, Oliver. *A Brief Introduction to Islamic Philosophy*. Cambridge: Polity Press, 1999.

———. *The Qur'an: an encyclopaedia*. Oxford: Taylor & Francis, 2006.

Leiken, Robert. *Europe's Angry Muslims: the Revolt of the Second Generation*. Oxford: Oxford University Press, 2012.

Lerner, Daniel. *The Passing of Traditional Society: Modernizing the Middle East*. London: Collier-Macmillan, 1964.

Levine, Joseph. "Intellectual History as History," *Journal of the History of Ideas*, vol. 66, no. 2 (April, 2005): 189–200.

Lewis, Bernard. *The Crisis of Islam: Holy War and Unholy Terror*. New York, NT: Random House, 2003.

———. *What Went Wrong? Western Impact and Middle Eastern Response*. London: Phoenix, 2002.

———. "Islamic Revolution," *The New York Review of Books*. Jan. 21, 1988.

Lia, Brynjar. *Architect of Global Jihad: The Life of Al-Qaeda Strategist Abu Mus'ab Al-Suri*, London: Hurst, 2009.

———. *The Society of the Muslim Brothers in Egypt: The Rise of an Islamic Mass Movement, 1928–1942*. Reading: Ithaca Press, 2006.

Lovejoy, Arthur, *The Great Chain of Being: A Study of the History of an Idea*. Cambridge, MA: Harvard University Press, 2001.

Lowry, Joseph Edmund. *Early Islamic Legal Theory: The Risāla of Muhammad ibn Idrīs Al-Shāfi'ī*. Leiden: Brill, 2007.

Lund, Aron. "Syria's Salafi Insurgents: The Rise of the Syrian Islamic Front," *Swedish Institute of International Affairs*, no. 17, 2013.

Maher, Shiraz and Amany Soliman. "Al-Qaeda confirms death of Bin Laden," *ICSR Insight*, 6 May 2011.

Maley, William. *The Afghanistan Wars*. Hampshire: Palgrave Macmillan, 2002.

Mandaville, Peter. *Global Political Islam*. Oxford: Routledge, 2007.

Mannheim, Karl, *From Karl Mannheim with an introduction by Volker Meja and David Kettler*. New Jersey: Transaction Publishers, 1993.

March, Andrew F. "Anwar al-Awlaqi Against Islamic Tradition," in Asma Afsaruddin (ed.), *Islam, the State, and Political Authority: Medieval Issues and Modern Concerns*. Palgrave Macmillan: New York, 2011.

McCants, William and Jarret Brachman, *Militant Ideology Atlas: Research Compendium*. Combatting Terrorism Centre: West Point, NY, 2007.

McCants, William. "The Lesser of Two Evils: The Salafi Turn to Party Politics in Egypt," Brookings Middle East Memo no. 23, May 2012.

———. "The Sources of Salafi Conduct." *Foreign Affairs*, Sept. 19, 2012.

———. *The ISIS Apocalypse: The History, Strategy, and Doomsday Vision of the Islamic State*. New York, NY: St Martin's Press, 2015.

Mdaires, Falah Abdullah al-. *Islamic Extremism in Kuwait: From the Muslim Brotherhood to Al-Qaeda and Other Islamist Political Groups*. London: Routledge, 2010.

Meijer, Roel (ed.), *Global Salafism: Islam's New Religious Movement*. London: Hurst, 2009.

———. "Yūsuf al-'Uyayrī and the making of a revolutionary salafi praxis," *Die Welt des Islams*, 47, 3–4, (2007): 422–459.

———. "Yūsuf al-'Uyayrī and the transnationalisation of Saudi jihadism," in Madawi al-Rasheed (ed.), *Kingdom without Borders: Saudi Arabia's Political, Religious and Media Frontiers*. London: Hurst, 2008.

Ménoret, Pascal. *The Saudi Enigma: A History*. London: Zed Books, 2005.

Michot, Yahya. "Ibn Taymiyya's "New Mardin Fatwa." Is genetically modified Islam (GMI) carcinogenic?" *The Muslim World*, vol. 101 (April 2011): 130–181.

———. *Muslims under Non-Muslim Rule. Ibn Taymiyya on fleeing from sin, kinds of emigration, the status of Mardin (domain of peace/war, domain composite), the conditions for challenging power; Texts translated, annotated and presented in relation to six modern readings of the Mardin fatwa*. Oxford: Interface Publications, 2006.

Middleton, Paul. *Martyrdom: A Guide for the Perplexed*. London: T&T Clark, 2011.

Moghadam, Assaf. *The Globalization of Martyrdom: al-Qaeda, Salafi Jihad and the Diffusion of Suicide Attacks*. Baltimore, MD: Johns Hopkins University Press, 2008.

———. "Motives for Martyrdom: Al-Qaida, Salafi Jihad, and the Spread of Suicide Attacks," *International Security*, vol. 33, no. 3 (Winter, 2008/2009): 46–78.

Mohamed, Mahfodz. "The concept of Qisās in Islamic law," *Islamic Studies*, vol. 21, no. 2 (Summer 1982): 77–88.

Molloy, Rebecca. "Deconstructing Ibn Taymiyya's views on suicidal missions," CTC Sentinel, vol. 2, 3, March 2009.

Moustafa, Tamir. "Conflict and Cooperation between the State and Religious Institutions in Contemporary Egypt," *International Journal of Middle East Studies*, vol. 32, no. 1 (Feb., 2000), 3–22.

Mowatt-Larssen, Rolf. *Islam and the Bomb: Religious Justification For and Against Nuclear Bombs*. Massachusetts: Belfer Center for Science and International Affairs, 2011.

Mubarakpuri, Safi ur Rahman Al. *When The Moon Split: A biography of Prophet Muhammad*. Riyadh: Dar-us-salam, 2002.

Musallam, Adnan. *From Secularism to Jihad: Sayyid Qutb and the Foundations of Radical Islamism*. Westport, CT: Greenwood Publishing, 2005.

Nafi, Basheer M. "Fatwa and War: On the Allegiance of the American Muslim Soldiers in the Aftermath of Sept. 11," *Islamic Law and Society*, vol. 11, no. 1 (2004): 78–116.

Najibabadi, Akbar Shah. *The History of Islam, Volume 3*. London: Dar-us-salam Publications, 2001.

Nasr, Seyyed Hossein, and Oliver Leaman (eds.), *History of Islamic philosophy*. London: Routledge, 1996.

Niblock, Tim. *Saudi Arabia: Power, Legitimacy and Survival*. Oxford: Routledge, 2006.

Nicolle, David. *The Great Islamic Conquests AD 632–750*. Oxford: Osprey Publishing, 2009.

Norton, Augustus Richard. "Thwarted Politics: The Case of Egypt's Hizb al-Wasat," in Robert Hefner (ed.), *Remaking Muslim Politics: Pluralism, Contestation, Democratization*. Princeton, NJ: Princeton University Press, 2005.

Nyazee, Imran Ahsan Khan. *Islamic Jurisprudence: Uṣūl Al-Fiqh*. London: International Institute of Islamic Thought, 2000.

Oishi, Etsuko, "Austin's speech act theory and the speech situation," *Esercizi Filosofici*, 1, 2006.

Opwis, Felicitas. *Maslaha and the Purpose of the Law: Islamic Discourse on Legal Change from the 4th/10th to 8th/14th Century*. Leiden: Brill, 2010.

———. "Islamic law and legal change: the concept of maslaha in classical and contemporary Islamic legal theory" in Abbas Amanat and Frank Griffel (ed.), *Sharia: Islamic law in the contemporary context*. Stanford, CA: Stanford University Press, 2007.

Orr, Tamra. *Egyptian Islamic Jihad*. New York, NY: Rosen Publishing Group, 2003.

Palonen, Kari. *Quentin Skinner: History, Politics, Rhetoric*. Cambridge: Polity Press, 2003.

Pankhurst, Reza. *The Inevitable Caliphate? A History of the Struggle for Global Islamic Union, 1924 to the Present*. London: Hurst, 2013.

Pape, Robert. *Dying to Win: The Strategic Logic of Suicide Terrorism*. New York, NY: Random House, 2005.

Pargeter, Alison. *The New Frontiers of Jihad: Radical Islam in Europe*. London: I.B. Tauris, 2008.

———. *The Muslim Brotherhood: The Burden of Tradition*. London: Saqi books, 2010

Patton, Michael. *Qualitative Research and Evaluation Methods*. London: Sage Publications, 2002.

Paz, Reuven. "Islamic Legitimacy for the London Bombings," *Global Research in International Affairs* (GLORIA), Project for the Research of Islamist Movements (PRISM), Occasional Papers, vol. 3, no. 4 (2005).

Pocock, J. G. A., "Foundations and moments," in Holly Hamilton-Bleakley, Annabel Brett, James Tully (eds.), *Rethinking The Foundations of Modern Political Thought*, (Cambridge: Cambridge University Press, 2006).

Quataert, Donald. *The Ottoman Empire, 1700–1922*. Cambridge: Cambridge University Press, 2005.

Rabi, Ibrahim M. Abu. *Intellectual Origins of Islamic Resurgence in the Modern Arab World*. New York, NY: State University of New York, 1996.

Rabil, Robert G. *Salafism in Lebanon*. Washington, DC: Georgetown University Press, 2014.

Rahman, Asyraf A.B. and Nooraihan Ali, "The influence of al-Mawdudi and the Jama'at al Islami Movement on Sayyid Qutb's Writings," *World Journal of Islamic History and Civilisation*, vol. 2, no. 4 (2012): 232–236

Ramadan, Tariq. *In the Footsteps of the Prophet: Lessons from the Life of Muhammad*. Oxford: Oxford University Press, 2007.

Ranstorp, Magnus. "Interpreting the broader context and meaning of Bin Laden's Fatwa," *Studies in Conflict & Terrorism*, 21, vol. 4 (1998): 324.

Rasheed, Madawi al-. *Contesting the Saudi State: Islamic Voices from a New Generation*. Cambridge: Cambridge University Press, 2010.

———. *A History of Saudi Arabia*. Cambridge: Cambridge University Press, 2010.

———. *A Most Masculine State: Gender, Politics and Religion in Saudi Arabia*. Cambridge: Cambridge University Press, 2013.

———. "Saudi religious transnationalism in London" in Madawi al-Rasheed (ed.), *Transnational connections and the Arab Gulf*. New York, NY: Routledge, 2005.

Rashid, Ahmed. *Taliban: The Story of the Afghan Warlords*. London: Pan Macmillan, 2001.

———. *Jihad: The Rise of Militant Islam in Central Asia*. New York, NY: Penguin Books, 2003.

———. *Descent into Chaos: The U.S. and the Disaster in Pakistan, Afghanistan, and Central Asia*. London: Penguin Books, 2009.

Reinhart, Kevin. "Like the difference between night and day." Hanafi and Shāfi discussions on Wājib and Fard,' in Bernard G. Weiss (ed.), *Studies in Islamic Legal Theory*. Leiden: Brill, 2002.

Riedel, Bruce. *The Search for al-Qaeda: Its Leadership, Ideology, and Future*. Washington, D.C.: The Brookings Institution, 2010.

Robinson, Adam. *Bin Laden: Behind the Mask of the Terrorist*. Edinburgh: Mainstream Publishing Company, 2001.

Rogerson, Barnaby. *The Prophet Muhammad: A Biography*. London: Hachette Digital, 2003. Kindle edn.

Roy, Olivier. *Globalised Ummah: the Search for a New Ummah*. London: Hurst, 2004.

———. *The Failure of Political Islam*. London: I.B. Tauris, 2007.

———. *Holy Ignorance: When Religion and Culture Diverge*. London: Hurst, 2010.

Rubin, Barry. *The Muslim Brotherhood: The Organization and Policies of a Global Islamist Movement*. London: Palgrave Macmillan, 2010.

Sageman, Marc. *Understanding Terror Networks*. Philadelphia, PA: University of Pennsylvania Press, 2004.

Said, Edward. *Orientalism*. London: Penguin Books, 2003.

Samat, Talib. *The 99 Most Eminent Names of Allah*. Kuala Lampur: Utusan Publications, 2001.

Schwartz, Michael. *War Without End: The Iraq War in Context*. Chicago, IL: Haymarket Books, 2008.

Sevea, Iqbal Singh. *The Political Philosophy of Muhammad Iqbal: Islam and Nationalism in Late Colonial India*. Cambridge: Cambridge University Press, 2012.

Shah, Niaz. *Islamic Law and the Law of Armed Conflict: The Conflict in Pakistan*. New York, NY: Routledge, 2011.

Shavit, Uriya. "The Wasaṭī and Salafi Approaches to the Religious Law of Muslim Minorities," *Islamic Law and Society*, vol. 19, no. 4 (2012): 416–457.

Sikand, Yoginder. "Sayyed Abul Hasan 'Ali Nadwi," in Ibrahim Abu-Rabi (ed.), *The Blackwell Companion to Contemporary Islamic Thought*. Oxford: Blackwell Publishing, 2006.

———. *Muslims in India Since 1947: Islamic Perspectives on Inter-Faith Relations*. London: Routledge Curzon, 2004.

Silke, Andrew. "Research on Terrorism: A Review of the Impact of 9/11 and the Global War on Terrorism," in Hsinchun Chen, Edna Reid, Joshua Sinai, Andrew Silke, Boaz Ganor (ed.), *Knowledge Management and Data Mining for Homeland Security, Series: Integrated Series in Information Systems*. New York, NY: Springer, 2008.

Sivan, Emmanuel. *Radical Islam: Medieval Theology and Modern Politics*. New Haven, CT: Yale University Press, 1990.

Sizgorich, Thomas. *Violence and Belief in Late Antiquity: Militant Devotion in Christianity and Islam*. Philadelphia, PA: University of Pennsylvania Press, 2009.

Skinner, Quentin. "Meaning and understanding in the history of ideas," *History and Theory*, 8 (1969): 3–53.

———. *The Foundations of Modern Political Thought*. Cambridge: Cambridge University Press, 2002.

Smith, Steven B., *The Cambridge Companion to Leo Strauss*. Cambridge: Cambridge University Press, 2009.

Steinberg, Guido. "The Wahhabi Ulama and the Saudi State: 1745 to the Present" in Paul Aarts and Gerd Nonneman (eds.), *Saudi Arabia in the balance: political economy, society, foreign affairs*. London: Hurst, 2005.

Sueur, James D. Le. *Uncivil War: Intellectuals and Identity Politics During the Decolonization of Algeria*. London: University of Nebraska Press, 2005.

Sykes, Percy. *A History of Persia, Volume 2*. Oxford: Routledge, 2006.

Tabarani, Gabriel G. *Jihad's New Heartlands: Why The West Has Failed to Contain Islamic Fundamentalism*. Milton Keynes: Author House, 2011.

Tal, Nahman. *Radical Islam in Egypt and Jordan*. Eastbourne: Sussex Academic Press, 2005.

The History of Ideas Club, *Studies in Intellectual History*. Baltimore, MD: The Johns Hopkins University Press, 1953.

Tibi, Bassam. *Islam's Predicament with Modernity: Religious Reform and Cultural Change*. Abingdon: Routledge, 2009.

———. *The Challenge of Fundamentalism: Political Islam and the New World Disorder*. Berkeley, CA: University of California Press, 2002.

Timani, Hussam S. *Modern Intellectual Readings of the Kharijites*. New York, NY: Peter Lang, 2008.

Toth, James. *Sayyid Qutb: The Life and Legacy of a Radical Islamic Intellectual*. Oxford: Oxford University Press, 2013.

Turner, John A. *Religious Ideology and the Roots of the Global Jihad: Salafi Jihadism and International Order*. Basingstoke: Palgrave Macmillan, 2014.

University of Chicago Press, *The Chicago Manual of Style, 16th edn: The Essential Guide for Writers, Editors, and Publishers*. Chicago, IL: University of Chicago Press, 2010.

Vidino, Lorenzo. *The New Muslim Brotherhood in the West*. New York, NY: Columbia University Press, 2010.

Voegelin, Eric, *The New Science of Politics: An Introduction*. Chicago: University of Chicago Press, 1987.

Wagemakers, Joas. "The enduring legacy of the second Saudi state: Quietist and radical Wahhabi contestations of Al-Walā' wa-l-barā'," *International Journal of Middle East Studies*, 44 (2012): 93–110.

———. "Framing "the threat to Islam": al-Walā' wa-l-Barā in Salafi discourse," *Arab Studies Quarterly*, vol. 30, no. 4 (Fall 2008): 1–22.

———. "A Purist Jihadi-Salafi: The Ideology of Abu Muhammad al-Maqdisi," *BJMES*, vol. 36, no. 2 (Aug. 2009): 281–297.

———. *A Quietist Jihadi: the Ideology and Influence of Abu Muhammad al-Maqdisi*. Cambridge: Cambridge University Press, 2012.

Warrick, Joby. *The Triple Agent: The al-Qaeda Mole who Infiltrated the CIA*. New York, NY: Vintage Books, 2011.

Watt, William Montgomery. *The Formative Period of Islamic Thought*. Oxford: Oneworld Publications, 1973.

———. *Islamic Philosophy and Theology*. Hoboken, NJ: Transaction Publishers, 2009.

———, *Islamic Political Thought*. Edinburgh: Edinburgh University Press: 1987.

Wehrey, Frederic, Theodore W. Karasik, Alireza Nader, Jeremy J. Ghez, Lydia Hansell, Robert A. Guffey. *Saudi-Iranian Relations Since the Fall of Saddam: Rivalry, Cooperation, and Implications for U.S. Foreign Policy*. Arlington, VA: Rand Corporation, 2009.

———. *Sectarian Politics in the Gulf: From the Iraq War to the Arab Uprisings*. New York, NY: Columbia University Press, 2014.

Wheeler, Brannon M. *Applying the Canon in Islam: The Authorization and Maintenance of Interpretive Reasoning in Hanafi scholarship*. Albany, NY: State University of New York Press, 1996.

Wickham, Carrie Rosefsky. *The Muslim Brotherhood: Evolution of an Islamist Movement*. Princeton, NJ: Princeton University Press, 2013.

Wiktorowicz, Quintan. "Introduction: Islamic Activism and Social Movement Theory," in Quintan Wiktorowicz (ed.), *Islamic Activism: A Social Movement Theory Approach*. Bloomington, IN: Indiana University Press, 2004.

———. "Anatomy of the Salafi Movement," *Studies in Conflict & Terrorism*, 29 (2006): 207–239.

———. "The new global threat: transnational salafis and jihad," *Middle East Policy*, vol. VIII, no. 4 (Dec. 2001): 18–38.

———. "Introduction: Islamic Activism and Social Movement Theory," in *Islamic Activism: A Social Movement Theory Approach*, Bloomington, IN: Indiana University Press, 2004.

———. *Radical Islam Rising: Muslim Extremism in the West*. Lanham, MD: Rowman & Littlefield Publishers, 2005.

——— "The Salafi Movement in Jordan," *International Journal of Middle East Studies*, vol. 32, no. 2 (May, 2000): 219–240.

———. *The Management of Islamic Activism: Salafis, the Muslim Brotherhood, and State Power in Jordan*. New York, NY: State University of New York Press, 2001.

———. *Islamic Activism: A Social Movement Theory Approach*. Indiana, IN: Indiana University Press, 2004.

Wiktorowicz, Quintan, and John Kaltner, "Killing in the Name of Islam: Al-Qaeda's Justification for Sept. 11," *Middle East Policy Council*, vol. X, Summer 2003, Number 2.

Wood, Graeme. "What ISIS Really Wants," *The Atlantic*, March 2015.

Wright, Lawrence. *The Looming Tower: al-Qaeda's Road to 9/11*. London: Penguin Books, 2007.

Wynbrandt, James. *A Brief History of Saudi Arabia*. New York, NY: Checkmark Books, 2010.

Yasushi, Kosugi. "Al-Manār revisited: the "lighthouse" of the Islamic revival," in Stéphane A. Dudoignon, Komatsu Hisao, Kosugi Yasushi (ed.), *Intellectuals in the Modern Islamic World: Transmission, Transformation and Communication*. New York, NY: Routledge, 2006.

Youssef, Michael. *Revolt Against Modernity: Muslim Zealots and the West*. Leiden: Brill, 1985.

Yusuf, Badmas Lanre. *Sayyid Qutb: A Study of His Tafsir*. Selangor: Islamic Book Trust, 2009.

Zayat, Montasser al-. *The Road to al-Qaeda: the Story of Bin Laden's Right-hand man*. London: Pluto Press, 2004.

INDEX

Battle of Nahrawan (658), 78
Battle of Qadisiyyah (636), 211
Battle of Siffin (657), 77
Battle of the Camel (656), 77
bayt al-ḥaram, 120
benefit, 130
Bentham, Jeremy, 61
bid'a, 13, 14, 27, 113, 200–2
bin Bayah, 'Abdallah, 86
bin Baz, 'Abd al-'Aziz, 8, 43, 103, 104, 119, 127–33, 136, 146, 150, 151, 152, 190, 192
bin Laden, Osama, 8, 15, 21, 42–6, 51, 52, 53, 56, 57, 58, 105, 134, 139–40, 152, 159, 189, 192, 195, 203, 204
bint Khayyat, Sumayyah, 39, 40
Blair, Anthony 'Tony', 24
blood money, 62
Boko Haram, 11
Bolsheviks, 198
Book of Jihad (Ibn Nuhaas), 33
Bosnian War (1992–5), 17, 18, 44, 45, 51
Boucebci, Mahfoud, 65
Brachman, Jarret, 9, 13
bughāt, 15, 47, 57, 76, 92
Burayda, Saudi Arabia, 136
Burma, 45
Bush, George Walker, 57
Byzantine Empire (c. 330–1453), 183

Cairo, Egypt, 35, 84, 90, 178
California-Arabian Standard Oil Company (CASOC), 127
Caliphate, 3–4, 31, 35, 38, 46, 53, 76–80, 88, 92, 116, 119, 169–70, 172, 174, 187, 193, 209
Calvert, John, 178
Cambridge School, 24–5
Camp David Accords (1978), 90
Canada, 9
capitalism, 177
Catholicism, 72
CBS News, 57
Central Asia, 41
charity, 72, 162
Chechnya, 17, 18, 45, 56
children, 57
Christianity, 39, 49, 72, 81, 94, 102, 104, 105, 118, 138, 150, 203
Churchill, Winston, 24–5
civil disobedience, 10
civilians, targeting of, 42, 49, 56–9
Clinton, William 'Bill', 44
collateral damage, 59
colonialism, 43, 169, 172, 180, 208
communism, 36, 41, 84, 152, 177, 194
concentration camps, 87, 181
Council of Senior Scholars, 9, 51, 104, 133
Crusaders, 44, 45, 50, 63, 64, 131, 140

Ad-Dalā'il fī Ḥukm Muwālāt ahl al-Ishrāk ('Abd al-Wahhab), 116–17, 118
dalālāt, 47
Damascus, Syria, 77, 84–5, 91
Dammam, Saudi Arabia, 35
dār al-ḥarb, 85, 87
dār al-Islam, 85, 87, 91
dār al-kufr, 91
Day of Judgement, 34, 39
Defence of Muslim lands, The ('Azzam), 33, 126
democracy, 10, 15, 42, 57, 75, 101, 175, 177, 188, 192, 198–200, 204–5
al-Dhahabi, Muhammad, 88

86–8, 103, 131, 151, 169–70, 175, 177, 178, 181–3
Muslim World League, 128
al-Musta'sim Billah, Abbasid Caliph, 35, 38
Mustafa, Shukri, 87, 90
al-Mustansir, Abbasid Caliph, 35
muwālah, 112, 137–8, 153

Nadwi, Abul Hasan 'Ali Hasani, 178–81, 185
Nagasaki, Japan, 52
Naguib, Muhammad, 86
el-Nahhas, Mustafa, 182
Naḥwa al-Nūr (al-Banna), 182
Najaf, Iraq, 105
Najd, Saudi Arabia, 115
namīma, 102
naṣīḥa, 76, 119, 132, 134, 132, 190–2, 195, 206
Nasser, Gamal Abdel, 86–7, 181
nation-state, 11, 125
nationalism, 84, 182, 194
Nazism, 25–6
neologism, 16, 18, 200
New World Order, 153
Niaz Shah, 46
Niblock, Tim, 117
Nida' al-Islam, 150
Nietzsche, Friedrich, 165, 176
Nigeria, 6
nihilism, 26–7, 46, 67, 107
niqab, 5
Noah, 121
Norway, 43
nuclear weapons, 52
Nūr ala al-darb, 150

obedience, 15, 34, 55, 80, 92–3, 113, 130, 139–40, 149, 164, 192–3, 196–7, 203, 205
Ogaden, Ethiopia, 45
Oman, 43
Omar, Mulla Muhammad, 4, 42, 134
al-Omar, Nasser, 188–9, 191, 195
Open Democracy, 24
oppressive rulers, 89, 94–101
Oslo Accords (1993), 44
Ottoman Caliphate (c. 1299–1922), 115–19, 172, 174
Oxford Dictionary of Islam, 195
Oxford University, 25

Pakistan, 21, 83, 96, 120, 138, 159, 175, 178
Palestine, 36, 44, 45, 51, 56, 126, 153–4, 159, 194, 207
Pankhurst, Reza, 170
Pape, Robert, 172
Pargeter, Alison, 16, 18
Paris, France, 53, 65
Permanent Committee for Scholarly Research and Fatwas, 7, 163, 200
permissive egalitarianism, 26, 27
Persia, 103, 183, 211
Philippines, 6, 45, 51
pilgrimage, 32, 35, 72, 162, 195
pious predecessors, 7, 158, 207
Plato, 23
poetry, 176, 177
political religion, 27
politicos, 9
polytheism, 14, 15, 34, 87, 101, 116, 117, 118, 121, 126, 129, 133, 145, 200, 205
Popper, Karl, 198
praxis, 12, 207
prayer, 32, 34, 72, 150, 162
predestination, 157
preserved tablet, *see al-lawḥ al-maḥfooẓ*
Punjab, 176, 177

ALLEN LANE
an imprint of
PENGUIN BOOKS

Recently Published

William D. Cohan: *Why Wall Street Matters*

David Horspool, *Oliver Cromwell: The Protector*

Daniel C. Dennett, *From Bacteria to Bach and Back: The Evolution of Minds*

Derek Thompson, *Hit Makers: How Things Become Popular*

Harriet Harman, *A Woman's Work*

Wendell Berry, *The World-Ending Fire: The Essential Wendell Berry*

Daniel Levin, *Nothing but a Circus: Misadventures among the Powerful*

Stephen Church, *Henry III: A Simple and God-Fearing King*

Pankaj Mishra, *Age of Anger: A History of the Present*

Graeme Wood, *The Way of the Strangers: Encounters with the Islamic State*

Michael Lewis, *The Undoing Project: A Friendship that Changed the World*

John Romer, *A History of Ancient Egypt, Volume 2: From the Great Pyramid to the Fall of the Middle Kingdom*

Andy King, *Edward I: A New King Arthur?*

Thomas L. Friedman, *Thank You for Being Late: An Optimist's Guide to Thriving in the Age of Accelerations*

John Edwards, *Mary I: The Daughter of Time*

Grayson Perry, *The Descent of Man*

Deyan Sudjic, *The Language of Cities*

Norman Ohler, *Blitzed: Drugs in Nazi Germany*

Carlo Rovelli, *Reality Is Not What It Seems: The Journey to Quantum Gravity*

Catherine Merridale, *Lenin on the Train*

Susan Greenfield, *A Day in the Life of the Brain: The Neuroscience of Consciousness from Dawn Till Dusk*

Christopher Given-Wilson, *Edward II: The Terrors of Kingship*

Emma Jane Kirby, *The Optician of Lampedusa*

Minoo Dinshaw, *Outlandish Knight: The Byzantine Life of Steven Runciman*

Candice Millard, *Hero of the Empire: The Making of Winston Churchill*

Christopher de Hamel, *Meetings with Remarkable Manuscripts*

Brian Cox and Jeff Forshaw, *Universal: A Guide to the Cosmos*

Ryan Avent, *The Wealth of Humans: Work and Its Absence in the Twenty-first Century*

Jodie Archer and Matthew L. Jockers, *The Bestseller Code*

Cathy O'Neil, *Weapons of Math Destruction: How Big Data Increases Inequality and Threatens Democracy*

Peter Wadhams, *A Farewell to Ice: A Report from the Arctic*

Richard J. Evans, *The Pursuit of Power: Europe, 1815-1914*

Anthony Gottlieb, *The Dream of Enlightenment: The Rise of Modern Philosophy*

Marc Morris, *William I: England's Conqueror*

Gareth Stedman Jones, *Karl Marx: Greatness and Illusion*

J.C.H. King, *Blood and Land: The Story of Native North America*

Robert Gerwarth, *The Vanquished: Why the First World War Failed to End, 1917-1923*

Joseph Stiglitz, *The Euro: And Its Threat to Europe*

John Bradshaw and Sarah Ellis, *The Trainable Cat: How to Make Life Happier for You and Your Cat*

A J Pollard, *Edward IV: The Summer King*

Erri de Luca, *The Day Before Happiness*

Diarmaid MacCulloch, *All Things Made New: Writings on the Reformation*

Daniel Beer, *The House of the Dead: Siberian Exile Under the Tsars*

Tom Holland, *Athelstan: The Making of England*

Christopher Goscha, *The Penguin History of Modern Vietnam*

Mark Singer, *Trump and Me*

Roger Scruton, *The Ring of Truth: The Wisdom of Wagner's Ring of the Nibelung*

Ruchir Sharma, *The Rise and Fall of Nations: Ten Rules of Change in the Post-Crisis World*

Jonathan Sumption, *Edward III: A Heroic Failure*

Daniel Todman, *Britain's War: Into Battle, 1937-1941*

Dacher Keltner, *The Power Paradox: How We Gain and Lose Influence*

Tom Gash, *Criminal: The Truth About Why People Do Bad Things*

Brendan Simms, *Britain's Europe: A Thousand Years of Conflict and Cooperation*

Slavoj Žižek, *Against the Double Blackmail: Refugees, Terror, and Other Troubles with the Neighbours*

Lynsey Hanley, *Respectable: The Experience of Class*

Piers Brendon, *Edward VIII: The Uncrowned King*

Matthew Desmond, *Evicted: Poverty and Profit in the American City*

T.M. Devine, *Independence or Union: Scotland's Past and Scotland's Present*

Seamus Murphy, *The Republic*

Jerry Brotton, *This Orient Isle: Elizabethan England and the Islamic World*

Srinath Raghavan, *India's War: The Making of Modern South Asia, 1939-1945*

Clare Jackson, *Charles II: The Star King*

Nandan Nilekani and Viral Shah, *Rebooting India: Realizing a Billion Aspirations*

Sunil Khilnani, *Incarnations: India in 50 Lives*

Helen Pearson, *The Life Project: The Extraordinary Story of Our Ordinary Lives*

Ben Ratliff, *Every Song Ever: Twenty Ways to Listen to Music Now*

Richard Davenport-Hines, *Edward VII: The Cosmopolitan King*

Peter H. Wilson, *The Holy Roman Empire: A Thousand Years of Europe's History*

Todd Rose, *The End of Average: How to Succeed in a World that Values Sameness*

Frank Trentmann, *Empire of Things: How We Became a World of Consumers, from the Fifteenth Century to the Twenty-First*

Laura Ashe, *Richard II: A Brittle Glory*

John Donvan and Caren Zucker, *In a Different Key: The Story of Autism*

Jack Shenker, *The Egyptians: A Radical Story*

Tim Judah, *In Wartime: Stories from Ukraine*

Serhii Plokhy, *The Gates of Europe: A History of Ukraine*

Robin Lane Fox, *Augustine: Conversions and Confessions*

Peter Hennessy and James Jinks, *The Silent Deep: The Royal Navy Submarine Service Since 1945*

Sean McMeekin, *The Ottoman Endgame: War, Revolution and the Making of the Modern Middle East, 1908–1923*

Charles Moore, *Margaret Thatcher: The Authorized Biography, Volume Two: Everything She Wants*

Dominic Sandbrook, *The Great British Dream Factory: The Strange History of Our National Imagination*

Larissa MacFarquhar, *Strangers Drowning: Voyages to the Brink of Moral Extremity*

Niall Ferguson, *Kissinger: 1923-1968: The Idealist*

Carlo Rovelli, *Seven Brief Lessons on Physics*

Tim Blanning, *Frederick the Great: King of Prussia*

Ian Kershaw, *To Hell and Back: Europe, 1914–1949*

Pedro Domingos, *The Master Algorithm: How the Quest for the Ultimate Learning Machine Will Remake Our World*